P9-CKH-223

How to

SURVIVE

—— *and* ——

THRIVE

in the

First Three Weeks of School

To my sister, Kathleen Ann Hoedeman, an extraordinary
middle school educator and a with-it teacher in every sense of the word

How to
SURVIVE
—— and ——
THRIVE
in the
First Three Weeks of School

ELAINE K. McEWAN

CORWIN PRESS
A SAGE Publications Company
Thousand Oaks, California

LIBRARY MSU-BILLINGS
WITHDRAWN

Copyright © 2006 by Corwin Press.

All rights reserved. When forms and sample documents are included, their use is authorized only by educators, local school sites, and/or noncommercial or nonprofit entities who have purchased the book. Except for that usage, no part of this book may be reproduced or utilized in any form or by any means, electronic or mechanical, including photocopying, recording, or by any information storage and retrieval system, without permission in writing from the publisher.

For information:

Corwin Press
A Sage Publications Company
2455 Teller Road
Thousand Oaks, California 91320
www.corwinpress.com

Sage Publications Ltd.
1 Oliver's Yard
55 City Road
London EC1Y 1SP
United Kingdom

Sage Publications India Pvt. Ltd.
B–42, Panchsheel Enclave
Post Box 4109
New Delhi 110 017 India

Printed in the United States of America

Library of Congress Cataloging-in-Publication Data

McEwan, Elaine K., 1941–
How to survive and thrive in the first three weeks of school / Elaine K. McEwan.
    p. cm.
Includes bibliographical references and index.
ISBN 1-4129-0453-6 (cloth)—ISBN 1-4129-0454-4 (pbk.)
  1. Effective teaching. 2. School year—Planning. I. Title.
LB1025.3.M356 2006
371.1—dc22

                               2005028709

This book is printed on acid-free paper.

06 07 08 09 10   10 9 8 7 6 5 4 3 2 1

Acquisitions Editor:	Robert D. Clouse
Editorial Assistant:	Jingle Vea
Production Editor:	Melanie Birdsall
Typesetter:	C&M Digitals (P) Ltd.
Copy Editor:	Marilyn Power Scott
Cover Designer:	Michael Dubowe
Production Artist	Lisa Miller

Contents

Preface

Whether you are an energetic novice, an exhausted veteran teacher, or a master teacher who is continually looking for ways to improve your craft, this book has the potential to help you notch up your effectiveness. *How to Survive and Thrive in the First Three Weeks of School* is based on a "big idea" represented by the following "equation": $3 + 3 = 33$. I call this set of numbers a *numerym*. [Note: Numeryms are similar to *acronyms* but use numbers rather than letters to communicate a complex idea, e.g., 24/7 or 9–11.]

My use of $3 + 3 = 33$ is an adaptation and expansion of a numerym coined in the early 1980s by an unknown staff member from the American Federation of Teachers' (AFT) Educational Research and Dissemination Division. At that time, $3 = 33$ was used to describe a body of research showing the impact of classroom management techniques established early in the school year (the first 3 weeks) on overall student achievement during the remaining 33 weeks of the school year (Emmer & Evertson, 1980). AFT personnel subsequently developed a teacher-training program that is still being offered by that organization (A. Gill, personal conversation, June 6, 2005). This idea is not a new one, but similar to essential habits for bodily health, like daily flossing and regular exercise, it needs to be revisited and reinforced periodically.

Principal Craig Spiers and his assistant, Tony Contos, administrators at Joliet Central High School (JCHS) in Illinois, adopted $3 = 33$ to communicate the importance of doing the "right things" during the first 3 weeks of the school year, after several JCHS teachers went through the training. Staff members know what the numerym means: Time invested in the beginning of the school year to teach routines and expectations will pay dividends in achievement later on. Craig explains the importance of $3 = 33$ this way:

> **When teachers at any level or in any subject haphazardly introduce, postpone, or skip the explicit instruction and mastery of important classroom procedures, they inevitably reduce or even eliminate the likelihood of high achievement for many of their students, as well as creating a downward spiral of frustration, exhaustion, and stress for themselves. (C. Spiers, personal conversation, January 10, 2005)**

I have personally witnessed the power of well-taught routines, rules, and rubrics in classrooms and schools where teachers and students are focused on learning and achievement is high. Conversely, I have observed what the absence of structure and expectations can do to lower teacher morale and depress student achievement. The central concept of $3 + 3 = 33$ is this: *Routines, rubrics, and rules (the 3Rs) taught and mastered at the beginning of the school year (3 weeks) result in a productive remainder of the school year (33 weeks).*

The numerym $3 + 3 = 33$ expresses the educational version of winning a game, match, or race during the initial minutes of competition. Teachers who spend the first 3 weeks of the school year intentionally teaching and then assessing their students' mastery of the routines, rubrics, and rules necessary to succeed in their grade levels or content areas are able to implement a full "academic press" during the remaining 33 weeks of the year. Not only do they survive and thrive professionally, their students soar academically. [Note: *academic press* is "the extent to which school members, including students and teachers, experience a strong emphasis on academic success and conformity to specific standards of achievement" (Lee, Smith, Perry, & Smylie, 1999).]

I call the educators who consistently implement $3 + 3 = 33$ *with-it teachers* (WITs). WITs are on top of, tuned in to, aware of, and in control of three critical facets of classroom life: (1) the management and organization of the classroom, (2) the engagement of students, and (3) the management of time (McEwan, 2002, p. 48).

The Goal of This Book: With-It-Ness for All Teachers

The goal of this book is to provide all teachers with the knowledge, skills, and motivation to become WITs. Of course, there are many other ways that teachers acquire with-it-ness: (1) through trial and error, (2) by taking a classroom management course during preservice training or working with a with-it supervising teacher, (3) in a teacher induction program that is accompanied by mentoring from a with-it teacher, or (4) in ongoing professional development and coaching. *How to Survive and Thrive in the First Three Weeks of School* offers you an additional way to observe and acquire with-it-ness: an opportunity to learn from dozens of WITs at every level (K–12) who generously share their own personal routines, rubrics, and rules toward the goal of helping you become a WIT.

Who This Book Is For

This book has been written for all K–12 teachers:

- Preservice teachers who are eager to learn as much as they can before stepping into their first official teaching position
- Recent graduates of undergraduate and graduate teacher-training programs who want to become WITs as quickly as possible

- Beginning teachers who are eager to make a difference immediately in their classrooms
- Alternative-career teachers who, although mature and successful professionals in other fields, need guidance in how to transfer their knowledge and experience to working with students
- Highly effective master teachers who are always eager to add tools to their teaching toolbox
- Experienced teachers who are feeling the pressures of standards-based instruction and assessment and are looking for ways to become more productive
- Teachers who are frustrated by the lack of discipline, respect, and motivation they see daily in their students
- Teachers who are demoralized by their lack of efficacy and want to feel empowered and energized once again

How to Survive and Thrive in the First Three Weeks of School will also be helpful to the following groups of educators:

- College and university professors in preservice teacher-training courses
- Administrators who provide professional development for teachers at all levels of experience
- Building-level and central office administrators who coach, mentor, supervise, and evaluate teachers
- Instructional coaches and mentors who desire to improve the performance of the teachers with whom they work

What With-It-Ness Is Not

Before you read further, let me clarify what with-it-ness is not. First, with-it-ness is not the *only* trait one needs to be a highly effective teacher (McEwan, 2002). The lack of with-it-ness, however, is one of the most common reasons why teachers at any level fail. Teacher dropouts are usually dedicated and hard-working individuals who care about kids and want to be effective but fail to thrive because they don't have a plan for how to accomplish what they and their students are expected to do.

Second, being a WIT does not mean you must be an automaton that reads from a prepared script and never has any "fun" in the classroom. Nor does being a WIT mean that you must run your classroom like a drill sergeant. You will discover as you meet the WITs in this book that each one puts a unique spin on with-it-ness to accomplish their stated goals. Although they may wear wacky costumes (Chesnutt), dance for their reading groups (Vitale), give their students "the hairy eyeball" (Lander), play musical chairs with honors biology students

(Robertson), or talk with the animals (Oosterbaan), they pursue their academic missions with dogged determination.

Overview of the Contents

How to Survive and Thrive in the First Three Weeks of School contains seven chapters. Each one presents vital information that will enable you to develop your own personalized 3 + 3 = 33 plan toward the goal of becoming a WIT.

The Introduction defines important terms and concepts and describes how the WITs were selected.

Chapter 1 describes how to establish a classroom environment that fosters student engagement. It explores a variety of ways to use classroom space and plan seating arrangements to enhance students' learning. You will find sample seating plans and room arrangements to stimulate your thinking about what will work best for you.

Chapter 2 focuses on the walls and bulletin boards of your classroom, discussing how to make your walls do the work of instruction while at the same time creating an aesthetically pleasing environment. It contains samples of posters from the classrooms of WITs at various grade levels and a menu of possible ways to use your walls to teach.

Chapter 3 examines precisely what kind of teaching models, moves, and approaches WITs use to teach the 3Rs, the important routines, rubrics, and rules that make their classrooms function like well-oiled machines.

Chapter 4 introduces dozens of organizational, academic, and social routines used by WITs. When mastered by students, these routines foster self-discipline and independence in your classroom, giving you more time and energy to teach.

Chapter 5 treats the subject of rubrics and shows how they can be used to raise expectations and ultimately student achievement, while Chapter 6 discusses how best to establish rules and choose rewards that build motivation and character. Finally, in Chapter 7, you will learn how to develop a personalized 3 + 3 = 33 plan for implementation in your classroom, whether at the elementary or secondary level. Examples are given from both levels.

In addition to the multiple routines, rubrics, and rules, you will also find advice, suggestions, and reflections from WITs regarding how they stay on top of, tuned in to, aware of, and in complete control of what's happening in their classrooms.

Special Features of This Book

How to Survive and Thrive in the First Three Weeks of School also contains a variety of special features—tips and ideas you can use tomorrow in your classroom:

- With-It Teachers' Roundtables—honest and practical observations from with-it teachers on the "big ideas" of each chapter
- Answers to frequently asked questions from both new and experienced teachers
- A With-It Teacher's (WIT's) List containing more than 200 time-savers, noise breakers, attention getters, silent signals, homework helpers, and menus to make it easier for you to convert your allocated teaching time to academic learning time

Acknowledgments

This book would not have been possible without the encouragement and support of dozens of highly effective principals throughout the country who generously identified and nominated the WITs in their schools and then encouraged them to complete a lengthy questionnaire regarding their classroom practices (see Resource B). However, in the end, the writing of this book depended on the collective wisdom and experience of close to 100 WITs from around the country. They devoted extraordinary amounts of energy and time to reflect on their teaching practices and write comprehensive answers. See Resource C for a complete list of the teacher contributors to this book.

I am appreciative of the following individuals who shared their wisdom by contributing answers to frequently asked questions: Cathie West, Joan Will, and Jeffery Lackney. Carol McCaig and Christine Steiner contributed the new teacher's perspective to the book. Debbie Hunsacker and Jeanette Jackson, experienced classroom teachers who now work with Reading First initiatives in Wyoming and Nebraska, contributed insights based on their frequent observations in primary classrooms.

A select group of WITs gave an extraordinary amount of their time and expertise to this book. They have inspired and instructed me throughout my writing. They are Judith Cimmiyotti, Susan Graham, Jay Pilkington, Michelle Perry, Darlene Carino, and Candace Darling.

A special thanks to Judith Cimmiyotti and Cathie West for their thoughtful reading of the manuscript in progress and for constructive feedback from their classroom and administrative perspectives.

Finally, I am profoundly grateful for the overflowing love, support, and encouragement I receive daily from my husband, business partner, and copy editor extraordinaire, E. Raymond Adkins. When deadlines loom and pressures mount, he is always there with a gentle word and a calming touch.

Corwin Press gratefully acknowledges the contributions of the following people:

Donna Adkins
Teacher
Louisa E. Perritt Primary School
Arkadelphia, AR

Roxie Ahlbrecht
Teacher
Robert Frost Elementary School
Sioux Falls, SD

Tyrone Olverson
Principal
Lincoln Heights Elementary School
Springdale, OH

Tim Persall
Principal
Arden Road Elementary School
Amarillo, TX

Kari Dahlquist
Principal
Creek Valley Elementary School
Edina, MN

Kathleen Thomas
Teacher
Caesar Rodney High School
Camden, DE

Laura Cumbee
Teacher
South Central Middle School
Cartersville, GA

Carrie Jane Carpenter
Teacher
Deschutes Edge Charter School
Redmond, OR

Denny R. Vincent
Principal
Muhlenberg North High School
Greenville, KY

Mark Murphy
Principal
Centennial Elementary School
Utica, NE

C. J. Huff
Superintendent of Schools
Eldon R–1 School District
Eldon, MO

Rosemarie I. Young
Principal/NAESP President
Watson Lane Elementary School
Louisville, KY

About the Author

**Elaine K. McEwan** is a partner and educational consultant with The McEwan-Adkins Group, offering workshops in instructional leadership, team building, and raising reading achievement K–12. A former teacher, librarian, principal, and assistant superintendent for instruction in a suburban Chicago school district, she is the author of more than thirty-five books for parents and educators. Her Corwin Press titles include *Leading Your Team to Excellence: Making Quality Decisions*; *The Principal's Guide to Attention Deficit Hyperactivity Disorder*; *How to Deal With Parents Who Are Angry, Troubled, Afraid, or Just Plain Crazy*; *The Principal's Guide to Raising Reading Achievement*; *Counseling Tips for Elementary School Principals* with Jeffrey A. Kottler; *Managing Unmanageable Students: Practical Solutions for Educators* with Mary Damer; *The Principal's Guide to Raising Math Achievement*; *Raising Reading Achievement in Middle and High Schools: Five Simple-to-Follow Strategies for Principals*; *10 Traits of Highly Effective Teachers: How to Hire, Mentor, and Coach Successful Teachers*; *Teach Them ALL to Read: Catching the Kids Who Fall Through the Cracks*; *7 Steps to Effective Instructional Leadership, 2nd Edition*; *Making Sense of Research: What's Good, What's Not, and How to Tell the Difference* with Patrick J. McEwan; *Ten Traits of Highly Effective Principals: From Good to Great Performance*; *Seven Strategies of Highly Effective Readers: Using Cognitive Research to Boost K–8 Achievement*; and *How to Deal With Teachers Who Are Angry, Troubled, Exhausted, or Just Plain Confused.*

Elaine was honored by the Illinois Principals Association as an outstanding instructional leader, by the Illinois State Board of Education with an Award of Excellence in the Those Who Excel Program, and by the National Association of Elementary School Principals as the National Distinguished Principal from Illinois for 1991. She received her undergraduate degree in education from Wheaton College and advanced degrees in library science (MA) and educational administration (EdD) from Northern Illinois University. She lives with her husband and business partner, E. Raymond Adkins, in Oro Valley, Arizona. Visit her Web site at www.elainemcewan.com where you can learn more about her writing and workshops and enroll in online seminars based on her books, or contact her directly at emcewan@elainemcewan.com.

Introduction

The essence of being an effective

teacher lies in knowing what to do to foster pupils'

learning and being able to do it.

—Kyriancou (1991, p. 1)

"Do you have any positive results yet?" I asked a high school principal who was implementing a ninth-grade drop-out prevention program.

"The numbers look good," she said, "but it was the day that Mr. McIntire's class taught itself that I knew we were onto something.

"I was scheduled to cover his first-period class so he could close on his new house," she explained. "But an emergency came up and I totally forgot."

When Mr. McIntire stopped in later to thank the principal for her thoughtful gesture, she had to confess that she had blown it.

"Who taught my class?" he asked, with a worried look, imagining 30 adolescents up to no good in the freshman wing.

Actually, Mr. McIntire's class taught itself. His students had mastered what he explicitly taught them during the first 3 weeks of the school year, and left on their own, they did what any well-taught class will do—followed his routines, rubrics, and rules to the letter. No one, not even the assistant principal who was doing an observation in the classroom next door, realized that Mr. M's class was flying solo. This incident is a perfect example of the "big idea" of this book—3 + 3 = 33—in action. Perhaps you doubt that *your* students are capable of the same level of self-direction, independence, and responsibility that Mr. McIntire's students displayed. However, you won't know until you implement 3 + 3 = 33 for yourself.

The "Big Idea" of 3 + 3 = 33

If you have played team sports or are a sports fan, you know the importance of effective coaching. Great coaches develop game plans. Their plans generally include practice routines for building basic skills, conditioning routines for developing strength and confidence, and set plays and strategies that team members have practiced to automaticity. When a game is close or the opposition puts on defensive pressure, players are able to draw on well-taught, intensively practiced routines mastered to perfection—how to inbound the basketball with only 3.1 seconds on the clock to make the game-winning shot, or how to create scoring opportunities when the other team has the ball and the clock is running down.

In your classroom, you are the "coach." You are responsible for developing a plan to maximize your students' academic success during the 36 weeks of the school year. In most states, standards and outcomes are prescribed in detail. But *how* you go about creating an environment to achieve those outcomes is up to you. You can either "wing it," or you can get "with-it." Teachers who wing it plan as they go. They are serendipitous and spontaneous. They go with the flow.

With-it teachers (WITs), on the other hand, are structured and organized. They are proactive pedagogues who know precisely how they want their students to "play" the academic game. Kounin (1970) coined the term "with-it-ness" and defined it as "overlappingness," the ability to multitask while teaching. Bullough (1989) later expanded the definition to include "the ability to simultaneously attend to a variety of stimuli and then to appropriately categorize what is observed and quickly respond in a way that will prevent disruption and maintain the flow of the lesson" (p. 47).

In *10 Traits of Highly Effective Teachers,* I expanded this definition of with-it-ness and included it as one of the ten traits of highly effective teachers: "the state of being on top of, tuned in to, aware of, and in complete control of three critical facets of classroom life: (1) the management and organization of the classroom, (2) the engagement of students, and (3) the management of time" (McEwan, 2002, p. 48). In the chapters ahead, I offer an even more expansive definition of with-it-ness: *the ability to preview, project, and predict the challenges and contingencies of an upcoming school year and proactively design a 3-week set of experiences to teach critical routines, rubrics, and rules that will prepare students for the rigors of mastering the desired content-area or grade-level outcomes.*

The premise of 3 + 3 = 33 is that the more consistently you teach your students the routines, rubrics, and rules (3Rs) of your classroom at the beginning of the school year (3 weeks), the more productive the rest of your year (33 weeks) will be. Instead of merely surviving the school year, you (and your students) will thrive. *You* will accomplish more because your students will be prepared to learn. *You* will have fewer discipline problems because your students will have mastered the rules. *You* will have more energy because your students will be carrying their share of the workload. Your principal will adore you. Parents will send you thank-you notes. Your colleagues will secretly envy you. But most important, your students will become high-achieving, self-reliant, independent, lifelong learners.

How to "Coach" Motivated and Attentive Students

There are at least three types of students in every classroom: (1) students who are attentive, motivated, and ready to learn; (2) students who could be attentive, motivated, and ready to learn, given a supportive classroom learning environment, and (3) students who have their own agendas and will readily take advantage of an unstructured and laissez-faire classroom to do what they please. Perhaps you have heard or even followed the advice given to teachers by some: "Don't smile until Christmas. Keep the kids guessing and on the edge of their seats, and you're guaranteed to be a successful teacher." There's absolutely no research to support the truth of this statement. But there are four research-based actions that *will* increase your likelihood of being a successful teacher: (1) Be proactive, (2) be nonassumptive, (3) be assertive, and (4) be instructionally relentless. If your goal is to have attentive, motivated, and high-achieving students, read on.

Be Proactive

There is no substitute for having a detailed plan as you head into any high-stakes, stressful, and complex endeavor, whether it is the first 3 weeks of a school year or the Super Bowl. Bill Belichick, three-time Super Bowl winning coach of the New England Patriots, is known for his meticulous preparation and planning. He believes that games are won before his players take the field (Hack, 2005). The Patriots' award-winning young quarterback, Tom Brady, is also proactive, described as "ritualistic in his approach and preparation" (Saraceno, 2005, p. 6C). WITs are exactly like Belichick and Brady: painstaking in their preparation and planning. The secret of their students' high achievement lies in their proactive approach. Proactive teachers instruct "carefully and strategically all that is required so that students will have the information necessary to behave appropriately [and achieve to their fullest potential]" (Kameenui & Darch, 1995, p. 3).

Be Nonassumptive

The biggest mistake many teachers make—both brand-new *and* experienced ones—is to launch into skills or content instruction without first teaching the 3Rs (routines, rubrics, and rules). They erroneously assume that their students *must* know how to line up, enter a classroom, study for a test, write a book report, greet the teacher, accept a compliment, organize a notebook, sharpen their pencils, or execute dozens of other routines, rubrics, and rules. Unless you explicitly model and explain the essential routines, rubrics, and rules for your classroom, the majority of your students will do what they have always done in the past.

Your goal is to be a nonassumptive teacher. My personal nominee for a Lifetime Nonassumptive Teacher Award is former UCLA basketball coach John Wooden. He is well known for his multiple NCAA national championships, but his approach to teaching the routines, rubrics, and rules of basketball to his teams is lesser known. The first thing Coach Wooden did each year was to conduct a clinic for his players on how to put on socks and tie shoes. He used that no-fail lesson plan: I Do, We Do It, You Do It, Apply It. Of course, most of the players on his teams were former high school basketball stars who had been putting on their socks and shoes for years. That wasn't the point. Wooden wanted his players to do it his way. He modeled how to "carefully roll the socks down over the toes, ball of the foot, arch, and around the heel, and then pull the sock up snug so there will be no wrinkles in it" (Wooden & Jamison, 1997, p. 60). He knew the importance of this simple routine to the health and well-being of his players' feet, and he wanted to make sure that an important game would never be lost because of painful blisters.

Take a moment to consider what specific student behavior (or lack thereof) is most problematic in your school. Then reflect on how you and your colleagues could design a lesson to teach students a better way to act—one that would produce long-term benefits, save time and energy by eliminating repetitious questions and answers, reduce noise or distractions, improve the quality of life for both students and teachers, and develop more responsible and independent learners. I asked participants in one of my workshops for their ideas regarding this issue, and Ryan Cross, Assistant Principal and Athletic Director of Fernley High School in Nevada, told the following story.

The biggest problem on our campus was the student parking lot. It was badly designed and covered with loose gravel. Attempts to regulate parking with concrete dividers only resulted in more creative parking formations by students. We had no money to upgrade the lot and countless memos to students and parents produced no improvement. Then a 100-year snowstorm created even more problems.

Back on the job after 5 snow days, Principal Sue Segura, her two assistants, Ryan and Pete Chapin, and the district's entire custodial staff donned safety vests and personally directed the parking of the students' cars according to a prescribed plan. The second morning, they repeated the process. On the third morning, they did it again. The custodial staff was growing a bit impatient, but the principal assured them that 4 days of supervised practice were needed for mastery. Sure enough, on the 5th day, every car was parked to perfection—without supervision.

Never assume that your students, no matter how old they are or how long they have attended your school, will figure out what you want them to do on their own. Even if you tell them what you want done or post announcements on flashing signboards, you may not get results. If you want your routines, rubrics, and rules to be habitually followed by your students, teach them explicitly and systematically, beginning on the first day.

Be Assertive

You may feel that being assertive and explicit with students, especially if you are a brand-new teacher, is too bossy or controlling. Never apologize, however, for being assertive in your classroom. Assertiveness is a mind-set that impacts the way you communicate (words) and behave (deeds) in your everyday (habitual) interactions with students. It is a positive, forthright approach to teaching that stands in stark contrast to less effective teaching styles characterized by aggressiveness or hesitancy. [The term *assertiveness* as used here should not be confused with the student management system, *assertive discipline*.]

Jill Aspegren is an assertive teacher. Here's how she describes her classroom environment and relationships with students:

> **I am in charge in my classroom. I make that clear from the beginning. When I step into my "teaching space," the area around my stool, I expect all talking to stop. I wait, but I do not speak until it is absolutely quiet and my students are attentive. I teach them to look me in the eyes, sit up straight in their chairs, and place their hands on their desks.**
>
> **My students respect my teaching time because I don't require absolute silence when they are working independently. I ask for a "workable" level of quiet, and my students respect that. Adults in offices rarely work in complete silence, so I don't expect that of my students. I am tough on them during the first few weeks of the school year. I take the time to teach them every little routine and idiosyncrasy of my classroom. But then I give them freedom to learn. I establish myself as the leader, but I also spend a lot of time developing relationships with my students. I ask questions about their lives, notice the small things they do, and give them lots of individual attention. I think it is the balance between my strength [assertiveness] *and* my willingness to enter into relationships that allows us to develop as a learning community.**

Be Positively Relentless

In my workshops, I humorously describe two categories of teachers: truckers and RVers. I came up with these labels based on two sets of experiences I've had: supervising teachers during my career as an educator *and* driving on the interstate highways of every state in the country during the past decade as a consultant. Each category of drivers has a unique approach to driving, not unlike their educational counterparts. The drivers of RVs are, for the most part, relaxed. They are free to meander, stop for leisurely lunches, or camp where the fishing looks good. On the other hand, truckers are bound by a schedule and tied to a destination. They have no time for serendipitous side trips.

Similar to their over-the-road counterparts, trucker teachers are constantly moving in the direction of their destination. They don't waste time, and their trips are carefully mapped every mile of the way. Here's what one trucker teacher had to say: "I think it's important to give children a sense of urgency . . . places to go, people to meet, things to do. I often tell my students, 'Life is full of deadlines, and our work is almost always evaluated on our ability to finish within a given time frame.'"

In contrast, RV teachers are unfocused and easily distracted. All teachers have moments of RV teaching. But when that approach is the norm, it's time to get back on the road. Trucker teachers are instructionally relentless.

The term *relentless* has two sets of meanings. There is the negative connotation found in adjectives like *punishing* and *ruthless*. But there is also a highly positive set of meanings that includes *uncompromising, persistent,* and *insistent.* WITs are instructionally relentless in the most positive sense. They refuse to give in or give up when it comes to teaching and learning. Kameenui & Darch (1995) call this mind-set "instructional tenacity" (p. 13). Unless you are *positively* relentless, your students will lose irreplaceable opportunities to learn.

The Research Support for 3 + 3 = 33

There is a substantial body of correlational research to support the worth of the concepts inherent in the 3 + 3 = 33 game plan. Tables I.1 and I.2 summarize a set of studies conducted from 1977 to 1983 on the topics of classroom management and effective instruction. While correlation research does not meet the "gold" standard of experimental (i.e., scientific) research as defined in the No Child Left Behind Act (NCLB), the consistent findings of these studies across many grade levels, schools, and locations make them noteworthy. Table I.3 condenses the findings of three major reviews of the research.

Table I.1 Correlational Research on Effective Classroom Management and Teaching

Researchers/ Authors	Topic	Instructional Practices Associated With Increased Student Achievement
Kounin (1977)	Characteristics of effective teachers	1. Teacher is able to deal with several things at once 2. Teacher judges quickly whether an event in the classroom is important or unimportant 3. Teacher exhibits an ongoing awareness of all that is happening in the classroom despite numerous distractions 4. Teacher times actions carefully for maximum effect 5. Teacher maintains group focus by giving attention to more than one student at a time 6. Teacher manages movement within the classroom by structuring student transitions
Emmer, Evertson, and Anderson (1979)	Teaching behaviors of effective teachers at the beginning of the school year	1. Teacher maximizes personal contact with students 2. Teacher monitors students' attitudes, behaviors, and work habits frequently 3. Teacher intervenes quickly to deal with behavior problems 4. Teacher ensures high levels of time on task 5. Teacher provides frequent and detailed feedback 6. Teacher structures activities and materials carefully 7. Teacher uses signaling systems during instruction 8. Teacher establishes clear routines and expectations 9. Teacher rehearses with the students the behaviors that match those expectations 10. Teacher reduces the structure as students master the routines
Emmer and Evertson (1980)	Effective management/higher achievement in JHS	1. Teacher develops a workable system of rules 2. Teacher systematically and thoroughly teaches rules and routines 3. Teacher carefully monitors pupil behavior and quickly stops inappropriate behavior 4. Teacher gives clear directions and holds students accountable 5. Teacher stops disruptive behavior, rarely ignoring it when it occurs 6. Teacher maintains high on-task rates during the first three weeks of school

Table I.2 More Correlational Research on Effective Classroom Management and Teaching

Researchers/ Authors	Topic	Instructional Practices Associated With Increased Student Achievement
Anderson, Everston, and Emmer (1979); Emmer and Evertson (1980); Emmer, Evertson, and Anderson (1980)	Classroom organization and effective teaching	1. Teacher analyzes the tasks of the first few weeks in detail and predicts what will confuse or distract students 2. Teacher presents rules, procedures, expectations, and assignments to students in a clear, detailed manner and establishes classroom routines 3. Teacher establishes a system of student accountability for behavior and academic work 4. Teacher consistently monitors student behavior and work and provides feedback on its appropriateness
Evertson (1982)	The power of teaching and reinforcing rules	Teachers who spend the first week teaching the rules, carefully monitoring, and consistently enforcing have fewer discipline problems during the year.
Emmer and Evertson (1980)	The power of having and teaching rules and consequences to students	Effective classroom managers have clearly defined rules and procedures to regulate the structure and flow of their classrooms. They explicitly teach students under what circumstances they can interrupt the teacher, when it is appropriate and not appropriate to be out of their seats, and when conversation is appropriate with fellow students.
Duckett et al. (1980)	Most effective approaches to classroom management	1. Teacher builds group cohesiveness and consensus 2. Teacher establishes academic emphasis 3. Teacher develops positive teacher-student and student-student relationships
Wise and Okey (1983)	The power of focusing on learning objectives	The effective classroom appears to be the one in which the students are kept aware of instructional objectives and receive feedback on their progress toward these objectives.

Table I.3   Reviews of Research on Effective Teaching

Researchers/ Authors	Topic	Instructional Practices Associated With Increased Student Achievement
Brophy (1999)	Synthesis of the principles of effective teaching	1. A supportive classroom climate 2. Curricular alignment 3. Thoughtful discourse (questions and discussion about "big ideas") 4. Scaffolding (the provision of help for struggling students) 5. Goal-oriented assessment 6. High and consistent expectations for achievement
Marzano, Gaddy, and Dean (2000)	Instructional approaches that improve student achievement	1. Identifying similarities and differences (e.g., comparing, classifying, creating metaphors and analogies) 2. Teaching summarizing and note taking 3. Reinforcing effort and providing recognition 4. Assigning homework and providing guided practice 5. Using nonlinguistic representations (graphic organizers) 6. Facilitating cooperative learning that is carefully structured and monitored 7. Engaging students in goal setting and providing feedback regarding progress 8. Generating and testing hypotheses 9. Activating prior knowledge
Walberg and Paik (2003)	Nine instructional practices that work in K–12 settings	1. Giving students feedback on homework 2. Focusing instruction on specific learning goals 3. Providing direct instruction to include sequencing of lessons, guided practice, and immediate feedback 4. Making connections between past and present learning and alerting students to the main ideas 5. Teaching learning strategies 6. Tutoring students one-to-one 7. Insisting that students master foundational concepts and skills before moving on to new learning 8. Teaching cooperative learning techniques and expecting students to work in cooperative learning groups 9. Combining approaches like tutoring, mastery learning, cooperative learning, and strategic instruction

Definitions You Need to Know

There are a variety of specialized terms used throughout this book. Some, although familiar in other contexts, will be used in new ways in the chapters ahead. Before you begin Chapter 1, take a few moments for a brief vocabulary lesson.

Routines

Routines are *desired patterns of behavior—procedures that are executed by either teachers or students.* Examples of routines that WITs regularly teach (i.e., model and explain) to lower elementary students include how to line up and how to sit quietly on the rug during direct instruction. Typical routines that all upper elementary and secondary students need for academic success include how to obtain assignments and class notes if absent or what to do immediately upon entering the classroom. WITs expect the procedures they teach to become habits their students can execute without thinking (e.g., what to do during a fire drill or lockdown, how to line up for dismissal at the end of the period).

Rubrics

The meaning of the term *rubric,* as used in this book and in the field of education generally, is more complex than the one-word definition you will find in any dictionary: *rule.* In schools, rubrics are *continuums of quality or completeness against which teachers and students measure and evaluate behavior and work products.* Classroom rubrics are clearly articulated expectations of teachers for students, of students for themselves, and students for teachers (if applicable). For example, a work product rubric might describe the qualities and characteristics of a paragraph, an essay, a bulletin board display, or an oral presentation, giving specific information about both the most acceptable and least acceptable versions.

Without rubrics, students are left to guess regarding what their work or behavior should look like. Motivated students must be mind readers to figure out what the teacher wants, and students who don't care will fill the standards vacuum with inappropriate work and behavior. Without rubrics, teachers are forced to be arbitrary in their evaluation of student work and behavior, creating feelings of uncertainty and anxiety in their students. Similar to routines, rubrics are often enhanced and supported by the use of teacher *prompts* and helpful *props.*

Rules (and Rewards)

Rules are *authoritative principles set forth to guide behavior in classrooms.* They constitute the code of conduct for both students and teachers. Along with rules often come rewards, *positive things that follow a desired response and act to encourage desired behavior.* Rewards are controversial in many circles, and we later explore a more comprehensive meaning of rewards that goes well beyond stickers and suckers.

How the With-It Teachers Were Identified

In the pages ahead, you will meet close to 100 WITs from around the country. They teach a variety of subjects and grade levels (K–12). The majority of respondents were nominated by their principals, who used the definition of a with-it teacher found earlier in this Introduction as their selection criteria. A smaller group of teachers was recommended by instructional specialists, literacy coaches, and consultants who had observed the WITs directly in their classrooms. In a few cases, I selected the teachers based on direct knowledge and observations of their teaching. In three instances, principals invited all of their staff members to complete the questionnaire and a small number of teachers out of the total faculty self-selected into the sample.

There were 341 nominations, and I sent the With-It Teacher Questionnaire, found in Resource B, to each one via e-mail. In some cases, technical difficulties resulted in returned e-mails, slightly reducing the number of the original sample. Ninety-seven teachers returned responses via e-mail, fax, and postal mail. For purposes of collating their overall responses and choosing specific quotation, examples, and vignettes, I divided the teachers into two grade-level groups: K–5 (Elementary) and 6–12 (Secondary). About 55% of the respondents fell in the elementary group and 45% fell in the secondary group. These percentages are nearly identical to the percentage of elementary and secondary teachers found in the 3.8 million teachers in the United States (Bureau of Labor Statistics, 2004–2005). The names and specific grade levels of the respondents are found in Resource C.

The length of each response varied widely; the questions were open-ended, and individuals were given the option to skip questions to which answers did not immediately come to mind based on their personal teaching practices. The length of the completed questionnaires ranged from 3 to 18 pages (8 ½" × 11" single-spaced typewritten pages in 12 pt. Times New Roman font). I queried more than 50% of the respondents, asking for more detail regarding specific classroom practices. They responded by sending seating charts, sample lesson plans, brochures, handbooks, rubrics, checklists, rating scales, PowerPoint programs, and photographs to me.

How With-It Teachers Teach

Given that the nominators (mostly principals and colleagues who knew the teachers and had observed them personally) selected possible participants

using a set of common criteria (i.e., my definition of a with-it teacher),
I expected to find common themes and practices among the respondents
regarding how they approached classroom management and instruction.
Furthermore, I expected to find that the classroom management and
instructional techniques of the WITs as reflected in their responses were
similar to those identified in teacher effectiveness literature as displayed in
Tables I.1–I.3. That was the case in both instances. The following beliefs,
words, and deeds are evident in the classroom management and instructional
techniques of WITs as reflected in their responses:

- They believe that all of their students are capable of learning if taught well.
- They believe they can teach anything to any child.
- They are consistent and predictable.
- They believe in routines and spend the first few weeks of school modeling
  and explaining these routines to their students, whether 5-year-olds or
  freshmen.
- They are self-disciplined and organized.
- They do not waste time.
- They model and use cooperative learning on a daily basis but consistently
  hold individual students personally accountable.
- They intentionally model and explain character traits they believe are
  important to success in school and in life.
- They intentionally model cognitive processing (i.e., their own thinking and
  problem solving).
- They inspire, motivate, and affirm their students.
- They are specific and consistent regarding their academic and behavioral
  expectations.
- They intentionally explain and model these expectations from the moment
  their students enter their classrooms in September.
- They do not threaten, patronize, or excuse their students.
- They are proactive and plan ahead.
- They are highly metacognitive, able to describe in great detail exactly what
  they do, why they do it, and what the results are.

Acronyms You Need to Know

Acronyms are used throughout the book as replacements for frequently repeated
words and phrases. This is a publishing convention that saves space and time,
as well as facilitating the reading process for you. *WIT* stands for with-it teacher,
and *WITs* stands for with-it teachers. *3Rs* stands for routines, rubrics, and rules.
To help you place the WITs in their respective grade-level contexts, I indicate
specific grade levels and content areas in the vignettes and examples, and in the

Roundtables and direct quotes, I use the following designations: *E* for Grades K–5 and *S* for Grades 6–12.

You will find a variety of figures (seating charts, floor plans, lesson plans, instructional materials, and rubrics) throughout the book. They are numbered consecutively within each chapter. For example, Chapter 1's figures are numbered 1.1, 1.2, and so on.

There are also tables (summaries of research or informational items related to the book). You have already encountered several of those in the Introduction. They are also numbered consecutively within each chapter. So in Chapter 1, for example, you will encounter Figure 1.1, Catherine's Floor Plan, and also Table 1.1, Research on Task Engagement.

What's Ahead?

In the chapters ahead, you will discover in more precise and specific terms exactly how you can become a WIT, a teacher who is able to survive and thrive based on how you teach your routines, rubrics, and rules during the first 3 weeks of the school year. You will have the collective wisdom of 97 with-it teachers to show you how to develop a $3 + 3 = 33$ plan for yourself. You will gain a new excitement and a growing sense of empowerment as you realize that you hold the keys to your students' academic success.

Chapter 1

Creating Spaces for Teaching and Learning

It is difficult, if not impossible, to separate

instructional activity from the physical environmental

setting within which it occurs.

—Lackney & Jacobs (2005, p. 1)

An aesthetically pleasing and fully functional classroom is your secret weapon in the ongoing battle to both close the achievement gap and raise overall student achievement. In fact, a current early childhood perspective based on the internationally acclaimed preschools in the town of Reggio Emilia, Italy, considers the environment to be "another teacher" (New, 2000).

No matter how old your students are, the physical environment of your classroom impacts their behavior and attitudes (Gump, 1987; McGuffey, 1982). In fact, most teachers believe that the cleanliness, orderliness, and character of their campuses influence not only their students' behavior (Lackney, 1996) but also their ability to teach.

The first step in developing your 3 + 3 = 33 plan is to visualize the physical layout in which you will teach and then design the optimum teaching and learning environment. (The 3 + 3 = 33 plan is described in complete detail in Chapter 7 if you are the kind of reader who needs to know how the book ends before you can start Chapter 1.) If you don't yet have your own classroom, let your imagination soar. However, once you are hired, be prepared to face reality. If you are currently teaching in a classroom that is hindering your ability to be a with-it teacher (WIT), think about what you have the power to change that will improve it.

This concept of the environment as a second teacher isn't applicable just to preschool classrooms in Italy. In an ideal world, all teachers would have state-of-the-art "second teacher" classrooms with functional furniture, ample storage, and wireless technology (Zernike, 2001). But in the real world, the responsibility for creating an inviting and workable learning space usually falls on *your* shoulders. In many instances, your mission may seem to be an impossible one. Even if you are faced with space more suited to storage than study, paint that is older than your great-grandmother, and furniture that is nailed to the floor, change the things you *can* change and cope with the things you can't. It's the first step in your journey toward becoming a WIT.

This chapter discusses two aspects of the classroom environment: (1) how to allocate and create classroom space that supports teaching and learning and (2) how, where, and with whom to seat students. But first, let's look at some of the challenges you will face.

The Challenges of Creating a Supportive Learning Environment

Regrettably, many aspects of your classroom environment are fixed. For example, the floor space and windows (or lack of) in your classroom can't be changed. Oh, new furniture *can* be purchased or requisitioned from a distant warehouse, and the thermostat *might* be able to be adjusted a degree or two. But those of us who have taught in aging and overcrowded buildings located in underfunded school districts can tell you: "What you see is usually what you get—at least for your foreseeable future."

High school teacher Marjorie Wood knows the feeling. She teaches Resource English on a campus with six buildings of varying vintages. Marjorie's building has been around for more than 100 years. She is realistic but not pessimistic about the drawbacks of her classroom. In a former incarnation, it was a science lab: Three gas jets still jut out of the floor as a reminder. With the typical can-do spirit of a WIT, Marjorie moved her desk over two of the jets and pushed a file cabinet over the third. "The pipes aren't that bad," she says. She does chuckle, however, when she reads books that recommend where to position the teacher's desk to maximize learning (Keller, 2004, p. 14).

Marjorie describes her classroom this way: "I have no control over the furniture in my classroom, and the placement of outlets and equipment for technology may have made sense to the electricians, but it's incomprehensible to me." Forget smart screens and whiteboards. Marjorie has a six-part slate board that opens like the pages of a book. It's a fabulous classroom for an antique lover, but how does a 21st-century teacher cope? With a healthy sense of humor and instructional tenacity!

Marjorie doesn't worry about the things she *can't* change. She's done the best she can with her environment, and as a "trucker teacher" (see the Introduction if you've forgotten the definition), she is focused on teaching her students how to apply learning strategies to mastering the challenging content of their academic classes (University of Kansas, 2005). Marjorie views these strategies as learning tools, and in keeping with that theme, she has placed an actual toolbox on the counter from which she frequently pulls out a tool to make a point. Posters containing prompts (questions or acronyms) cover her walls to remind students how to apply the strategies in various contexts. Marjorie is a WIT.

It's up to you to make your space work, even with all of its limitations! In Marjorie's case, it was as simple as buying the toolbox, hanging up a few posters, pushing the desks into groups of four, and planning her lessons. Of course there are those teachers whose classrooms are more spacious and well appointed. Their options for beautification seem endless, and they decorate and furnish with a passion. Primary teacher Carol Howell falls into that category:

> **I enjoy making my classroom comfortable with potted plants, lamps, and an old rocking chair. I have the good fortune of having wonderful windows with high ceilings. I put up the blinds and leave the windows unobscured. Natural light is refreshing. My classroom is filled with children's art—both framed and unframed. Even our agreed-upon classroom rules are illustrated by students.**

The extent to which Carol goes in her quest to create a warm and inviting classroom is rarely possible at the middle or high school levels where classrooms are smaller and students are bigger. But that doesn't let secondary teachers off the hook completely.

Middle school teacher Val Bresnahan is fascinated with the Chinese art of feng shui and for good reasons. Special education teachers often get the leftovers when it comes to classroom assignments, and they need all the help they can get. [Note: Feng shui is pronounced *fung shway* and is the art of positioning objects (e.g., furniture, plants, pictures) in one's surroundings to enhance the flow of energy in a space or in one's life.]

Val explains her educational approach to feng shui:

> **Before school starts, I spend time in my classroom envisioning the teaching I will be doing and the students with whom I will be working. I arrange the room so it is not only visually appealing and balanced but works well for instruction. Sometimes, once the actual students arrive, what I planned**

doesn't work, so I have to rethink my vision. The classroom has to be balanced, though.

For 7 years of my teaching career, I shared a classroom with another special ed teacher *and* a music teacher. There were four pianos in the room (two in the middle) and a set of three-tiered risers adjacent to my desk. There were 32 desks that had to be positioned just the way the music teacher wanted them. This just did not work for me. I was not as effective as I could have been because I couldn't design space that met the learning needs of my students. I did not realize what a powerful effect the environment had on me until this year, when I have my own, albeit much smaller, classroom.

Even though Val's new classroom *was* formerly known as the broom closet, it belongs to her, and she has been able to add plants, arrange the furniture, *and* use the walls to meet both her and her students' needs.

Val isn't the only WIT who is fascinated by feng shui. Third-grade teacher Michelle O'Laughlin became interested in this ancient art after she had her home rearranged by a feng shui consultant. She immediately applied one of the principles at school by positioning her desk diagonally facing the door, in what is called a "Welcoming Position." She draped it in colorful fabric, placed a plant on the corner closest to the door, and waited for reactions. "You wouldn't believe how many comments I've received," she reports. Although feng shui is one of the more unusual approaches to arranging classroom space, its principles frequently have some basis in common sense or accepted principles of design. But if the concept is a little too far out for you, don't worry. It isn't the only way to think about arranging your classroom.

How to Allocate, Arrange, and Use Classroom Space

School architects and designers call the creation and re-creation of classroom space by teachers *placemaking.* You are a *placemaker,* an individual who creates a place that supports teaching and learning to the greatest extent possible. There are two approaches to designing and utilizing space in schools: (1) territorial and (2) functional (Lackney & Jacobs, 2005).

The territorial approach, as its name implies, is based on "individual ownership" of space and furniture. Students *and* teachers have desks in which to store their materials, and if students move around in the classroom, they take their desks or chairs with them. In contrast, functional arrangements partition the physical space into interest areas or learning centers available to all students such as would be found in the typical early childhood classroom or a school with open classrooms where students move freely from place to place. For example, in a functional classroom, the activities in which students are engaged dictate their physical location. During small-group instruction, they may move to a table at the back of the room. During a read-aloud, they sit on a carpeted area. In a territorial setting, students engage in the same kinds of activities but remain with their desks.

The pendulum has swung back and forth over the years regarding the preferred way to design space. My take on this issue is this, after watching an entire district tear down walls in several buildings (including a high school) and then rebuild them several years later after teacher and parent complaints overwhelmed the administration: It's not an either-or decision. All classrooms (and schools) need *both* territorial (private) *and* functional (group) spaces for teachers *and* students.

Q and A

Kelly Neumeister (E): How can I create a more spacious feeling in my small classroom?

Jill Yates (E): In order to use space efficiently and accommodate the frequent changes of pace in my instructional day (from independent to partner to small-group to large-group activities), I prefer the fewest possible pieces of furniture in the classroom. I have a desk for each student, three tables for small-group activities, art and computer centers, one small couch, and a large number of low bookcases. I learned during my first 2 years that my "teacher" desk and the extra tables in the room only collected piles of paper. In addition, they impeded the flow of traffic as we moved our desks around. So I got rid of them. My priority space is a large carpeted gathering area on the floor, and we spend a lot of time there. If you have too many cubbies, corners, and tables, it creates a cramped and cluttered atmosphere.

Elementary teachers generally have more flexibility to create both kinds of space and to do it on a more permanent basis. Their classrooms are larger, often lending themselves to the creation of homey, family-like atmospheres. In addition, elementary teachers usually work with one group of children all day, allowing more opportunities for using a variety of functional spaces. In contrast, secondary students travel to and from various functional centers (e.g., band room, technology center, science and computer labs), so their specialist teachers can enjoy territorial spaces especially designed for their content areas.

If you are feeling a bit confused about how teachers in self-contained classrooms create both territorial and functional spaces for their students, let's visit a classroom to see how it's done. Second-grade teacher Catherine Clausen handles multiple territorial and functional spaces with an ease that belies the complexity of its design. Her classroom floor plan is shown in Figure 1.1.

Student desks are grouped in fours (called *table groups* because the four desks form a flat table surface when pushed together), but there is also a mini-U of eight desks at the front of the room, where students who need extra help or supervision during direct instruction can be close to the teacher's watchful eyes. Students seated in the U face the least distracting area of the classroom for independent work. Students do have their own *personal* desks (i.e., they are in charge of their own books and supplies) but also enjoy the flexibility of moving to other places and working with students other than their tablemates throughout the school day.

During reading and math, one of the table groups is turned into a teaching station for Catherine or a volunteer. The students who are seated there know that from time to time, they will have to find an empty desk or workspace in the classroom. These shifts in seating during the day give students opportunities to practice making wise choices. Developing students' decision-making skills is one of Catherine's goals, and she and her class often reflect on what has gone well during independent work periods as well as what needs improvement.

"If I were to have a group that for some reason couldn't learn to make wise choices about where to sit," Catherine says, "I would have assigned seating all day long. But I let the tether out as far as I can and still maintain a climate of focused thinking and learning." Lest you get the impression that Catherine's space-shifting routines somehow magically happen, she hastens to explain, "I teach all of my procedures [routines] *explicitly* at the beginning of the year and we practice, practice, and practice some more." Additional information about Catherine's routines will be found later in the book.

Although secondary WITs have fewer options when it comes to designing their environments, they manage to be every bit as creative as Catherine is in second grade. Middle school social studies teacher Jay Pilkington arranges his classroom in five rows of four to six desks, an ostensibly "old-fashioned" seating plan. But Jay's utilization of this plan is flexible and functional.

Each row has a designated leader (the student in the first seat) and a caboose (the student in the last seat) who perform certain duties. Jay uses the five-row format (with an even number of students in each row) to support

Figure 1.1 Catherine's Floor Plan

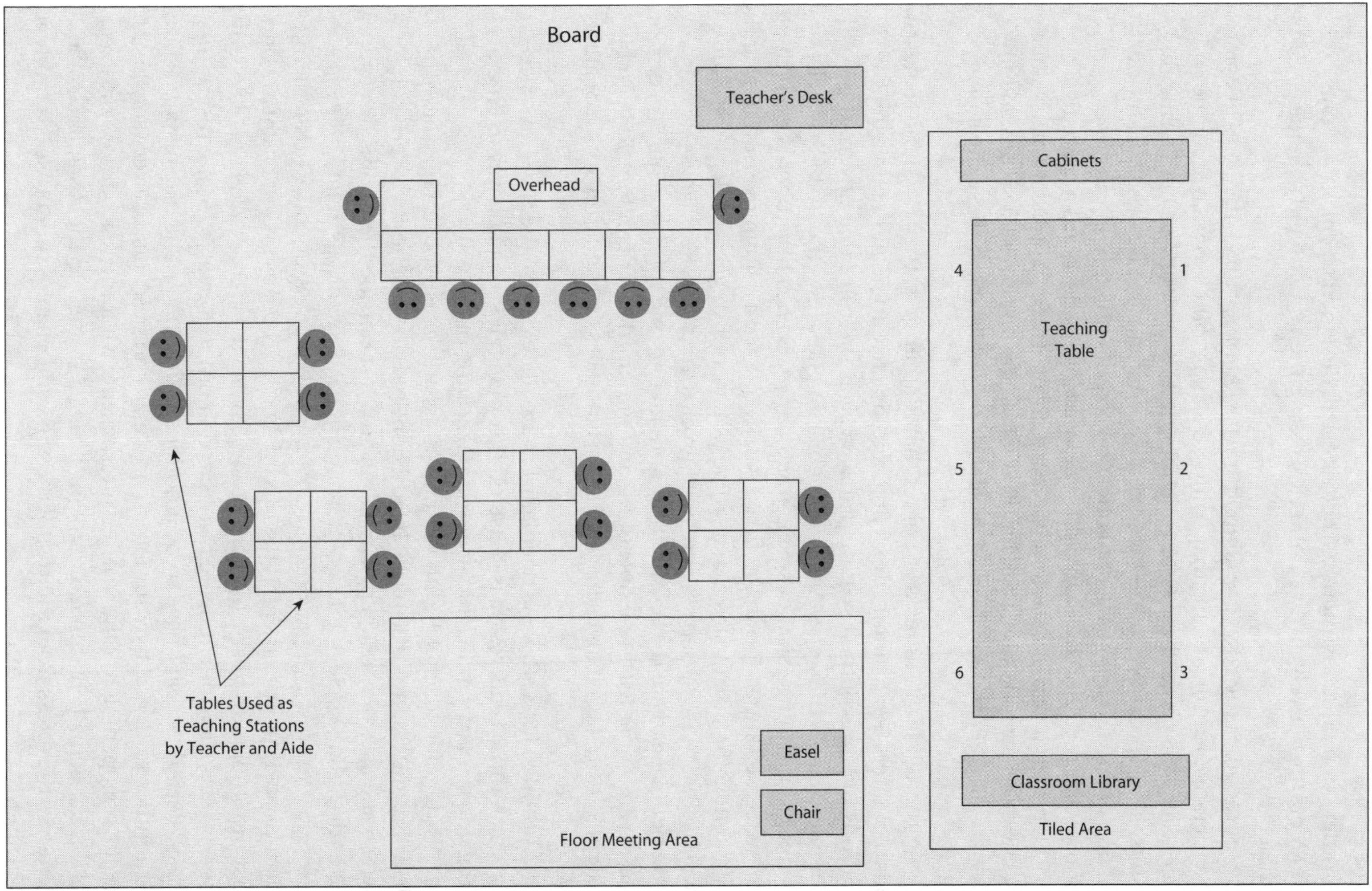

SOURCE: Reprinted by permission of Catherine Clausen.

a variety of unique instructional activities, all designed to ensure that his students are actively involved and processing the content and "big ideas" of his subject.

Sometimes the rows break up into pairs. At other times the rows become cooperative learning teams that compete against other rows in a unique version of the game show *Family Feud*, titled "Row Feud" by Jay. During this unusual cooperative-competitive exercise, students can be observed furiously taking notes, finding answers to questions, and ultimately sharing and comparing their findings. On another day each row becomes a piece of a cooperative "jigsaw" as students prepare group presentations on an assigned section of a textbook unit. Still another small-group activity, also designed by Jay, is called "Read, Revel, and Reveal." More details about these intriguing activities can be found in Chapter 4.

Although Jay's students are older than Catherine's, they need the same kind of intense explaining, modeling, and practice to help them master the various nuances of their seating plan as well as the rules that govern the learning games they play. An avid baseball fan, Jay views the first few weeks of school as the fall version of spring training. He teaches his students everything they need to know during the first 3 weeks to have a winning season during the remaining 33. Jay explains that at some point during every week, the students will be able to work in pairs and small groups, *and* play Row Feud—a competitive activity that is one third note taking, one third pop quiz (everyone has to answer at least one question), and one third just plain fun! To keep his lineups fresh, Jay changes his seating assignments each quarter with a Seating Chart Lottery.

Although Jay's students definitely have assigned seats, the physical space in which those seats reside is constantly changing. It's a unique way to create functional space within a highly territorial seating plan.

Sixth-grade teacher Judith Cimmiyotti creates space for teaching and learning and also for discipline. In addition to space around the overhead, which she calls her "teaching circle," an area just outside the door is designated as a "discipline circle." "I don't intermingle teaching and discipline," she explains, "especially in a whole-group setting. If I have students who are being disruptive, I speak to them in the discipline circle because I don't want anyone but the student to hear what I am saying. I believe it creates a feeling of security, not only for the student being disciplined in private but also for the rest of the class, since they don't have to be emotionally drawn into the disciplinary action of another student. Many students, particularly adolescents, are very sensitive to what is happening to others, often internalizing what the teacher says or does as if it has actually happened to them. Taking a student to the discipline circle removes the stress from the rest of the class and enables them to focus on their learning."

In addition to allocating, arranging, and utilizing classroom space, WITs must also determine how, where, and with whom their students will sit.

How, Where, and With Whom Your Students Sit

The First Decision: Arranging Your Furniture

In the ideal school, you would be able to request tables (some round and some rectangular) and chairs for cooperative work, a half dozen study carrels for the increasing numbers of students who need their own "office space" in which to work, and enough desks for all students to have individual seating during direct instruction and test taking.

JoAnne Deshon's third-grade classroom has the right kind of furniture and enough space to make any teacher happy. She has arranged the room in territorial pods of six desks (for five students, with the extra desk holding supplies, book tubs, and the ever-present box of tissues). See her seating plan in Figure 1.2. There is also ample room for functional space: a table for quiet work behind a bookshelf, a table near the writing area for peer conferences, a large rug for read-alouds, and three computers, with two chairs at every computer. At test-taking time, students move their desks into rows. [Note: While this arrangement requires one student in each pod to turn his or her chair to see the teacher, whiteboard, or screen, JoAnne notes that she chooses the students who sit in these seats carefully and is sensitive about where she stands during direct instruction. When she has more than 20 students, some of the supply desks become seats for students, or she forms a smaller pod of three students.] JoAnne is fortunate. She has the space and the furniture she requires to implement the seating arrangement that works best for her teaching and the learning needs of her students.

Remember, there are no right or wrong answers when it comes to choosing furniture. The success of *what* you do ultimately depends upon *how* you do it. The next section addresses some critical issues to consider when it comes to choosing a seating plan for your students.

The Second Decision: Developing Your Default Seating Plan

The secret to becoming a WIT is to find the optimum way to work with the furniture that's been supplied in the room to which you've been assigned. The second decision to make is how you will arrange the desks or tables to begin the school year. This seating arrangement becomes your *default* seating

Figure 1.2   JoAnne's Seating Plan

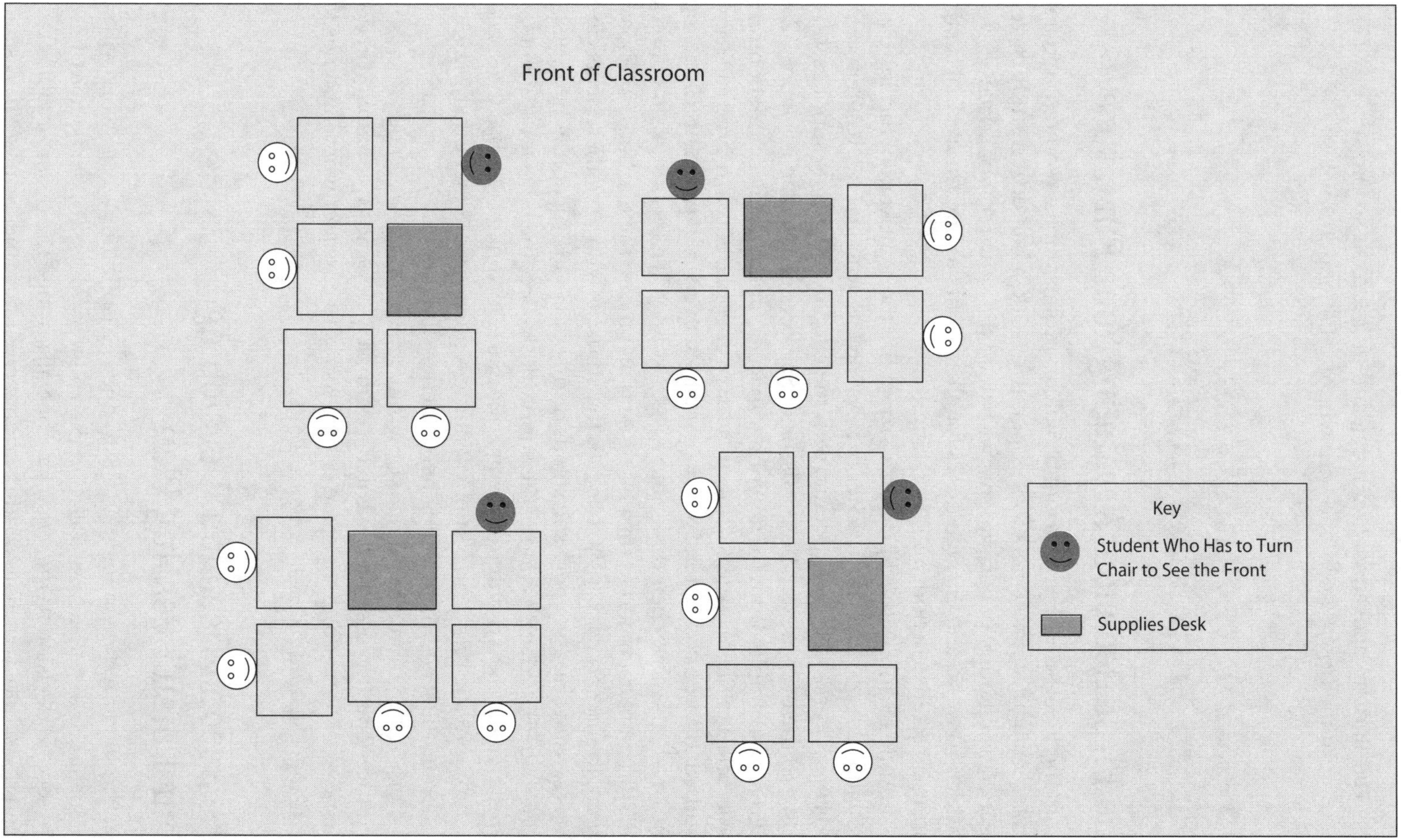

Front of Classroom

Key

Student Who Has to Turn
Chair to See the Front

Supplies Desk

plan, the one to which your students will ultimately return at the end of the day or period or after you have completed a specific instructional activity. If you plan to have a seating chart (and it is a good way to learn students' names unless you label their desks or give them name tags on the first day), the default seating plan is the one to which their names will be assigned. For example, Catherine's default plan is the four-desk table group shown in Figure 1.1 while Jay's default plan is the five-row configuration described earlier.

Consider the following questions as you think about what will work best for you and a typical class of students. Choose a seating plan that builds on your strengths as a teacher.

1. What teaching methodologies do you plan to use (direct instruction, group discussion, centers, cooperative learning, paired discussion)?
2. What types of assignments and tasks do you expect students to do (individual, group, partner, written, spoken)?
3. Are your learning outcomes more process or product oriented? Or both?
4. Are you trained to teach your students the routines they need to be successful in a cooperative seating plan?
5. What is the optimum placement of seating for students to see the screen, board, TV, or teacher without having to move their heads or their bodies?
6. Do you expect students to move their desks into different configurations based on specific activities you will use on a regular basis?
7. Do you have a lesson plan for teaching your students *how* to move their desks and then how to put them back in their original spots?
8. What kinds of materials are needed to support your seating arrangement and will they be community or personal materials?
9. Have you been trained in how to use cooperative learning techniques so that you can model and explain to your students the skills they require to be successful interdependent learners?
10. Do most of your students have the maturity levels and social skills to handle a default cooperative seating arrangement?
11. How many students in your classroom need some type of preferential seating to meet special learning needs (e.g., ELL, learning disabilities, autism, physical disabilities, or ADHD)?
12. How many students will have the services of a full-time instructional aide? Where will you seat that individual to maximize learning for everyone?
13. How many students are struggling academically and require ongoing one-to-one attention?

14. What are the major sources of ambient noise in your classroom (e.g., heating or cooling fan, lavatory, door to the hallway, an open classroom or team-teaching setting)? Have you sat in every seat to see if students' ability to hear will be compromised in any particular location? Are there students with hearing impairments that may need a classroom amplification system?

15. How much flexibility do you have for the creation of permanent functional spaces (e.g., comfortable reading nook with rug for stories, several study carrels for private "office space" for students, kidney-shaped table for small-group instruction, technology area for computers)?

16. Are there any safety hazards that must be considered when placing the furniture (e.g., cords, plugs, pipes, doorways)? Are all room exits clear in case of emergencies?

17. Is there plenty of space for you and your students to move about the room without bumping into each other or furniture?

18. Is there enough room for students to move their desks into various configurations throughout the day?

19. How quickly can you move to each of your students to answer questions or give individual help?

20. Is there enough room for privacy during test-taking situations?

21. Can you see everything that is happening from every vantage point in your classroom? (These questions were developed with advice and input from Jill Yates.)

Even after you have painstakingly prepared a seating chart for the first day of school based on your answers to the preceding questions, you may have to change it. What works for someone else, what you were told in your education classes, or even what has worked for you in the past may not work at all with a particular group of students.

Third-grade teacher Julie Elting says, "Until this school year, I've had tables with four students sharing a table. I began the year in clustered groups, but I have a very chatty class, and a lot of my students have focusing issues. I've had to change to rows with all of the desks facing the front whiteboard area. Although it seems rather old-fashioned, it works for this particular class."

Even students who will eventually be able to handle the distractions of sitting close to other classmates may need a full series of modeled lessons and lots of practice before their cooperative efforts will be productive. Many WITs begin the year with desks in rows, and some have found that for certain subjects and certain groups of students, learning is maximized when their desks remain that way for the entire year *unless* specific cooperative learning activities are planned.

Diane Pope teaches high school math in a small classroom. She likes the pod arrangement but finds that it limits her ability to move quickly to students who need help, a high priority in her algebra, honors math analysis, and AP calculus classes. Also, because she gives so many short quizzes, she is sensitive to her students' almost daily need for privacy.

The current conventional wisdom regarding how students *should* be seated in all classrooms clearly favors the pod arrangement (i.e., a small cluster of from two to four desks) or five to six students at a table in both elementary (Patton, Snell, Knight, & Gerken, 2001) and secondary schools (McFadyen, 2005). Furthermore, there is a large body of research showing the academic benefits of cooperative learning (Johnson, Johnson, & Holubec, 1994).

However, when students are working on independent assignments rather than true collaborative projects, group seating can have its downsides. Table 1.1 summarizes a body of research in which comparisons were made between the time on task and engagement of students (ranging in age from 7–14 years) sitting in rows (or pairs in which no student sat opposite another working on the same surface, and the teacher could have eye contact with every student without any having to turn more than 90 degrees) and students sitting in pods or at tables facing each other.

First-grade teacher Jill Yates speaks for many of her colleagues when reflecting about seating arrangements: "When I graduated from college, I believed that a classroom with traditional rows rather than cooperative groups was an indicator of inferior teaching and classroom management. I had the false impression from my teacher training that all students did better in a maximum cooperative state. This mistaken idea did not take into account factors like the learning and behavioral characteristics of students with special needs. Now I teach to a variety of different learning styles during every day, and I am very comfortable using not only the two extremes (students at individual desks in rows and students in groups of six at tables) but also everything in between. What's important is the freedom to be flexible enough so that I can reach all of my students in a given school year."

All of the WITs use cooperative learning in their classrooms as one of a repertoire of instructional models, but they also use a variety of seating plans throughout the school day. They readily move or ask students to move desks into various arrangements depending on how they are teaching, what kinds of processing activities are planned following direct instruction, and the types of instructional tasks that will be assigned to students.

WITs maintain multiple places in their classrooms for students who need their own space, either temporarily or permanently. They often begin the year in rows with assigned seats, move to pairs, and then move to cooperative groups *after* they have *taught* their students the routines, rubrics, and rules of cooperative learning. They never assume that their students will intuit how to learn cooperatively with classmates. They teach them how to do it.

Table 1.1 Research on Task Engagement of Students in Two Different Seating Arrangements

Authors	Treatment	Findings
Single Research Studies Axelrod, Hall, and Tamms (1979) Wheldall, Morris, Vaughan, and Ng (1981) Wheldall and Lamm (1987) Yeomans (1989) Hastings and Schwieso (1995)	Single research studies were conducted with students between the ages of 7 and 14 years in schools located in England. In all of the studies, time-on-task data were collected during two different 2-week periods in which the seating arrangements were alternated between two designs at various times of the day.	The studies show that the classroom practice of sitting students in groups to undertake individual tasks makes work difficult for most of them and especially difficult for the most distractible. The studies also show that alternative arrangements result in substantial improvements in students' engagement with their work. Matching the seating arrangement to the task is critical.
Reviews of Research Merrett (1994) Hastings, Schwieso, and Wheldall (1996)	The first design had students seated in groups around flat-topped tables or desks drawn together to form working surfaces. The second arrangement had students seated in rows of desks (i.e., any arrangement that did not require students to sit opposite one another, work on the same surface, or have to turn their heads more than 90 degrees to make eye contact with the teacher during direct instruction).	"All too often there may be a mismatch between the collaborative setting of the group and the individual learning tasks given to pupils. The result is that the setting may distract pupils from their work" (Alexander, Rose, & Woodhead, 1992, para. 96).

Q and A

 Judith Cimmiyotti (S): What are the important things to keep in mind when seating students who are hyperactive and distractible?

Elaine: Figuring out where to seat distractible students requires creativity and flexibility. What works for one student may fail with another and what works today with a child may not tomorrow. But there are some standard accommodations that all teachers can employ (McEwan, 1998, pp. 115–131).

- Seat students where most visual distractions are behind them (e.g., in front row with back to rest of class). Remember, however, this seating arrangement could have its disadvantages because students will lose the opportunity to pick up visual cues from classmates regarding appropriate attending behaviors and what books and materials are being used. Consider a seat near the front rather than in the front row as an alternative option.
- Seat students away from potential distractions, such as heaters, air conditioners, high traffic areas, pencil sharpeners, windows, water coolers, noisy classmates, and doorways.
- Seat students near the teacher as well as appropriate role models. Avoid isolating students unless they self-select this option.
- Post classroom expectations and rules in highly visible places, and if necessary, post more specific expectations or to-do lists on students' desks.
- Create a stimuli-reduced area that all students may use (e.g., study carrels in a corner of the room). Encourage students to self-select this environment as they feel the need.
- Permit students to stand, move between two desks, or sit at a round table and move from chair to chair while working.
- Provide task-oriented breaks for selected students (e.g., to run errands, water plants, or distribute materials).
- Provide exercise breaks to relieve the "wiggles." Encourage students to use seat isometrics, such as pushing feet down on floor or pulling up on the bottom of the chair.
- Don't place distractible students face-to-face and elbow-to-elbow with classmates during independent study periods. Even responsible adults find it hard to resist off-task behavior in close quarters.
- Permit students to use earplugs or headphones to block auditory distractions during tests or independent seatwork.

- Allow for a higher level of restlessness and movement on the part of hyperactive students during your lessons than would normally be acceptable to you. If you are personally sensitive to distractions and movements, associate stillness with attentiveness, or believe that students are purposely annoying you, discipline yourself to focus your attention in another direction (unless students are distracting other students).

The Third Decision:
The Placement of Individual Students

In addition to selecting or eliminating furniture *and* deciding on an overall seating plan, you must also consider the needs of the students who don't readily fit into your preferred seating plan. Your ultimate goal is to have every student engaged, on task, and learning. Sonia Brettman frequently has numerous students with special needs included in her middle school classes. "Recently I had 10 students in my class with special needs," she related. "Two of them had full-time aides and required seating on the outside edge of the tables of four so their aides could sit, stand, or kneel next to them and not be in the sightlines of other students. Two students were autistic and needed placement near the door so they had less distance to travel and fewer distractions on the way to their desks. In my cooperative groups of four, I try to balance ability and needs, but that year I had more than one low student per group (there was a severely dyslexic student reading at the second-grade level and two students with Aspberger's syndrome). So I placed a second child in each of the two groups that had an aide, and the aide worked with the whole group as appropriate."

With-It
Teachers' Roundtable

CLASSROOM SEATING

Elaine: Let's talk about the first day of school. Do your students have a choice of where to sit?

Bobbie Oosterbaan (E): I assign my kindergarten students to a table on the first day. They need the security of "their place" to work. Then I adjust assigned seating throughout the year to help students build cooperative learning skills with their classmates.

Jean Piazza (S): My students are free to choose where they want to sit. We discuss the importance of students managing themselves, knowing what works for them as well as what distracts them, and I encourage them to make wise choices so they can be successful.

Julie Elting (E): I ask my students for input about seating. In fact, some of them came up with the idea to have all of the students' desks face the board rather than facing each other.

Laurie Anstatt (E): I begin the year with rows of single desks in order to reinforce the expectation that students are responsible for their own learning. Once they learn our routines, I group them with partners.

Elaine: How do you rearrange your seating for all of the different things that go on in your classrooms?

Jill Aspegren (E): I move desks all the time. The arrangement of the desks coordinates with the rhythm of my teaching. My students know what kind of lesson is coming up based on the way I ask them to position their desks.

Elaine: What's the most important thing about a seating arrangement to you?

Paula Hoffman (S): Seeing my students' eyes. When I see their eyes, I can tell whether or not they're "getting" it. If they aren't, I can easily walk into the center of the group to help individual students, answer questions, or clarify confusion.

Catherine Clausen (E): Getting to my students quickly is the most important thing to me. With a U-shape, I can get to them quickly as well as foster whole-class discussion *and* focus during direct instruction.

Elaine: What options do you have available for those students who need alternative seating?

Larry Snyder (S): I have a study carrel in the back of the room for students that need to get away from classroom distractions. And I also have tables across the back of the room for students to go to if they need a change of scenery. Plus I have a music stand in the back of the room for students who can't sit still for an entire class period.

Michelle O'Laughlin (E): I have a designated quiet work corner, which is simply a student desk near mine that faces the wall. Students know that this is a place they can go if they are feeling distracted by their neighbors.

Elaine: How do your seating arrangements meet the needs of students who require individualized help?

Figure 1.3 **Darlene's Seating Plan**

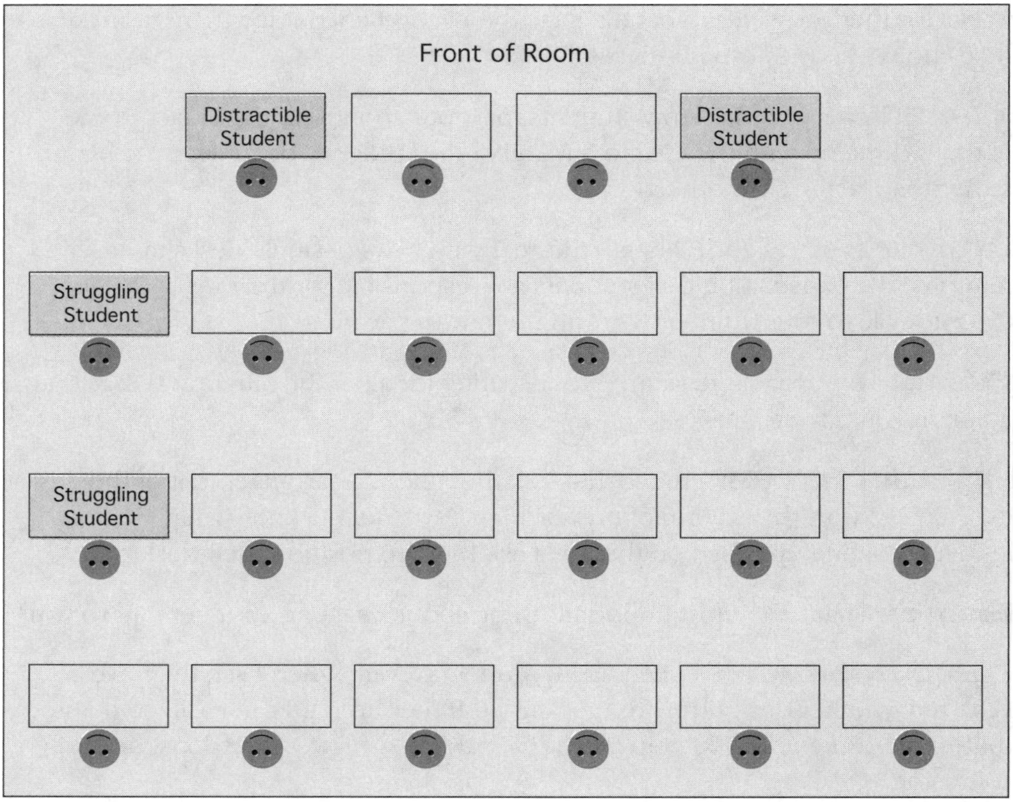

SOURCE: Reprinted by permission of Darlene Carino.

Darlene Carino (E): My students are seated in four horizontal rows facing forward toward the whiteboard. Students who require preferential seating are seated in the front row. I place the students who need constant attention from me on the ends of the rows. Within the rows, I seat students next to someone of a differing ability so they can help each other. (Darlene's seating plan is shown in Figure 1.3.)

Candace Darling (E): I arrange the desks in pairs facing the front of the room. There is an aisle in the middle for easy access to all of the students, and everyone has a partner to help if needed. (Candace's seating plan is displayed in Figure 1.4.)

Elaine: What about the students who are chatty when they're sitting close to others?

Bobbie Oosterbaan (E): I place the responsibility for creating a quiet workroom on the individual student. If a particular student's enthusiasm is *verbally overflowing*, I ask, "Is this a quiet place to work?" The student in

Figure 1.4 Candace's Seating Plan

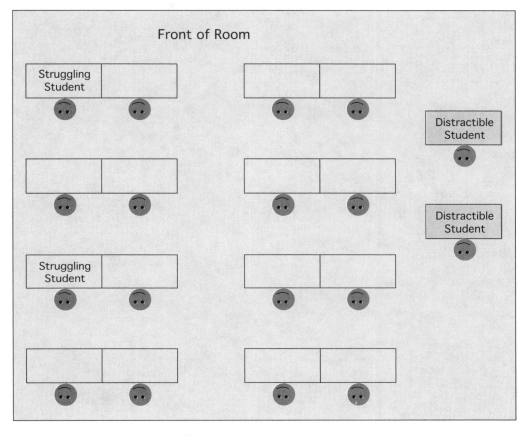

SOURCE: Reprinted by permission of Candace Darling.

question generally regains their composure quickly. However, if a student needs more than two reminders, I simply say, "Please find a quieter place to work."

Elaine: Thank you for your insights and proactive responses. Being a WIT means thinking ahead so you can help your students think ahead.

What's Ahead?

In addition to creating spaces for teaching and learning, WITs also design walls and bulletin boards that support instruction. Just ahead, we'll explore the various ways that WITs make their walls work for them as "second teachers."

Chapter 2
Creating Walls That Work

I've learned over the years that although my classroom

needs to be a welcoming place that is ready for my

students on the first day, it doesn't have to be perfect.

I deliberately stop tweaking things several days before

school begins. This approach provides time for me to

mentally walk through the lesson plans for the opening

days of school and also to rest.

—Darla Ryser (E)

Once you have envisioned your classroom space and chosen a seating plan that complements your teaching style, curriculum, and the special needs of your students, your next step is to make your walls work for you, hopefully as a "second teacher." Begin with the time-honored rule of design you may have learned in Art Appreciation 101: Form follows function. Roughly translated, this means that your walls should not be overdecorated and distracting but rather should serve specific instructional purposes. Primary reading resource teacher Joanne French explains it this way: "Since the goal of my walls is to engage students, I strive for functional and interactive bulletin boards that are simple (uncluttered), attractive (colorful), and stimulating without being distracting."

High school Spanish teacher Susan Graham follows the same set of rules:

> **I like simple and colorful decorations, and because I teach a foreign language where we learn numbers, colors, and days of the week, my room can resemble a primary classroom. I put up posters that contain simple Spanish vocabulary and display Mexican realia like sombreros and piñatas as well. [Note: *Realia* are concrete objects from the everyday world that are used during instruction in order to make language comprehensible (Florida State University, 2005).] I also have Spanish-language children's books available on a counter for students to check out.**

Middle school teacher Jerry Jesness is at the opposite end of the decorating continuum from Susan. Although they both teach Spanish, Jerry's classroom is functional, if not particularly aesthetic. He admits, "I'm afraid you're asking the wrong person about classroom decor. I realize that it's important in elementary school. Fortunately, when I taught at that level, I had an instructional aide who was happy to take charge of such things. Currently my walls are covered with instructional items like maps, lists of common prepositions, irregular verbs, and commonsense rules for organizing essays."

Susan would no doubt find Jerry's classroom too sparse for her tastes. In fact, she gently chides some of her secondary colleagues for not recognizing the importance of an aesthetically pleasing classroom:

> **I think high school teachers undervalue and underestimate the importance of a decorated classroom. Lots of high school classrooms are depressing to be in because the teachers think the students are too old for decorations. It's very simple to make a room more pleasant to be in and still maintain an "adult" environment. Personally, I think it's important to "finish" bulletin boards instead of just putting up posters anywhere and having the bulletin boards look unbalanced. Simple background paper and border make a huge difference.**

Middle school history teacher Larry Snyder agrees: "I believe in a colorful room, with many displays and bulletin boards. I post motivational proverbs, class rules, daily assignments, and a school news section that my students regularly update. I want them to take ownership of our classroom."

Can you be a WIT if you're not artistic? The answer is *yes,* and in the pages ahead, I hope to encourage even the most reluctant "decorators" to realize the worth of adding a little color and excitement to otherwise bland and boring classrooms.

Given today's standards-based focus, classroom walls at every level *must* support instruction and enhance learning. Principals are encouraged to "walk the walls" of their schools looking for evidence of learning objectives, procedure steps, whole-class brainstorming efforts, cooperative group work with multiple names attached to a work product, and student work centers in which something from every student is displayed (Downey, Steffy, English, Frase, & Poston, 2004). If you think you don't have the talent to pull it off, engage parent volunteers to put up backgrounds or enlist students to sign up for bulletin board duty. Assign a class committee to create motivational posters that support your learning outcomes. If you're a computer whiz, trade talents with a fellow teacher who's artistic: "I'll develop a template for your weekly quizzes if you'll get my bulletin boards ready for student work displays."

With-It-
Teachers' Roundtable

USING YOUR WALLS WISELY

Elaine: As I visit classrooms around the country today, I see bulletin boards that are more outcome focused and learning centered than those I remember from 20 years ago. How do *you* decide what to put up on your walls?

Michelle Perry (E): My first-grade colleagues and I feel that everything we display in our classrooms *must* be purposeful.

Elaine: It would seem that not only are today's walls more purposeful, they are also developed collaboratively with students.

Shannon Coombs (E): On the first day of school, I ask my first and second graders to close their eyes and picture what they would like their classroom to look like. Together we make a list of the things we want on the walls. The room belongs to everyone, not just me.

Elaine: When I was a classroom teacher, there was a lot of pressure to have everything perfect on the first day. I'm delighted to see the trend that enlists students in a collaborative effort.

Kelly Paul (E): I am amazed at the amount of time some teachers spend putting up elaborate bulletin boards. I wonder what they give up in order to find the time. I also wonder how the students can feel any ownership of the classroom if the teacher does *all* of the work.

Elaine: Are your bulletin boards really empty on the first day of school?

Val Bresnahan (S): Absolutely. I start each year with bare walls. I'm sorry to say that some of my middle school colleagues never do fill their vacant bulletin boards. But my students and I "build" our walls together. We start by formulating our classroom rules together, and that's the first thing we post.

Bobbie Oosterbaan (E): I don't worry about decorating my walls before students arrive, either. I put up the framework for several key categories and add titles such as Quality Work Wall, The Write Stuff, Numbers Count, and Working Words. I do explain to parents (since this is kindergarten) that "something is coming" and that their children will be involved in creating their own environment.

Carol Robertson (S): I feel OK about my empty bulletin boards, now that I know Bobbie's boards are empty, too. Actually, I leave my walls unadorned for the same reason—so I can display examples of student work. My only major *decoration,* if you can call it that, is a large four-color poster that functions as the organizational structure for all of the cooperative lab work we do in my classes. (Take a look at Figure 2.1.)

Elaine: I'm delighted to hear that high school teachers like Carol and Marty display student work in their classrooms.

Marty Pope (S): Not only do I believe that it's important to display student work, I think you also have to keep the walls fresh. I'm positive you can actually kill brain cells with sterile walls and bulletin boards that don't change for 9 months.

Elaine: Once the school year gets going, how do you keep your walls up to date when there are so many more pressing responsibilities?

Sue Plaut (S): I make the whole process as painless as possible. I use wrapping paper as backgrounds for my bulletin boards. Then, rather than stapling individual pieces of student work to the board, I tack string to the bulletin boards and attach student work to the string with mini-clothespins I found at the fabric store. This way I don't have to remove staples and worry about tearing the background paper or the students' work. Actually, whenever possible, I have kids put up and take down their own work.

Bobbie Oosterbaan (E): I use parent volunteers! I take photos of many finished bulletin boards to give the parents a template to follow.

Phyllis Chesnutt (S): My students participate in changing the classroom decor. This fosters pride and ownership. Most of what I display on the walls is their work. I feel that displaying assignments is one more opportunity for students to "publish" their work.

Elaine: Do students actually pay attention to your wonderful walls?

Figure 2.1   Carol's Cooperative Learning Poster

Materials Monitor

Red is the color of this quadrant. The "red" team member is in charge of procuring and managing materials for the table.

Cheerleader

Green is the color of this quadrant. The "green" member of the team is in charge of encouraging and affirming fellow team members.

Expert

Yellow is the color of this quadrant. The "yellow" member of the team is in charge of finding the answers to team members' questions and making sure that everyone thinks and writes clearly.

Moderator

This quadrant is blue. The "blue" member of the team makes sure that everyone does their fair share and helps keeps the group on task.

Sue VanderNaald-Johnson (S): Students need to be trained to "read" the room to assist them in completing their assignments and taking tests. This is a readily available resource if they are taught how to use it.

Michelle O'Laughlin (E): At the beginning of the year, I conduct a classroom tour with my students and talk about the different areas. Students always notice the two blank places above the windows and the coat hooks. These spaces are reserved for the display of their work.

Marjorie Wood (S): I actively teach the content of the walls to my students at the beginning of each semester and then periodically as needed. Sometimes students need a friendly reminder of the rules or the grading scale, so I go back and review the applicable posters.

Rhonda Carpenter (E): I create scavenger hunts that "force" my students to read the walls. For example, I might ask them to find three strategies on the west wall that they can use to solve a math problem or find some "rich" words on the south wall that they can use in their stories.

Elaine: After hearing you describe how your students use the walls, I think I'm safe in saying that you do indeed have "second teachers" in your classrooms.

How With-It Teachers Use Their Walls to Support Learning

WITs use their walls as organizers, reminders, motivators, affirmers, encouragers, textbooks, and learning resources. If *you* want to be a WIT, trash those torn posters and get rid of the outdated memos. Cover your blank bulletin boards with burlap, fabric, wrapping paper, canvas, suede, or any other covering that provides texture, color, or drama to your classroom. Then, "deck your walls" with meaningful and challenging student work. In many schools, student work overflows into the hallways.

Q and A

 Elaine: As an administrator, how much importance do you place on a well-decorated classroom?

 Cathie West, Principal: An exceptional-looking classroom does not *always* equate with exceptional teaching; nevertheless, *all*

of the exceptional teachers that I have known have had sensational-looking rooms. When I cross the threshold of these remarkable learning spaces, something takes hold and draws me in.

But if teachers focus only on making impressions, they will miss the most important reason to craft an inviting learning space. These stunning rooms become teaching tools in the hands of insightful teachers. Bulletin boards announce new themes, giant to-do lists help children keep track of assignments and daily events, and labels show students where to find supplies and how to keep things organized. There are charts that tell students their groups for workshop time, graphs that track progress toward classroom goals, and displays of students' best work. I love visiting thoughtfully constructed classrooms where teaching and learning are evident, where beautiful surroundings give rise to a serene feeling, and where students thrive academically and socially. Do I place importance on a teacher's room environment? Absolutely!

At George Elementary School in Jackson, Mississippi, walking the hallway walls is an adventure in learning. Before students' work can be displayed outside classrooms, it is evaluated by teachers and students using their Standard for Displayed Work (the following is the 2005 version):

- Student work products must be directly related and representative of required state learning outcomes, and the competency and learning objective to which the work is related must be posted.
- Student work products must be legible, neat, attractive, and clean. No sloppy handwriting or misspelled words are permitted.
- Student work products must be related to a central theme even if different assignments or projects are displayed.
- The overall presentation must be creative and attractive, using bright colors and several types of media. No dull and dreary assignments in pencil on ragged notebook paper are permitted.

You and your students may want to develop a similar rubric for publishing their work. If you're wondering exactly what WITs do put on their bulletin boards, consult the menu of more than 100 possible items found in the WIT's List in Resource A.

WITs use their walls to accomplish the following learning purposes: (1) to teach collaboration and cooperation, (2) to create learning communities, (3) to affirm and celebrate the individuality of their students, (4) to communicate their missions, (5) to build vocabulary and inspire excellent writing, (6) to provide information not found in textbooks, (7) to serve as instructional aids, (8) to practice and review required skills and content, (9) to share their values with students, and (10) to motivate and inspire students.

Use Your Walls to Teach Collaboration and Cooperation

Bridget Rigg-Anderson and her fourth graders work collaboratively to create nearly everything that appears on the walls of their classroom, and although the bulletin boards are empty (except for backgrounds and titles) at the beginning of the school year, they don't stay that way for long. Bridget explains:

> **We decide together what to hang on the walls, based on our learning needs. For example, the first thing we did this year was to brainstorm a list of "strong" verbs. Then we added a tombstone surrounded by "dead" verbs (e.g., *was, is,* and *am*) along with some words that we decided to put to rest in our writing (*cool, awesome, nice, good*). I knew my students understood the purpose of our decor when early in the year several parents visited prior to a field trip. Students took great delight in pointing out the lists we had created. But more important, the students explained the purpose of the work and how they used it on a regular basis.**

There needs to be balance in the color scheme and accents used. Some teachers overdo the decorating, thinking that students need lots of color to be stimulated and interested in learning. I believe that my teaching should stimulate the children more than the surroundings.

—Susan Biltucci (E)

Use Your Walls to Create Communities of Learners

Val Bresnahan's middle school resource students evidenced an ownership of their classroom's walls that surprised even their teacher. She packs the period from start to finish with a range of activities, and in spite of Val's instructional relentlessness, the class didn't always make it through the entire agenda every day. That sometimes meant losing track of unfinished items. Val says, "This concerned the students, if you can believe that."

On their own and without input from the teacher, the students devised a practical and impressive solution: a to-do list with a weekly spreadsheet on which the class could check off items as they were completed. Val laminated a to-do list (see Figure 2.2) and mounted it in a prominent place in the classroom. She says,

Figure 2.2   **Room 200 To-Do List**

	M	T	W	TH	F
1-minute think, 3-minute write, 2-minute share					
Red word spelling drill					
Red word written spelling test					
Sound drill					
Spelling sentences					
Build-a-sentence					
Tell about words you heard					
Word bucket word					
Workbook practice					
Stories for fluency practice					
Fluency builders (words)					
Paragraph write/rewrite					
Idioms					
Novel read					
Grammar practice					
Language! Reader					

SOURCE: Reprinted by permission of Valerie Bresnahan.

After we complete each activity, we check it off on the appropriate day using a vis-à-vis pen. This ensures that we don't shortchange any activity. At the end of the week, a student transfers what we have completed to an 8.5" × 11" duplicate of the poster. This functions as a permanent record for me. The poster is then cleaned off and readied for the upcoming week.

Val's students are mastering a critical real-world skill: the importance of setting goals and being accountable for completing them in a timely way. WITs use their walls to create vibrant communities of learners.

Use Your Walls to Affirm and Celebrate the Individuality of Your Students

On the second day of school, Sue Plaut's middle schoolers make "Getting to Know Me" posters. All of the posters go up by the end of the first week of school and stay there until after back-to-school night. She says, "I make sure that whenever parents come to my room (e.g., back-to-school night or parent-teacher conferences), they will see *their* child's work displayed. I believe that kids, parents, *and* administrators would much rather see students featured on the walls than pristine bulletin boards created by teachers."

Oh, the things that can be taught from one little wall are amazing.
    –Barbara LaMastus (E)

In Kathy Hoedeman's middle school math and science classroom, students make Birthday Bumper Stickers during the first week of school. The 12" × 4" pieces of construction paper, which bear students' names, birth dates, and any decorations or symbols they choose to describe themselves, are mounted in categories by month on the back wall. They serve two purposes: (1) to remind students to properly acknowledge one another's birthdays when they occur and (2) to illustrate frequency tables when that topic is studied in math.

Use Your Walls to Communicate Your Mission

WITs take every opportunity they can to reiterate their values regarding education and their personal teaching missions. In Jill Aspegren's fourth-grade classroom, her decor acts as a second teacher:

I use my bulletin boards, wall space—even hooks from the ceiling—to communicate my message: *This is a busy and active workspace*. I always display all of the students' art and writing projects—not just selected ones. I want my classroom to be a "community of learners." I love the energy that a bright and colorful environment provides. I display two of my favorite mantras in prominent places: (1) "You will shine like stars here" and (2) "A school should be the most beautiful place in any village—so beautiful that the greatest punishment is to not be welcomed inside." I love my classroom and communicate this to my students.

Use Your Walls to Build Vocabulary and Inspire Excellent Writing

Jennifer Dunn decorates her second-grade classroom with what she calls "juicy word" charts. They aren't fancy (a large piece of colored butcher paper on which students write big words they encounter in their listening and reading), but they pack a powerful punch when it comes to motivating students to discover and use "big" words. When they find a juicy word, students are expected to write it on one of the charts, first in *pencil* and then, after the word has been checked in the dictionary and corrected (if needed), in marker. Jennifer says, "I'm not the only one who is teaching and using big words! My students constantly refer to these charts as they use 'juicy words' in their writing assignments."

First-grade teachers Candace Darling, Michelle Perry, and Darlene Carino have come up with a new twist on the word wall concept. They call it "Word Wizard," and the "wizard" is a student who becomes a human word wall for the day. Their morning routine includes a read-aloud that is related to the current theme in their reading series, a recent holiday, or a topic from another curricular area (both fiction and nonfiction are used). After choosing the read-aloud for the day, the teachers share the responsibility of identifying three vocabulary words, describing how they are used in the text, and writing a child-friendly definition of each word. Once the story has been read and the words have been discussed, a Wizard for the day is chosen. Wizards wear their word cards with definitions on a necklace and carry a sign indicating they would like to be asked about their words. Wizards must provide definitions of their words to anyone who asks. If you're short of word wall space, put your students to work. The "human word wall" idea could also be used to review vocabulary related to any classroom theme, test, or unit. Once worn, the words are hung on the vocabulary wall, and points are awarded to students who are "caught" being a "Word Wizard" (using the word in writing or conversation). See Figure 2.3 for a sample set of words and definitions from a Dr. Seuss story.

Use Your Walls as a Supplementary Textbook

Bulletin boards can serve as the textbooks you may not have. High school social studies teacher Rose Bender explains: "For one of my American History courses, I assign a project called Lost and Found. Students are expected to research Americans (with special emphasis on African Americans and Hispanic Americans) who have contributed in important ways to our society, culture, or government but somehow have been forgotten by the authors of our history book. Students create posters and do presentations to the class about their chosen individuals. The posters are then displayed in the classroom where everyone is expected to read and take notes on their contents, to be tested for on the midterm exam." WITs recognize the value of having students construct learning materials that can serve as supplementary textbooks.

Use Your Walls as Instructional Aids

One way to use your walls as "second teachers" is to label objects and locations in your classroom. In the lower grades, labels can teach new words, help students find important classroom supplies, and even teach students the names of their classmates. In multicultural classrooms where several languages are spoken, label in two or more languages. Trying to learn words in other languages can give students whose only language is English an appreciation of the efforts of their English Language Learner classmates. In the upper grades, labeling becomes more sophisticated.

In her sixth-grade classroom, Judith Cimmiyotti posts the four main directional points on the walls before school begins, in anticipation of the mapping skills unit scheduled during the first month of school. But she leaves them up all year. She explains, "We are constantly comparing, contrasting, and relating where we are to locations around the world." WITs never miss an opportunity to connect new information with prior learning.

Use Your Walls to Teach Character

Kindergarten teacher Barbara LaMastus is unequivocal regarding the importance of character-building: "Without a doubt," she says, "the most important thing on our walls is the class motto: 'Today I will use good manners and treat others the way I want to be treated.'"

Figure 2.3   Word Wizard Poster

Oh, the Places You'll Go!
by Dr. Seuss

succeed

enemies

slump

"And will you succeed?"

to do well or to get what you want

"On you will go though your enemies prowl . . ."

someone who wants to hurt or harm you

"And the chances are, then, that you'll
be in a slump."

a sad depressed state

47

SOURCE: Adapted and reprinted by permission of Darlene Carino, Candace Darling, and Michelle Perry.

She continues, "We stand and repeat this motto each day as part of our morning routine. My philosophy is that the development of good character is, by far, the most important thing I can strive for in my students. Our character words poster reminds me and my students of the Tyson Tigers' Character Words (see Figure 2.4).

Michelle O'Laughlin sums up the rules in her third-grade classroom in just two words: Safety and Respect. After brainstorming examples of safe and respectful behaviors, students create posters with an acrostic poem using the words *safety* and *respect*. The posters decorate their walls for the first month of school and are used almost daily as Michelle helps students enlarge their understandings of what these words mean in terms of their attitudes and behavior.

Use Your Walls to Let Students Know What You Value

Although high school teacher Thomas Leighty displays material related to the content of his courses (U.S. History and Criminal Justice), he also believes in conveying his personal ideals and values through his classroom decor, even if it is not specifically related to his subject matter. He says, "I love to read, and so I put up posters that promote reading."

Allan Reichenbach, high school math teacher, is a photography bug. He confesses that he is not very adept at creating traditional bulletin boards, but he does have his own unique artistic talent: photography. So he decorates his classroom with enlarged photos he has taken of scenic views and zoo animals around the country, frequently using them as conversation starters with his students. "I feel this is another way to relate to them—to be more than just their math teacher," he says.

Q and A

 Elaine: How does color affect students' behavior and learning?

Jeffery A. Lackney, PhD, AIA: Experimental research on how color impacts students' attitudes and behavior is limited, and conclusions are mixed regarding its influence on achievement. But color should certainly be seen as an environmental variable that contributes to sensory stimulation and attending. In the laboratory, color has been found to affect changes in mood and emotional state, psychomotor performance, muscular

Figure 2.4   The Tyson Tigers' Character Words

Responsibility:	Being accountable for my behavior
Perseverance:	Continuing to do something in spite of difficulties or obstacles
Kindness:	Having a friendly, good-natured attitude toward others
Compassion:	Feeling for another's need and helping that person without expecting anything in return
Dependability:	Being trustworthy to do what I say I will
Work:	Not being lazy in the tasks given to me
Generosity:	Having an unselfish attitude and willingness to share with others
Thankfulness:	Being grateful and saying so
Friendliness:	Knowing, liking, and accepting other people just the way they are
Manners:	Behaving in ways that show good character
Determination:	Continuing on, regardless of the circumstances
Obedience:	Doing what I am told with a happy, submissive spirit
Forgiveness:	Treating someone as though they never hurt me
Honesty:	Always having truthful words and ways
Love:	Having a great affection of the mind and heart
Orderliness:	Having neatness, tidiness, proper behavior; lawfulness
Patience:	Waiting with a happy spirit
Contentment:	Being happy with what I have
Optimism:	Having a happy outlook that everything will turn out for the best
Thoughtfulness:	Having consideration of others; courtesy
Self-Control:	Doing something even when I do not feel like it
Tolerance:	Accepting others and their beliefs even when I do not agree
Courage:	Standing up for what I believe in; bravery
Respect:	Having a high or special regard for others; honoring one another
Enthusiasm:	Having a strong, positive feeling of excitement
Humility:	Having an absence of pride or self-assertion; modesty
Punctuality:	Being on time for the requirements of life
Attentiveness:	Paying heed or care
Joyfulness:	Having delight, happiness, gladness
Confidence:	Having trust; a feeling of assurance or certainty

SOURCE: Adapted by permission of Lola Malone.

activity, rate of breathing, pulse rate, and blood pressure. Warm colors (yellows, reds) are associated with slight elevations in blood pressure in children, while cooler colors (greens, blues) caused slight drops in blood pressure. Optical stimulation by the use of warm colors and brilliance of lighting will cause increases in muscular tensions, respiration rate, heart action, blood pressure, and brain activity. Cool colors and dim lighting bring about reverse effects, such as muscles relaxing more and sleep being facilitated. We can assume, then, that people (including students) feel most comfortable and relaxed in environments that simulate natural conditions. But vivid color used appropriately can help teachers draw students' attention to what is important to notice. Posters and instructional aids that you want to stimulate brain activity and "arousal" should be in bright colors, like reds and yellows, to grab students' attention. However, carpets and area rugs in too-bright or garish colors may draw your students' attention away from what's really important. The wise use of color to transform a depressing atmosphere into one that is pleasing and appropriately stimulating may well have a positive effect on both student attitudes and behavior (Cohen & Trostle, 1990; Read, Sugawara, & Brandt, 1999; Zentall, 1986).

Use Your Walls for Practice and Review

If there's something your students absolutely *must* master, put up a poster and use it for daily practice and review. Not only will a display remind your students of what they need to know, it will also remind you to refer to it periodically for a quick practice session. First-grade readiness teacher Nancy Raihall posts the following charts in her classroom: Number Words, Color Words, Pairs of Opposites, Pairs of Rhyming Words, Months of the Year, and Days of the Week. Nancy's students use these charts daily in an activity held just before snack time. Here's how it works:

> **Each student receives a baggie filled with a set of laminated cards that goes with one of the charts. For example, for students receiving a set of number words, the task is to put the cards in order from 1 to 10 (using the reference chart if needed), raise a quiet hand, read them to me, and then pick a snack. Snack Time definitely motivates my students' usage of the walls.**

WITs recognize the importance of review and practice when their students need total mastery.

Figure 2.5   The Hopes and Dreams of Jenny's Students

This year my hope or dream is to . . .

Have friends	Be the learning queen
Be a good listener	Learn how to tell time
Complete my work	Get good grades in school
Write bigger words	Take my time with my work
Be better at sitting	Learn better than last year
Get on the honor roll	Work well with other students

Use Your Walls to Inspire and Motivate

High school English teacher and learning strategies coach Jean Piazza has a large banner stretched across one wall of her classroom. "I frequently use it to challenge my students to think for themselves," she explains. It says, "Do I Dare to Disturb the Universe?" (Cormier, 1974).

Sixth-grade teacher Judith Cimmiyotti has chosen a William Ward (2005) quotation to inspire and motivate her students: "If you can imagine it, you can achieve it. If you can dream it, you can become it."

High school math teacher Diane Pope writes a different inspirational or motivational quote on her board every day. "I don't always mention the quote before class, but my purpose is either to inspire my students or make them think. I have many students who copy down the quote, and if I don't get it written, they ask for it first thing. That quote is part of the routine." Diane goes to one of the many Internet quotation sites or Google's A Famous Person to see what they said that might motivate her students.

Jenny Hoedeman's second graders each articulate a hope or dream for the new school year and then write it in a tracing of one of their hands. Their hopes and dreams remain on a bulletin board for the year, to inspire, motivate, and remind them daily of their goals. Figure 2.5 contains just a few of their hopes and dreams.

What's Ahead?

In the next chapter, we shift our attention away from the physical aspects of your classroom and focus on precisely *how* WITs teach the 3Rs (routines, rubrics, and rules) during the first 3 weeks of the school year. We examine a variety of teaching moves, models, and approaches that WITs use to get the results they do with their students.

Chapter 3

How to Teach the 3Rs

Routines, Rubrics, and Rules

The key to success is making sure your students are comfortable with even the most basic routines so that your attention can be on teaching skills and content, not repeatedly explaining simple tasks.

—Rhonda Carpenter (E)

Now that you have designed your classroom space, crafted your seating plan, and decorated your walls, let's examine what WITs do differently when they teach. Although WITs look the same as other teachers when they are having coffee in the lounge or walking down the hallway, the minute they close their doors and begin to teach, they say and do things very differently from their less effective colleagues.

Why are WITs more successful than other teachers? Why are *they* able to get results year after year, regardless of the demographics of their students? The answer is simple. They excel at maximizing *academic learning time* (ALT) for all of their students and providing *interactive learning time* or direct instruction for those students who need teaching tailored to their specific needs (Saphier & Gower, 1997, p. 64). ALT is the amount of time students are successfully engaged in academic tasks and moving toward specified goals at appropriate levels of difficulty.

All teachers have the same amount of *allocated time* (AT) in which to teach, but WITs value and use time differently than their less effective colleagues, especially at the beginning of the school year. They invest their precious minutes of AT during the first 3 weeks to teaching their students the 3Rs (routines, rubrics, and rules). During the first 3 weeks of school, they might well have these words posted outside their classrooms: *Do not disturb: 3R lesson in progress.*

How to Maximize Academic Learning Time

The WITs who contributed to this book shared dozens of ways to maximize ALT, not only during the first 3 weeks of the school year but also in the 33 weeks thereafter. Although they encounter the same roadblocks to achievement that other teachers do, they have devised a variety of ways to go over, under, through, and around these roadblocks. They have discovered how to cut down on wasted time with time-savers and signals, reduce excessive and unproductive noise with noise breakers, and increase student time on task with attention getters. The following sections contain just a sample. Consult the WIT's List in Resource A for more than 200 field-tested ideas from the 97 WITs who contributed to the book.

Time-Savers

WITs refuse to let valuable ALT slip away and are constantly looking for ways to maximize it. They are able to motivate students to work more efficiently, thereby giving them more time for instruction. Here are just a few of the ways they squeeze out extra time on task:

- They never look the other way when their students are idle. They teach routines so that students are always productively engaged.
- They hold students accountable for completing homework.
- They convey a sense of urgency and academic press in their classrooms, always giving their students *enough* time to finish but never time enough to waste.
- They find volunteers to help them with repetitive tasks so they can focus on teaching.
- They often utilize the time before the day or period begins to engage their students in academic tasks.
- They teach bell to bell.

Signals That Silence Students

Another way WITs maximize ALT is by using signals that enable them to get their students' immediate attention, a technique that is essential if students are engaged in animated conversations in their cooperative groups. WITs have devised some ingenious ways to quiet conversational students in an instant. These include snapping, clapping, stomping, waving, or clicking—signals that never fail to get their students' attention. WITs can simply wave a hand and magically silence the room to convey essential information or even to impress visitors to their classrooms.

Kindergarten teacher Paula Larson has devised a Quiet Game that keeps her students silently engaged for up to 10 minutes if an emergency arises that she needs to handle. (You can find Paula's game in the WIT's List in Resource A along with other teachers' versions of a Quiet Game.) In order to qualify as a WIT, you *must* teach your students at least one or two fail-safe signals that will quiet them and gain their attention instantly on field trips, during assemblies, in the event of emergencies, or when important visitors arrive in your classroom.

Noise Breakers

As you may have guessed, noise breakers are the opposite of noisemakers. And we all know who makes the most noise in classrooms—active, motivated, and conversational students. To keep students' voices from becoming overly boisterous, WITs play classical music, wind chimes, and xylophones. Sandi Seckel (E) even plays a rainstick, a hollow bamboo instrument that is filled with rice and seeds. When Sandi turns it slowly upside down, the rice and seeds fall to the other end, making a sound that resembles falling rain. Mary Koster (S) rings a "deci-bell" to remind students that their voices are exceeding the acceptable decibel limit. See the WIT's List for a description of how Mary teaches the "deci-bell" routine to her students.

WITs know the importance of having calm and productive work environments, but they also recognize the value of having their students process information and work cooperatively with their peers—particularly as the content grows more challenging. However, even veteran WITs experience a measure of frustration with exactly where to draw the line between productive conversation and noise. They are constantly trying new approaches. Perhaps some of their noise breakers will help *you* keep your noisemakers under the legal decibel limit.

Attention Getters for Off-Task Students

Although WITs encounter students in their classrooms who are disengaged, off task, distracted, or just plain disinterested, they never give up on them. They use every trick they can think of to keep off-task students on task. Here are just a few of them:

- Whisper a reminder to pay attention in an off-task student's ear.
- Make eye contact with off-task students and even give them a little wink to let them know you've caught them daydreaming.

- Put a sticky-note reminder on the desk of a misbehaving student.
- Use the names of students who aren't paying attention in math examples and problems, like Allan Reichenbach (S) does.
- Give students the look your mother gave you when you misbehaved. One WIT calls it "the hairy eyeball," and others refer to it as "the look" or "the evil eye." Whatever you call it, start perfecting a stare of total disgust and disappointment with your students' inability to stop talking and start paying attention.

Attention Getters for Whole-Group Instruction

WITs constantly monitor the attention of all students during whole-group instruction and frequently adjust their approach when they see too many daydreamers and nap takers.

- Mary Koster gives her middle schoolers a brain break when she sees them getting antsy. Sometimes she displays an optical illusion on the overhead to help students exercise a different part of their brains for 60 seconds. Or she might suggest that students move their right legs in a clockwise circle while making the number 6 in the air with their right hands.
- Carol Robertson is always ready to stop for a quick think-pair-share (Kagan, 1993) or partner reading activity when she sees her biology students beginning to fade.
- When the majority of Dave Wilkie's third graders grow inattentive, he begins talking to the walls or windows pretending that they are giving him the attention his students are not. Dave finds that humor (at his own expense) always revives sleepy students.

Most of my routines are focused on time. I urge my students to make use of their time. I help them see that we have precious little time in comparison to the size of the big wide world waiting to be discovered around us.
—Jill Aspegren (E)

Grab your highlighter or some sticky notes and head to the WIT's List (Resource A) for ideas you can implement tomorrow. Begin to assimilate some of the more than 200 time-savers, noise breakers, and attention getters into your repertoire of teaching behaviors, a few at a time, in the coming weeks.

How to Become a With-It Teacher

Just ahead is a road map for you to follow as you take the next step (and this one is a giant leap upward) toward becoming a WIT.

- First, discover *how* WITs actually teach the 3Rs to their students during the first 3 weeks of school and then commit to doing the same in your own classroom.

- Second, explore the most common teaching models and approaches so that you can select those that are appropriate for bringing your students to the mastery of your grade level, or content area's outcomes during the remaining 33 weeks of the school year.
- Third, identify a set of generic teaching moves that are essential to employ on a daily basis, no matter what model or approach you choose to use, and begin to intentionally incorporate and practice them.

The terms *routine, rubric, rule,* and *reward* were defined earlier (see the Introduction), but there are several additional terms you'll need to know to become a WIT: *teaching move, teaching model* or *approach,* and *instructional activity.*

Teaching moves are generic teaching actions, the things teachers do and say during instruction. There are 16 moves that WITs skillfully blend into the seamless act of teaching, and you'll hear about each one in more depth from the teachers themselves. For a preview of the teaching moves and their definitions, see Table 3.1.

Table 3.1 Teaching Moves

Move	Description
Explaining	Providing verbal input about what will happen in a lesson, what the goals are, why it's being done, how it will help students, and what the roles of the teacher and the students will be during the lesson
Giving Directions	Providing unambiguous and concise verbal input that seeks to give students a way to get from where they are at the beginning of a lesson, task, or unit to the achievement of a specific task or outcome; providing wait time for students to process directions, time for students to respond, and opportunities to ask clarifying questions
Modeling	Thinking aloud regarding cognitive processing (e.g., making connections with prior knowledge to something that is read in the text), demonstrating, acting out, or role-playing behaviors and actions (e.g., acting out different ways to receive a compliment given by a peer)
Reminding	Causing students to remember or think regarding something that has previously been taught; restating something that has been previously taught in a novel way to ensure remembering
Guiding Practice	Leading students through a supervised rehearsal of a skill, process, or 3R (routine, rule, or rubric) to ensure understanding, accuracy, and automaticity

(Continued)

Table 3.1 (Continued)

Move	Description
Scaffolding	Providing instructional support (e.g., further explanation, modeling, coaching, or additional opportunities to learn) at students' independent learning levels that enables them to solve problems, carry out tasks, master content and skills, or achieve goals that would otherwise be impossible without teacher support
Coaching	Asking students to think aloud, cueing them to choose strategies that have been taught (e.g., cognitive strategies for comprehension, problem-solving strategies in math, organizational or social strategies), delivering mini-lessons when needed, and providing feedback to students
Attributing	Communicating to students that their accomplishments are the result of effort, wise decision making, attending to the task, exercising good judgment, and perseverance, rather than their intelligence or ability
Constructing Meaning	Working collaboratively with students to extract and construct multiple meanings from conversations, discussions, and the reading together of text
Motivating-Connecting	Generating interest, activating prior knowledge, and connecting instruction to the real world or the solution of real problems
Recapping	Summarizing what has been concluded, learned, or constructed during a given discussion or class period, as well as providing statements regarding why it is important and where it can be applied or connected in the future
Annotating	Adding additional information during the course of reading or discussion—information that students do not have but need in order to make sense of the discussion or text
Assessing	Determining both formally (through testing) and informally (through questioning) what students have learned and where instruction needs to be adjusted and adapted to achieve mastery
Facilitating	Thinking along with students and helping them develop their own ideas, rather than managing their thinking, explaining ideas, and telling them what and how to do something
Redirecting	Monitoring the level of student attention and engagement and using a variety of techniques, prompts, and signals to regain or redirect students' attention and focus on the learning task, transitioning students from one activity to another with minimal time loss
Affirming	Encouraging, praising, or rewarding students' actions, attitudes, thinking processes, verbal statements, and work products

Teaching models are "particular pattern[s] of instruction that [are] recognizable and consistent . . . [and have] particular values, goals, a rationale, and an orientation to how learning shall take place" (Saphier & Gower, 1997, p. 271). Models of teaching are often associated with particular theorists or researchers. For example, Roger and David Johnson (Johnson et al., 1994), along with Robert Slavin (1978), are the most well-known scholars who have conducted research on the cooperative learning model. Teaching approaches, on the other hand, are commonly accepted patterns of instruction, such as lecture or recitation.

Instructional activities are the plans and procedures that teachers make and follow for the purpose of instruction—the specific things that teachers and students *do* during instruction.

If all of these definitions are making your head spin, here's an example to help you sort out the critical attributes of each term. Jay Pilkington teaches middle school social studies. As a new teacher, he used the lecture approach almost exclusively in his classroom. He did a lot of talking and telling, with very discouraging results. His students weren't mastering the content, and he was stressed and exhausted. Jay wisely decided to try a new *teaching model,* a research-based one that provided opportunities for students to cognitively process the course content with classmates: cooperative learning (Johnson et al., 1994; Kagan, 1993).

Jay quickly realized, however, that in order to use this popular model effectively, he would have to explain, demonstrate, and facilitate his students' mastery of the 3Rs of cooperative learning—before he could begin teaching social studies. He also discovered that he needed some motivating *instructional activities* that fit his content, learning objectives, and time frame; the schoolwide expectations; *and* his middle school students. Hoping to engage his students' interest, he came up with three: Row Feud; Share 'n' Compare; and Read, Revel, and Reveal.

Jay also added some new *teaching moves* to his repertoire. He no longer stands in front of his podium "talking" and "telling." He is now facilitating, affirming, motivating, coaching, and constructing, among other essential moves.

If you decide to use cooperative learning in your classroom, first familiarize yourself with the cooperative learning model and then teach your students the 3Rs they need, to take full advantage of this powerful way to teach. Because Jay's students have learned how to work together to find answers and share responsibilities, their brains (i.e., working memories) are totally available to cognitively process what they are reading, hearing, and discussing. They are able to make connections to prior knowledge as well as to extract and construct multiple meanings from the text and discussion. Sounds exciting, doesn't it? Just remember, it all begins with mastering the 3Rs. If you would like your classroom to function like Jay's, read on.

> I continually stress to my students that any time we lose is lost forever. There is no getting that time back.
> —David Wilkie (E)

How With-It Teachers Teach the 3Rs

Although WITs are eclectic and situational in their approaches to teaching, using a variety of teaching models, all of the 17 teaching moves, and dozens of motivating instructional activities, they approach the first 3 weeks of school in a more single-minded fashion. They focus specifically on four of the teaching moves: explaining, giving directions, modeling, and guiding practice.

- *WITs explain.* To explain is to give students verbal input about what the routine, rule, or rubric is, what its purpose is, why it's important, how it will help them in completing assignments (getting along with classmates, learning more, etc.), how it will help the teacher (giving more time to work with individual students who need help), how it will improve life in the classroom (students will have time for computer games or silent reading), and possibly bring benefits later in life (the option to go to college, earn more money, or get a better job). WITs are explicit. They use plain language, express themselves clearly, and do not infer, imply, or assume. They spell it out.
- *WITs give directions.* They provide unambiguous and concise verbal input that gives their students road maps to get from where they are at the beginning of a lesson to the achievement of a specific task or outcome. Their students are never in doubt about what to do next. That means increased ALT.
- *WITs model.* They engage in observable behaviors, act out scenarios, or role-play examples and nonexamples for their students and also think-aloud about what is going on in their minds. They never just *explain* and *give directions.* They also *show.*
- *WITs guide students in ample amounts of practice.* They do not fast-forward directly from their explanations of the 3Rs to handing out complex assignments that require mastery. Instead they guide students in practicing the 3Rs until they are sure that mastery has been attained.

Irrespective of the age of their students, the subjects they teach, or where in the country they work, WITs are on the same page when it comes to *how* they teach the 3Rs during the first 3 weeks of the school year. They explain, give directions, model, and guide practice. They leave nothing to chance. They don't rush to implement a plan for which their students aren't ready. In fact, middle school language arts teacher Phyllis Chesnutt advises, "Maintain structure at the beginning until your students have mastered the routines they need to handle less-structured activities."

Q and A

Q **Elaine:** You're nearly finished with your first year of teaching. What do you know now that you wish you'd known at the beginning of the year?

A **Christina Steiner (E):** I wish I had realized earlier how important it is to be consistent. Consistency is the only way to establish one's authority [assertiveness] as a teacher. I learned, although slowly, that it was the systems and routines I put in place that made my classroom run smoothly. Once the routines were taught and mastered, I rarely needed to raise my voice.

With-It
Teachers' Roundtable

TEACHING THE 3RS

Elaine: What's your approach to teaching the 3Rs to your students?

Susan Graham (S): I explain my procedures very carefully the first time so students will get the routine. But that's never a guarantee that everybody has it. So I re-explain it as often as necessary. Recently I've spent *more* time on teaching my routines *more* thoroughly so that they are *really* mastered at the beginning of the year. (Susan's class routine and the review exercises she uses while teaching it can be found in Chapter 7.)

Nancy Finch (S): After I explain what the routine is, then I model it, and of course, I always provide opportunities for my students to practice.

Laramie Hudson (E): I work each routine into my plan book at the beginning of the year. You can't teach them all at once. I model, then I have students practice the routine immediately. I review the routines all year, especially when we haven't used a routine for a while.

Carol Robertson (S): One of the most important sets of rules and routines I teach is lab safety. I explicitly explain each rule and routine and then guide the students in the creation of a lab safety booklet. I do a lot of modeling.

Shannon Coombs (E): I use a modeling lesson design based on the work of Madeline Hunter that was developed in my district. (See Table 3.2.)

Table 3.2   Shannon's Modeling Lesson Design

Step	Description
Anticipatory Set/ Lesson Focus	Teacher activates the background knowledge and experiences of students in order to build connections to the current lesson
I Do/You Watch	Teacher models how to do what the students will be expected to do by the end of the lesson
I Do/You Help	Once again the teacher models with the help of the students
You Do/I Help	Students perform the task under the guidance of the teacher
You Do/I Watch	Students complete the task independently while still under the teacher's supervision
Closure	Teacher summarizes the purpose and possible applications of what was taught and gives a homework assignment if applicable

SOURCE: Adapted by permission from a modeling lesson design based on the work of Madeline Hunter and developed by the staff of the Douglas County (NV) School District.

Lyssa Sahadevan (E): I teach all of the routines in my classroom using the "I do it, we do it, you do it" lesson design, which sounds similar to the plan Shannon mentioned. Once a routine is established, the rest is smooth sailing.

Darla Ryser (E): I have a similar lesson plan that I follow. (See Table 3.3.)

Sue Wyman and Michele Engelsiepen (E): We physically show our students every step of what we expect them to do—even in the bathroom! Of course we don't actually use the bathroom, but we do walk our students through knocking on the door, turning the light on, closing the door, using a little bit of paper, flushing, washing hands, and turning out the light.

Elaine: What's the most effective way to get students to *master* the 3Rs?

Marty Pope (S): Through practice. The brain loves the unique and the novel, but the brain also requires structure.

Stacy Shires (E): The best way to teach primary-school-age children classroom routines is to model and then practice them regularly.

Elaine: How important is it to explain the reasons for having certain rules and routines to students?

Catherine Clausen (E): Giving the reasons and logic for what you're doing is a very important part of explaining. We have discussions about how various routines help us learn, and we also model what life in our classroom will look like using our rules and what life would look like without the rules. Then we follow up with more discussion.

Table 3.3   Darla's Mini-Lesson for a Classroom Routine

Anticipatory Set	*State the Goal/Aim: "Today you're going to learn how second graders return to their desks when they leave the computer center or rug."*
Teacher Models: Part 1	Teacher models or role-plays why it is important by showing what it doesn't look like: "What would happen if I weren't careful and ran to my desk? (If you feel comfortable, act it out.) Then discuss with students some of the outcomes: It wouldn't be polite; it wouldn't be safe; someone could get hurt, and so on.
Teacher Models: Part 2	Teacher models or role-plays what it does look like: "That's why it's important to learn a better way. Let me show you." Teacher stands up and, without talking or touching anyone, goes to sit at the teacher's desk. "Think about what you saw." Teacher goes back and discusses with students what they observed: "It was quiet. The teacher walked. Everyone was safe."
One Student Models	"Andy, will you show everyone how you can stand up and, without talking or touching anyone, walk straight to your desk?" As Andy models, teacher compliments him and brings everyone's attention to the key points that have already been mentioned and any others that are pertinent.
Two Students Model	"Brianna and Chris, will you show everyone how you can stand up and, without talking or touching anyone, walk straight to your desks?" As they model, teacher compliments them and comments on the key points.
Small Group Models	"Table Group 1, show us how you can stand up and, without talking or touching anyone, walk straight to your desks." As they model, teacher again compliments them and mentions the important points.
Whole Class Models	Although the whole group would rarely leave the rug all at one time to avoid unnecessary traffic jams, teacher practices it here. "You are doing a terrific job. Now let's see if the rest of you can do it as quietly as the others did. Stand up and, without talking or touching anyone, walk straight to your desks." Again teacher compliments them and highlights the important points.
Feedback	Teacher is enthusiastic, positive, and provides specific feedback to teach or correct behavior. If someone doesn't follow the procedure correctly, teacher assumes that they just need more practice.
Practice	Teacher repeats the steps (all or part) each time the routine is used until it is mastered. Teacher repeats the steps occasionally throughout the year to review, for new students and for consistency. Teacher also playfully practices the routine with a stopwatch to determine students' best time.
Reflections	Teacher chooses an appropriate group time to reflect with students about the routine and to remind them of the reasons for the routine. "Who remembers why we need a routine for going to our desks? Is it working?" Teacher discusses and listens for suggested improvements from students.

SOURCE: Reprinted by permission of Darla Ryser.

Elaine: Do you feel that it's worth all of the time you spend?

Tara Vitale (E): I have learned that the more time I put into teaching my routines, the more successful my school year will be.

Jay Pilkington (S): It *is* a lot of work and repetition, but I am convinced that if you take the time at the beginning of the year to verbally explain, model, and practice classroom routines, things will really start to roll in a positive way as the year progresses. When your students know your routines, everybody's life is easier. Many students at this age need structure and appreciate having it in class. Not only does this help with class flow and organization, it also helps with classroom behavior management *and* reduces discipline problems.

Q and A

 Teffany White (Sp. Ed.): When you have just 30 minutes to work with a child who is low in reading, how can you make the most of that time?

Joan Will, Reading Coordinator: There are eight essentials to making every minute count when you have only 30 minutes in which to raise a student's reading level:

- Make your teaching diagnostic. Know exactly what the student needs and respond directly to that need. Make sure the student has no misconceptions or misunderstandings.
- Make your instruction intensive and explicit. If the session is during school hours, the student is missing something else. It should not be reading instruction in the classroom. Your session should be in addition to classroom reading instruction.
- Make your session fast-paced. Make every minute count. There should be no downtime in the 30 minutes.
- Keep the student actively engaged. Students should be reading and writing, not just listening and watching. Don't do the work for the student. Expect the student to work hard during the 30 minutes.
- Make the session multisensory. For example, rather than just visually showing students a card and asking them to respond with the sound, have them write the letter while saying the sound to lock it in their memory.

- Scaffold instruction. Students should not be doing independent work in a 30-minute session.
- Include guided reading. Show students how to apply skills and strategies so they can use them in classroom assignments.
- Read as much of the time as is possible. Struggling readers don't read nearly enough.

How With-It Teachers Choose Their Teaching Models

WITs don't just choose *a* model. They employ a variety of teaching models and approaches every day in their classrooms. Rhonda Carpenter (E) does it all. "I plan my day in such a way that there are opportunities for students to work cooperatively with each other [cooperative learning], independently [direct instruction], and as a whole class [inquiry]. I also build in time to have a one-to-one conference with each student [nondirective teaching]."

Rhonda has skillfully managed to include all four categories of teaching models into one school day: (1) social (cooperative learning), (2) behavioral (direct instruction), (3) information processing (inquiry or inductive thinking), and (4) personal (nondirective teaching). When you hear educators trying to make a case for using only one model, think of Rhonda.

Some theorists put teaching models in two categories: direct and indirect. Use direct instruction if you need to teach "facts, rules, and action sequences"; use indirect instruction if you want to teach "concepts, patterns, and abstractions" (Borich, 2000, p. 229). *Discovery learning* and *constructivism* are other terms used to describe indirect instruction.

Catherine Clausen compares direct and indirect instruction in her second-grade classroom this way. "A constructivist approach [i.e., indirect, inquiry, or discovery learning] brings a sense of wonder and curiosity to all that we do. But often, a constructivist approach in isolation is inefficient and ineffective, just as a direct instruction approach in isolation can become dry and less than inspiring. However, when these models are used together, they can help students get the information they need to be successful *and* nurture the higher-level thinking skills they require to become thoughtful, curious, and engaged learners."

In Catherine's classroom, students experience both indirect *and* direct instruction. Indirect instruction comes in the form of "investigations," brief dips into topics often of the child's choosing (Hoyt, 2002). Students become near experts on topics by researching from various books and other sources they choose. They then present what they have learned in a two-page informational text format. The final product includes various features found in informational texts: diagrams, some paragraphs on their subject, some bulleted facts in specific categories, a few fun or weird random facts, and usually an acrostic poem.

Direct instruction comes in the form of the *Open Court* (2005) reading program. It provides best-practice think-alouds (scripts) printed front and center in the teacher's guide to the anthology. Catherine's job is to make the provided scripts her own, adding her personal enthusiasm and tweaking the teacher's guide prompts to make them more natural. She uses direct instruction with lots of choral responding and practice to teach blending and decoding, and while Catherine concedes that some teachers may find it boring, she loves the excitement that comes from watching her students unlock the code and become fluent readers.

WITs utilize and adapt a variety of different methods. They are situational teachers, if you will, able to select the model or approach that best meets the demands of their content, their students, and their learning outcomes and then execute it successfully with students. They are able to move back and forth with ease along a continuum of teaching models that ranges from teacher centered at one end to student centered at the other, but they are always subject centered no matter how they are teaching.

WITs do it all: (1) They use multiple models and approaches; (2) they continually add to and refine their repertoire of teaching models; (3) they choose an approach or model that best fits the content, the level of their students, and the objective they wish to achieve; (4) they develop their own unique models of teaching that specifically apply to their students and area of teaching; and (5) they carefully consider new approaches that are introduced to them by evaluating research and examining results. High school social studies teacher Thomas Leighty summarizes the importance of being eclectic this way: "When teachers have multiple models in their arsenal, they have fewer discipline issues, students are more actively engaged, and more learning occurs."

How With-It Teachers Use the Teaching Moves

Whatever subject they are teaching or model they have selected, WITs employ at least 17 different teaching moves. Listen to their descriptions of how they execute each of the moves.

Explaining

Providing verbal input about what will happen in a lesson, what the goals are, why it's being done, how it will help students, and what the roles of the teacher and the students are during the lesson

Marjorie Wood (S): At the beginning of the year when I describe my Strategic English class to students, we discuss what makes a learning community. We talk about appropriate times to offer help (such as spelling a word or lending a pencil, etc.). We talk about how to help one another feel comfortable in a classroom where it's OK to make mistakes without the fear of being teased. We go over the syllabus for the course and review the units to see how they're connected to the "big picture." We discuss the idea that we are all unique learners, and with one another's help, we'll all become better readers and writers.

Michelle Perry (E): I always explain *why* I am doing something and try to relate what I am teaching to my students' lives.

Joanne French (E): I explain to my students why we have the routines we do. If they understand the reasons we do things, they will become more involved.

Val Bresnahan (S): Everything I do is designed to enhance my students' learning. I always try to tell them the "why" of what we do.

Paula Hoffman (S): On the first day of school, I work with my students to develop our routines so that everyone feels like they have a say in how the classroom operates. We determine the expectations of the class, our academic routines, our requirements for success, and even our nonacademic routines.

> I model from day one what I expect students to do because I don't like to waste time. Children don't want to waste time either. They get bored and restless just like adults. Boredom creates chaos. Chaos results in less time for learning.
> —Susan Willingham (E)

Modeling

Thinking aloud regarding one's cognitive processing (e.g., making connections with prior knowledge to something read in the text) or acting out or role-playing behaviors and actions (e.g., acting out different ways to receive a compliment given by a peer)

Kathy Amacher (S): I regularly model my own personal problem solving and comprehension of text by verbalizing what is going on in my mind during those processes.

Sharyn Genschmer (E): Each time we work in cooperative groups, I model the desired behavior for students. I generally provide specific examples of what kinds of conversation I expect to hear.

Sara Wiles (E): Not only do I model examples, but I also act out nonexamples in a really dramatic way. For example, I exaggerate inappropriate behavior and then model how I would go about correcting my behavior. When I introduce my signal for getting students' attention, I ask them to talk loudly (much louder than usual), and then use the signal to see how quickly they respond.

Michelle Perry, Darlene Carino, and Candace Darling (E): We use the first few weeks of school to teach all of our routines. We show students how to pick up their morning work quietly, where to put it when it is done, and how to use each of the centers in our classrooms. We model the correct way to do things during each component of our day. We follow this up by having several students role-play various scenarios, both correctly and incorrectly.

Rose Bender (S): Whenever I have a class that needs to develop note-taking skills, I model for students on the overhead or whiteboard precisely what they should be writing down in their notebooks as a result of something I have said. In the beginning weeks of the school year, I am more deliberate about writing notes out for them, and as the year goes by, I am able to just "speak" notes to them to get them to listen and take notes without relying on the overhead or whiteboard. I always collect students' notebooks to see whether they are getting the critical ideas from my lectures and our discussions.

Giving Directions

Providing unambiguous and concise verbal input that seeks to give students a way to get from where they are at the beginning of a lesson, task, or unit to the achievement of a specific task or outcome, including the provision of wait time for students to process directions as well as time and opportunities to ask clarifying questions

Jill Aspegren (E): I do not leave anything to chance. I give precise directions for sharpening pencils, using glue, putting paint in a bowl, cleaning a paint brush, and even how to leave it to dry. I am fanatical about these things during the first weeks, and then I never have to mention them again.

Darlene Carino, Candace Darling, and Michelle Perry (E): Before each assignment, we give slow, careful directions in small chunks. Then we ask students to repeat the directions back to us once or twice. This saves time in the end because we don't have to give directions over and over again.

Marjorie Wood (S): In addition to giving verbal directions, I also put up an overhead with the specific expectations for each routine, written out in a step-by-step format.

Scaffolding

Providing instructional support (e.g., further explanation, modeling, coaching, or one-to-one time) at students' independent learning levels that enables them to solve problems, carry out tasks, master skills or content, or achieve goals that would otherwise be impossible without teacher modeling, prompting, and support

Melissa Bock (E): I use many approaches in my teaching, depending on the needs of my students and the task at hand. I differentiate my instruction using flexible grouping within my second-grade team as well as small-group instruction throughout the day. I use tiered lessons in which I provide different assignment rubrics to students, depending on their levels. I strongly believe that students learn better when I am teaching to their levels. You can't expect every child to learn at the same pace, and I don't believe in leaving students behind.

Coaching

Asking students to think aloud, cueing them to choose strategies that have been taught thus far (e.g., cognitive strategies for comprehension, word attack strategies for decoding, problem-solving strategies in math, organizational strategies for completing a research paper, or social strategies for working in cooperative groups) as well as delivering mini-lessons when needed and giving feedback to students

Sharyn Genschmer (E): I expect my students to explain their thinking whenever they answer a question. I usually follow up their answers with these questions: "Why did you choose that answer? How do you know?"

Kathy Hoedeman (S): When we check homework together, students must show me they're listening and reflecting on what they've done by making notes to themselves on their papers. I often collect homework and just check for "evidence of checking." This is also noted when I do a journal collection at the end of a chapter. They are encouraged to write notes to themselves about why they made an error or what they could have done better. I make a big deal about kids who do this well, often telling them I would rather see homework with notes all over it than a perfect paper.

Reminding

Causing students to remember or think about something that has previously been taught; restating something that has been previously taught in a novel way to ensure remembering

Stacy Shires (E): I post recess rules (written in large type) on the back classroom door (the door students use when going to recess), so they are the last thing they see before leaving the classroom. I remind the students, as they are lining up, to review the rules.

Darren Lander (S): I explain and consistently remind students of the rules and enforce them. Inconsistency is my (our) greatest tendency and it is also our greatest enemy in teaching self-discipline.

Guiding (Practice)

Leading students through a supervised rehearsal of a skill or process to ensure understanding, accuracy, and ultimately mastery

Lori Taylor (E): For knowledge and skills that I want my students to retain, I use a lot of repetition. For example, if I am introducing new vocabulary, I go over the definitions before reading the story. Then as we encounter the words in the story, I stop and check for understanding of the meanings. After reading, we review what we have read along with the meanings of our new words. Then during the day, I call on different students to give the definitions out loud at least three or four more times.

Attributing

Communicating to students that their accomplishments are the result of effort, making wise choices, attending to the task, exercising good judgment, and perseverance, rather than their intelligence or ability

Judith Cimmiyotti (S): I believe in sending positive messages constantly. I have quotations posted, to which I often refer: "Do your best and never give up," "If you don't try, you will never know," "Focus on your goal, visualize your goal, achieve your goal!" and "Your character really counts."

Catherine Clausen (E): I teach my students about brain research and let them know that *they* are the masters of their learning. They have the power to grow dendrites and to become smarter. I let them know that brain researchers have said that the top of a person's head actually warms up when there's lots of learning going on and then have them touch the tops of their heads. We will stop every now and then to check the tops of our heads. The kids love knowing they are truly their own masters when it comes to learning.

Constructing Meaning

Working collaboratively with students to extract and construct multiple meanings from conversations, discussions, and text

Bridget Rigg-Anderson (E): I recently taught my class reciprocal teaching (RT) (Palincsar & Brown, 1984). After individually explaining, modeling, and practicing the clarifying, questioning, predicting, and summarizing cognitive strategies individually, the students worked in cooperative groups to read expository text. [Note: The four strategies are used together in the reciprocal teaching model.] They love RT, and I love listening to them clarifying their thinking for each other, questioning one another, and commenting on each other's observations about what they have read.

Motivating and Connecting

Generating interest, activating prior knowledge, and connecting instruction to the real world or the solution of real problems

Phyllis Chesnutt (S): My students don't just write to turn in assignments or projects. They write for a variety of audiences so they can publish, share, and regularly display their work around the school. Students create personal newsletters, children's books, articles for school newsletters, and poems for contests.

Michelle O'Laughlin (E): I motivate students using my personal experiences as a mountain climber. I have pictures of mountain climbers, with motivational phrases posted on all four walls. One of my posters is of the Colorado Trail, a 471-mile trail between Denver and Durango, which I am in the process of completing. I continually explain how I set goals, overcome setbacks, and work toward completion. I want to inspire my students to try challenging things in their lives.

Recapping

Summarizing what has been concluded, learned, or constructed during a given discussion or class period, as well as stating why it is important and where it can be applied or connected in the future

Jay Pilkington (S): I use a prompt I created called "Freeze for Your Intelligence" (FFYI) during group work, games, and reviews for tests. My purpose is to let students know that what I am about to say is very important knowledge for them to have. Sometimes it's a critical concept they need to know for an upcoming test, new information I want to connect to the current discussion, or something they should write down in their notes. Upon hearing me say, "FFYI," students stop what they are doing or saying and give me their undivided attention. After I share the important information and we have done any necessary discussion or clarifying, I say, "thaw," and students go back to what they were doing.

Christine Gabriele (E): After every lesson, my students and I think aloud together (reflect) on what has gone well in the lesson, what they have learned, and what questions they still have that we can answer together. I find that taking 2 minutes at the end of a lesson is extremely informative for me, and also puts into words for the students what has happened.

Annotating

Adding additional information during the course of reading or discussion—information that students do not have but need in order to make sense of what they are learning

Barbara LaMastus (E): We [my students and I] look at the United States map and the globe and recite the name of our city, state, country, continent, and planet every day. Sometimes we even talk about the solar system and our galaxy. We find our city and state on the map and look for our neighbors, Canada and Mexico. I always note that several of our classmates used to live in Mexico. We find the oceans, the Great Lakes, and the Mississippi River that flows on the border of our state. We pull out the globe and find India, because that is where one of our classmates was born. Every day we add a little more information to the discussion as we develop a sense of our place in the world. I want my students to understand that they are part of something huge, grand, and exciting!

Assessing

Determining what students have learned and where instruction needs to be adjusted and adapted by assessing, both formally and informally

Kathy Amacher (S): One of the fastest ways to find out either *what* students know or *how* they are thinking is to use individual dry-erase boards. I write a math problem on the board and the students work the problem on the dry-erase boards. I can quickly scan the room and award a point to all of the students who have the correct answer.

Mary Koster (S): All of my students have red, yellow, and green index cards that are ringed together in a clip. When I am explaining something or they are working in cooperative groups, I'll stop and say, "Show me what you know." They hold up the card that reflects their stage of learning:

Green means, "I get it!"

Yellow means, "I'm unsure."

Red means, "Stop! I need help."

Facilitating

Thinking along with students and helping them develop their own ideas, rather than managing their thinking, explaining ideas, and telling them what and how to do something

Kathy Hoedeman (S): When my students are working in cooperative groups, I circulate, kneel beside individual students or a group, and facilitate where necessary, complimenting as I go. They always seem to have a sense of how important their interactions are. Even groups who come and ask to be changed at the start seem to end up being grateful for lessons learned, friendships formed.

Redirecting

Monitoring the level of student attention and engagement and using a variety of techniques, prompts, and signals to regain students' attention and focus on the learning task or to transition students from one activity to another with minimal time loss

Marty Pope (S): After every 10 minutes of instruction, I provide 2 minutes for my students to reflect on and process the information. The reflection can be written or shared with a neighbor. "What were the three most important points I just made? Turn to your neighbor and discuss." Or "Jot down the point you do not agree with." This helps students to remain engaged in what we're doing without my having to continually remind them to pay attention.

Affirming

Encouraging, praising, or rewarding students' actions, thinking, work products, or verbal statements

Barbara LaMastus (E): We give three hip-hip-hoorays for special achievements! We also do the "The Dance of Joy," but that is reserved for only the grandest of accomplishments. Celebrating the successes of ourselves and others is a very generous way of living. "Generosity" is one of our character words. Wouldn't the world be a more glorious place if our children learned to be happy for others instead of being jealous of others' accomplishments? In my classroom, I try to establish an "all for one, one for all" spirit in everything we do.

What's Ahead?

In the next chapter, we'll take a look at the first of the 3Rs—routines. You are no doubt aware of the many organizational routines that help you increase your academic learning time. But you'll also discover a variety of academic and social routines that when taught to your students can help your classroom function more effectively.

Chapter 4

Routines That Develop Self-Discipline

Rather than rewarding those students who are

responsible and organized with praise, good grades,

and success, I do everything I can to teach every student

to be successful.

—Kathy Hoedeman (S)

This chapter is about teaching students three kinds of classroom routines: (1) organizational, (2) academic, and (3) social. Routines aren't the most exciting aspects of classroom life to the average teacher, but to WITs, they are the foundation of effective instruction. In much the same way that a foundation ceases to be obvious after a building's completion, the routines you establish will eventually be invisible to visitors to your classroom. They will only see a well-rehearsed and finely tuned group of students engaged in learning. On the other hand, knowledgeable educators will know instantly that you are the architect who designed the entire structure, an incomparable WIT!

You will recall from the Introduction that a routine is *a desired pattern of behavior—a procedure that is habitually executed by either students or their teachers.* Here's how to tell the difference between organizational, academic, and social routines, although as you begin to develop and teach your own routines, you will find that the categories inevitably overlap to some extent.

Organizational routines serve to help you manage the movement of students and paperwork in humane yet efficient ways. *Academic routines* include both the teaching moves you routinely make and the learning procedures your students regularly employ that ensure success for all. Finally, *social routines* are the behavioral patterns that keep interpersonal communications and relations in the classroom on a positive and productive plane. All three categories of routines are essential to maximizing academic learning time and increasing student achievement.

Organizational Routines

The business of school involves moving hundreds of bodies from place to place *and* transporting reams of paper, stacks of books, bins of materials, and carts of equipment from here to there. If you want to be a WIT, you must develop efficient and effective ways to expedite the movement of students and "stuff" in and out of your classroom while at the same time remaining totally focused on teaching and learning. Thoroughly taught and mastered organizational routines enable you to achieve this goal.

The number of times students come and go daily from their self-contained elementary classrooms is astounding. Whole classes pass in and out of their rooms nearly a dozen times daily, and that doesn't include the individual students and small groups who travel to speech, music lessons, reading, or special education teachers and tutors. In addition, most primary students move about their classrooms constantly, stopping at various centers to complete academic tasks while their teachers are meeting with small groups.

In middle and high schools, students are also on the move all day long. In addition to the six to eight periods or blocks to which they travel, students are frequently in and out of the building for extracurricular activities; on and off buses for athletic competitions; and in and out of showers, bathrooms, and locker rooms. To further complicate the movement of these more mature students, they are often all moving through the hallways at the same time with sometimes limited supervision. Whenever students need to go from here to there, the goal of WITs is to have them get where they're going quietly, safely, independently, and as quickly as possible. To achieve that goal, your students need to master multiple organizational routines.

In addition to the movement of students, there are monumental organizational challenges posed by the daily paper shuffle in schools. Students bring notes, money, and homework to school, all of which need to be handled by the teacher and other staff members. Teachers in turn pass out newsletters, permission forms, homework assignments, and graded papers in prodigious quantities to students. Some must be kept and filed, some must be taken home for parental signatures, and some must be completed and returned to the teacher. In addition to the paper shuffle, there are books, materials, supplies, and equipment that need to be organized, stored, retrieved, used, and put back.

In addition, time literally vanishes during transitions between the multiple instructional activities that occur in a day or period. In an average class, where a transition routine has not been mastered by students, one transition (e.g., from a cooperative learning activity to a period of class discussion) can steal between 5 to 10 minutes from your ALT. Multiply the number of minutes by the number of transitions that occur during a day to compute how much ALT disappears on a daily basis. To maximize ALT in the midst of all of the shuffling paper and moving bodies, you *must* create a variety of specific organizational routines, teach them to your students, and then discipline yourself to use them, too.

First, let's consider the most essential organizational routine—getting *all* of your students through your classroom door every day, into their seats, and cognitively engaged in the learning objectives for the day as expeditiously as possible. This is known as the *beginning-of-the-day* or *-period routine*. It consists of a list of things you require and expect your students to do every morning (or period) when they come into your classroom.

It may contain one or more of the following items, depending on the grade level: (1) exchanging greetings with the teacher and fellow students; (2) stowing outerwear, lunches, and book bags; (3) reading the daily schedule on the board; and (4) completing a warm-up or "bell-work" assignment shown on the overhead. WITs realize that for this beginning-of-the-day routine to run smoothly every morning, students will need explicit instruction for each of the subroutines. Figures 4.1–4.3 show some sample routines used by WITs at various grade levels.

The goal is to make your beginning-of-the-day or -period routine a habit during the first 3 weeks of school. Some schools develop a set of routines that all teachers use, and if that is the case in your school, your job will be much easier because the routines you teach will be reinforced and practiced in every classroom. If no buildingwide routines are in place, you're free to design and implement your own.

The precise steps *you* choose to include in your beginning-of-the-day routine are not as important as the fact that you design a routine that meets your needs and those of your students, teach it to them, and then *follow it every day*.

Designing a beginning-of-the-day routine is only the first of many routines to be tackled. The next most important routine to develop is one that is seldom mentioned in most classroom management texts—a transition time routine. Transition time is how long it takes you and your students to wind up one activity and start another. In a self-contained classroom there are multiple transitions during the day:

- Students remain at their seats and change from one subject to another or from one kind of activity to another.
- Students move from their seats to an activity in another part of the classroom.

(Text continues on page 81)

Figure 4.1 Beginning-of-Day Routines for Grades K–2

Kindergarten

Students walk into the classroom and put away their personal belongings.

Students each pick up a happy ticket (tickets like those used at carnivals and fairs) and write their names on the backs of their tickets.

Students put their happy tickets into their happy pockets (pockets on a chart hanging on the wall) and have a seat in the circle (Litz).

[Note: Happy tickets are part of the teacher's behavior plan. Students collect and exchange their tickets for rewards and privileges.]

First Grade

1. Students enter classroom and place their color-coded homework folders and notes in a labeled cart.

2. Students sign up for lunch by placing their attendance clip next to the picture of their lunch choice. (There is a labeled picture card for each menu choice.)

3. Students sharpen their pencils.*

4. Students retrieve morning work from a basket labeled "Morning Work."

5. Students put their names on their "Morning Work" papers.

6. Students choose two "just-right books" from their book baskets.

7. Students go to the rug for our morning meeting to greet each other, share, hear about the news for the day, and engage in a quick activity to set the tone for the day (Carino, Darling, & Perry).

Second Grade

1. Students empty their backpacks and hang up their outerwear.

2. Students place their emptied home folders (a folder specifically designed to send messages, newsletters, and flyers home to parents) in their personal mailboxes.

3. Students place notes from parents and completed homework assignments in the teacher's basket.

4. Students place their snacks in their desks.

5. Students sharpen two pencils and place them in their desks* (Kennedy).

*Some WITs run pencils through an electric pencil sharpener prior to students arriving at school.

Figure 4.2   Beginning-of-Day Routines for Grades 3–6

Third Grade

1. Teacher greets students at the door. Students know not to interrupt the teacher's greetings of other students unless there is a high-level emergency.

2. Students walk in the door, put reading homework in the green basket, math homework in the blue basket, reading log in the yellow basket, and any notes in the "notes from home" basket.

3. Students take things out of their backpacks and stack them in the corner of the room to avoid clutter.

4. Students sharpen their pencils.*

5. Students sit down and start their morning board work.

6. Teacher walks into the room and says, "Good Morning, Boys and Girls," and they chorally respond, "Good Morning, Miss Mariano."

7. Teacher collects the homework baskets (the homework is already sorted out) and records it on a homework clipboard while the students listen to the morning announcements and work on their independent morning work.

8. Students place their finished morning work into the red basket and read silently if they finish early (Mariano).

Fourth or Fifth Grades

1. Students enter the classroom.

2. Students put their homework in the basket and check off their names on the list.

3. Students sharpen their pencils.*

4. Students do two sections of math review.

5. Students read silently (Hudson).

Sixth Grade

1. Teacher greets students with a handshake and personal message at the door.

2. Students empty their backpacks, put them away, and greet the students in their pod.

3. Students read the assignment written on the board and begin working on it (Cimmiyotti).

*An alternative to students sharpening their pencils individually is to have one or two students perform the task at the end of each school day to save time. Some teachers prefer to run pencils through an electric pencil sharpener prior to students' arrival.

Figure 4.3 **Beginning-of-Period or Beginning-of-Block Routines for Secondary Level**

High School Reading and Writing Workshop (Special Education)

1. Students enter the classroom, get their materials, and begin working immediately on their board work.

2. The daily routine is written on the board. Students have a daily sheet they are expected to complete. It contains
   - Today's goal
   - Today's agenda
   - Section for notes
   - Section for homework assignment (Swiney).

Middle School Math and Science

1. Students approach classroom and check the door for the list of materials that are needed for the class that day. If they do not have the needed materials, they go back to their lockers to get them.

2. Teacher stands in hallway outside of classroom and greets students. They are expected to say, "Good morning Mrs. H."

3. Teacher and students make eye contact and teacher "takes students' temperatures" for that day.

4. Teacher takes attendance during this time.

5. Students check the board for their to-do list that morning.

6. When students have finished all of the to-do items, they read silently (K. Hoedeman).

High School Biology

1. Students check the board for a homework assignment and copy it into their daily planner.

2. While teacher takes attendance, the materials monitors from each cooperative team pick up the team folders, pass out any graded work to team members, and place team members' homework in the designated folder. They then return the folders to the trays for their class periods.

3. Teacher begins class (Robertson).

Figure 4.4   Transition Routine

1. Quietly (no talking) put away materials that are no longer needed.

2. Consult the agenda to determine the next activity, needed materials, and location.

3. Quietly (no talking) gather materials needed for next activity and quickly move to the new location (if applicable).

4. Begin working (if applicable) or wait quietly (reading a just-right book) until the teacher signals it's time to begin.

- Students move from learning center to learning center throughout the classroom.
- Students move from somewhere else in the classroom back to their seats.
- Students leave the classroom to go outside or to another part of the building.
- Students come back into the classroom from outside or another part of the building (Paine, Radicchi, Rosellini, Deutchman, & Darch, 1983, p. 84).

The recent move to block scheduling at the secondary level, while creating opportunities for teachers to vary instructional approaches and activities, has also increased the number of transitions, always potential time wasters. Efficient transitions demand a high degree of involvement and commitment by both students and teachers. Students need to follow the steps for an efficient transition, and teachers need to have their materials prepared, a minute-by-minute plan in place, and an alertness to monitor the transition and praise those students who are on task during that time. (See Figure 4.4 for an example.)

Q and A

Elaine: What do you do to help adolescents who just can't seem to get organized?

Kathy Hoedeman (S): Being responsible and organized is a big part of success in sixth grade. Over the years I've watched successful students in an attempt to identify some behaviors that I could then teach to those students who do not do these things. One thing I've noticed is that successful students come into the classroom with a "ready to learn" attitude. This is evident from the moment they walk in the door. They have the materials necessary to succeed on any given day. So one thing my partner and I do is list the materials needed for the day outside our classroom door on a whiteboard. In the beginning of the year, the list is very specific: "Blue math journal, green science journal, binder reminder, SSR book, pencil, checking pen and highlighter, calculator." Later in the year I am able to simply write "The Usual" and list only the special things (e.g., coloring supplies, signed math test). If students still have problems remembering their materials, we make a checklist and tape it inside the student's locker door. With the right routines and practice, I can teach organizational and academic routines to almost any student.

Imagine that your day is off to a fantastic start with a smashing beginning-of-the-day routine, and you are orchestrating efficient transitions between instructional activities for maximum efficiency. Now it's time to think about an end-of-class routine (like the one shown in Figure 4.5) that will take you and your students out of the classroom on a high note.

Once you have developed routines to start and end your day or class periods and discovered how to squeeze more instructional time out of transitions, you're on your way. You will, however, need to develop many more organizational routines before you'll be worthy of the WIT designation. "How many?" you ask. As many as are necessary to build a solid foundation for learning and orchestrate

Figure 4.5   **End-of-Period Routine for Grades 5–12**

1. Students copy assignments as written on the overhead, LCD screen, flip chart, or board into their daily planners or assignment notebooks.

2. Students collect the materials needed to do the assignments and stack them on top of their desks.

3. Students clean up their desk and floor areas.

4. Students complete assigned class jobs (if applicable).

5. Students collect backpacks and clothing (if applicable).

6. Teacher and students summarize or recap the "big ideas," essential questions, or learning objectives of the day or period.

7. Students complete their Exit Slip (a sticky note or 3" × 5" card on which they have written a summary statement of the class, a question about something they don't understand, or the answer to a question posed by the teacher).

8. Students wait for teacher's signal to exit the classroom.

9. Students give their Exit Slip to the teacher and say good-bye.

NOTE: WITs place copies of their routines in a Substitute Folder to ensure time on task when they are absent.

a smoothly functioning classroom. Check out the possibilities on the menus for both elementary and secondary classrooms found in the WIT's List (Resource A). Then choose specific routines that fit your grade level, students, and teaching approaches.

With-It
Teachers' Roundtable

ORGANIZATIONAL ROUTINES

Elaine: What is the best way to establish routines with students?

Judith Cimmiyotti (S): The most effective way to establish a routine is to have students practice it, even when the process might seem mundane. Sixth-grade students are no different than third-grade students. They thrive on knowing what is expected.

Joanne French (E): I'm very fussy about my students keeping their desks organized. We have random desk checks, and I reward organization. I believe that my students need this kind of instruction and guidance. It makes an impact on time, instruction, and learning.

Laurie Anstatt (E): Teaching all of my routines takes a big chunk of time in the fall. I teach the routine and we practice it. I put up a chart at the front of the room that contains the list of things students have to do in the morning to be considered "ready." There are places on the chart for students to initial each day that they complete every task. When all of the spaces are filled in, the class receives a reward.

Elaine: You obviously have the expectation that every student is going to master your routines.

Olga Litz (E): Many teachers assume that kindergarten students can't follow written directions. My written directions at first include more pictures than words, but as the year progresses, students are able to follow written directions quite successfully. There are teacher check points, where students have to show their work before they move on to the next job. Every student is held accountable for their learning and is responsible for completing assignments.

Elaine: How long does it take to get everything down pat?

Judith Cimmiyotti (S): I believe that if teachers take the first 3 weeks to establish the climate they want, they will save themselves a great deal of work later down the line. I spend the first 3 weeks establishing my classroom procedures, guidelines—and most important, establishing a climate of classroom respect for one another.

Elaine: What's the most important organizational routine?

Joanne French (E): The beginning-of-the-day routine—when students first enter the room. My students arrive at different times, and they all want my attention the minute they walk into the classroom. How do I get them all into the room and working independently for 10 minutes? By teaching them a routine.

Elaine: What's the most important part of your beginning-of-the-day routine?

Julie Elting (E): Wake-up work. My colleagues and I have used this term for years. Sometimes I call it a *brain warm-up*. It consists of work that is on my students' desks when they come into the classroom. (See Figure 4.6.)

Elaine: How do you keep from losing time during transitions?

Kathi Kennedy (E): When I can minimize student movement (except for moving to a new spot for instruction), I have more time for teaching and learning. Students definitely do not need to visit their backpacks or the pencil sharpener during the day.

Academic Routines

Academic routines are the daily actions in which you and your students engage in the course of teaching and learning. Teachers' academic routines include the *moves* and *scripts* (i.e., actions and words) you employ during instruction. Students' academic routines are the moves and scripts that students execute when they are working at learning in the classroom. When you have acquired and perfected a repertoire of academic routines, you will be able to monitor how well your students are attending and understanding, modify lessons in progress, and deal with minor disruptions, all without missing an instructional beat.

As your students begin to master the critical academic routines of your grade level and classroom, they will be able to work more confidently and independently. WITs identified the following categories of academic routines that they find particularly helpful:

- Mnemonic devices
- Songs, rhymes, and chants
- Role-playing and skits
- Using homework for instruction

Figure 4.6   Wake-Up Work: Teffany's 4 Squares

1.	**2.**
Solve this problem:	Underline the verb in each sentence:
Ted bought two burgers for $1.75 each.	1. The boy was thinking of where he put his pen.
He gave the clerk $5.00. How much change will he get back?	2. When did your teacher throw away the papers?
3.	**4.**
Find a spelling word that rhymes with	Answer in a complete sentence: What does the word *debris* mean?
1. House _____	_____
2. Frown _____	_____
3. Found _____	_____
4. Mouth _____	_____
5. Loud _____	_____

SOURCE: Reprinted by permission of Teffany White.

- Grouping
- Cognitive processing of text, lecture, and discussion
- Games
- Problem-solving scripts and prompts
- Beginning-of-class work (e.g., bell-work, do nows, wake-up work, etc.)
- Checking for understanding
- Cooperative learning routines

Here are some examples of how WITs use these routines in their classrooms:

Mnemonic Devices

Mnemonic devices are favorite academic routines for teaching students how to memorize important information. WITs use acronyms to help students remember strategies like COPS (capitalization, organization, punctuation, and spelling), PQ3R (preview, question, read, recite, and review), and KWL-Plus (K = What we, *k*now, W = What we *w*ant to learn, L = What we *l*earned, and Plus = Developing a resource organizer and summarizing statement about what was learned).

They use acrostics like *Does McDonald's Sell Hamburgers Before Dawn?* (divide, multiply, subtract, check, bring down) to help students remember the steps in the division process (A. Graham) and visualization as described by Susan Graham in the following section to help students memorize vast quantities of new vocabulary.

Susan Graham (S): Have students fold a blank piece of paper into four equal sections once or twice. [There need to be enough sections to accommodate the number of new vocabulary words you expect your students to learn in a week.] Then guide students in the following process:

1. Write one new word, divided into syllables to aid in decoding if applicable, in each folded section.
2. Write a student-friendly definition of the word dictated by the teacher.
3. Draw a picture to aid in remembering what the word means.
4. Draw a smaller picture to serve as a pronunciation clue.

Research indicates that if students draw a picture or "mental map" (see Figure 4.7) of a word (or anything they want to learn), they are likely to remember it seven times longer than if they just memorize it in a rote fashion (Rose & Nicholl, 1997).

Songs, Rhymes, and Chants

Bobbie Oosterbaan (E): I use songs (especially rounds), rhymes, and chants to enhance memory, concentration, and coordination before beginning to teach

Figure 4.7   Memory Builder for Learning Vocabulary

People have a 96% retention rate when they study a big picture of the definition of the word with a small picture of how the word sounds. For example, in Spanish, *pato* is duck, and here is a picture of a duck and a pot.

You don't have to be an artist to use this mnemonic device. You need only 30% of a picture to tell what it is. Can you tell what the following picture is?

If you draw your own picture or "mental map" of anything, not just Spanish vocabulary words, you will remember it seven times longer than memorizing it without any associations (Rose & Nicholl, 1997).

SOURCE: Adapted and reprinted by permission of Susan Graham.

intensive content lessons. Chants that build familiarity with the alphabet, letter sounds, vowels, grammar, and math skills help to synchronize the class and get their minds ready to learn more challenging content.

Role-Playing and Skits

Carol Robertson (S): My students sometimes have a hard time visualizing processes on a molecular level, so we write Readers' Theater skits for molecular characters. One particular skit is about Petunia the Proton and Ed the Electron as they go through splitting up, rejoining briefly, splitting up again, and so on, until their final reunion in a taxi cab.

Using Homework for Instruction

Kathy Hoedeman (S): My least favorite part of teaching math is checking homework. Whether I collect it and check it on my own or we check it together in class, I often find it boring. However, I do believe it's an essential academic routine—an opportunity for me to find out where students need clarification and further instruction. Students need to know whether or not their practice the night before was done well. So I have a number of academic routines that revolve around homework that make it run smoothly. When we check it together in class, students know that three things have to be out on their desks: (1) their journals open to the assignment for the day, (2) their textbook open to the assignment page, and (3) a checking pen. The checking pen is one of the items I require each day in class (pencil, checking pen, and highlighter are three "musts" every day). During the first few weeks of school, I often have my pockets full of Smarties or Jolly Ranchers. When I say, "Let's get ready to check homework," students know they need to get out those three things. The first two cooperative groups in which all four members are prepared will get candy. Soon the routine is automatic, and I phase out the treats.

To keep the grading of homework interesting, Kathy has come up with a menu of ways to grade homework that hold her students accountable without putting her on overload. You'll find the complete set of tips in the WIT's List in Resource A under the heading Homework Helpers.

Grouping and Differentiation

Yvette Wallace (E): I have assigned all of my students to flexible groups of four to six, based on their instructional needs in math and reading. On 3 days of the week, math and reading are taught in a center-type approach. Each group meets with me for instruction at their instructional level, works on an independent project at their independent level, or meets with a trained volunteer who executes a lesson I have written for that group. This is as effective in math as it has traditionally been for reading. Students get more individualized attention, guidance, and monitoring from experienced readers and mathematicians.

Cognitive Processing of Text and Discussion

Yvette Wallace (E): I call this routine "Tell a Neighbor," and I use it to ensure that all students have an opportunity to process concepts and ideas. Rather than asking a question outright and calling on just one student to answer it (leaving other minds to wander), I ask students to talk about an idea or share the answer to the question with a neighbor, before I ask for a volunteer. This routine results in more talking and thinking than I could ever have anticipated. It also trains students to listen to one another. After they "tell a neighbor," I often call on someone to tell us about a good idea they heard from a neighbor.

Games

Susan Biltucci (E): Games are one of my favorite academic routines! I have created a Jeopardy game on the computer that I frequently use as review at the end of a social studies chapter. My son and I developed a template so I can add new questions for each social studies or science unit chapter and then save them on a CD.

Jay Pilkington (S): Row Feud is a note-taking and discussion activity formatted like the television game show *Family Feud.* My version is a combination of note taking, a pop quiz (everyone is required to answer one question), and spirited competition. Here's how it works. I prepare a set of questions (five, to go with the number of rows I have in my seating plan) and notes (answers and additional material I want to make sure the students have mastered) for the part of the chapter that has been assigned as homework reading. First students write the five questions into their social studies notebooks. Then each team (row) is randomly assigned one of the five questions, and away we go.

Problem-Solving Scripts and Prompts

Darla Ryser (E): I use the following problem-solving routine and its accompanying prompts to help students describe in writing how they have solved a problem. I provide instructional support throughout the year, and by the end of the year, students are following the steps and writing responses on their own.

1. Identify the problem or question: *I don't know* _____.
2. Identify and label the variables and important words in the problem: *I do know* _____. Be sure to list or tell the variables and important words.
3. Brainstorm possible methods (ways) to solve the problem: *I could* _____.
4. Choose a method to use: *I'm going to* _____, *because* _____.
5. Use the method and tell step by step what was done: *First, I* _____. *Then, I* _____. *Next, I* _____. *Finally, I* _____.
6. Tell the solution: *I found that* _____.
7. Check to make sure that the solution solves the problem. Check the problem or question you wrote in 1 with the answer you gave in 6.

SOURCE: Adapted from the Kent, Washington, School District Writing Curriculum by Darla Ryser and reprinted with permission.

Do Now, Bell Work, Activators, Brain Work

WITs give many clever names to the assignments their students are expected to complete the minute they enter the classroom in the morning or at the beginning of a class period. Some use commercially prepared materials like Daily Oral Language, Math, or Geography. Others come up with their own ideas based on state standards. To maximize ALT, use these activities to review what you did the day before or to practice knowledge or skills that need to be routinized. Beware of letting these opening activities become mundane and just one more thing you have to get students to do. Unless they are connected to the students' world and the material that needs to be mastered, they will become time wasters.

Thomas Leighty (S): It's extremely important to have an opening independent activity every day. At the beginning of each U.S. History class, my students find a cartoon or brief reading passage related to the lesson on the overhead, along with one or two questions to answer. In my criminal justice classes, students listen to a police scanner and take notes.

Checking for Understanding

Dennis Szymkowiak (S): All of my colleagues (Mundelein High School, Illinois) and I use Entrance and Exit slips on a daily basis to check for student

Figure 4.8   **Entrance and Exit Slip Routine**

1. Choose the format of the slips (e.g., preprinted teacher-designed form, 3" × 5" note cards, 3" × 5" slips of paper, or sticky notes).

2. Choose the prompt (e.g., questions, reflections, vocabulary).

3. Make two slips available to students at the beginning of every day or class period: one to fill out during class to leave with the teacher as they exit (Exit Slip) and one to fill out at home to bring with them to the next class period (Entrance Slip).

4. Collect the slips every day at the beginning and end of class and make sure that students see or hear you using what they have written to inform your instruction or impact their grades.

SOURCE: Reprinted by permission of Dennis Szymkowiak.

understanding and to give us information to keep instruction at the right level of difficulty (see Figure 4.8). Here's the way the routine works in my English classroom. I use 3" × 5" note cards (or paper cut down to that size) for students to respond to the prompt or prompts I give to them. When students have a reading assignment for homework, the prompt for an Entrance Slip might be to write down three questions they have as a result of their reading. Questions work with both fiction and nonfiction, and they are a good readiness activity for student discussion. Quickly reading students' questions before class gives me an immediate understanding of the nature and extent of individual and group comprehension. If all of the questions are of a literal nature, a lesson I've planned at a higher level will need to be modified. Likewise, if students' questions reveal a deeper or more critical understanding, I can move the lesson to a higher level.

WITs are masters at assessing how well their lessons have gone and how they need to adjust instruction. A menu of ways to check for students' understanding can be found in the WIT's List under the heading Checking for Understanding.

Cooperative Learning

Thomas Leighty (S): Cooperative learning is one of the mainstays of my teaching. This approach gives students of varying strengths and abilities the opportunity to work together to solve problems. I also believe that if you put students in friendly competition with one another occasionally, it causes them to study more and work harder. Cooperative learning is research based, always a plus if you want to raise student achievement.

Jay Pilkington (S): Read, Revel, and Reveal is a cooperative learning activity in which small groups prepare oral presentations on different parts of a chapter. Each group does the following:

a. Reads their assigned part of the chapter

b. Revels in the information by discussing the main points of their section and identifying the critical information that needs to be presented to the rest of the class; they prepare an "infoposter" that presents that information in any style they choose: outline, timeline, bulleted list, chart, web, Venn diagram, or acrostic poem

c. Reveals the important information by presenting and discussing their "infoposter" to the rest of the class

Social Routines

Social routines encourage positive social behavior and include *all of the behavioral patterns related to interpersonal communication and relations with others, both peers and teacher.*

Sometimes the routines are one-to-one, such as the social routine used by Kathy Hoedeman that was described in an earlier chapter. She expects her sixth graders to greet her face-to-face every day before they enter the classroom. For many students, this is a difficult assignment. They would prefer to sneak in the door unnoticed, but Kathy insists on their mastery of this very simple social routine—one that will be a part of their interpersonal communication skills for the rest of their lives.

In other instances, the routines are part of a larger classroom or school model, such as the establishment of a learning community like that found in Dennis Szymkowiak's high school English classroom. Dennis begins establishing a learning community during the first week of school, but he knows that this concept must be revisited and reroutinized at critical points during the year. He says,

> **Community is something that needs to be redefined and reestablished at various times during the year. If a new student transfers in or moves to my class from another one, the community needs to be reestablished. If a student leaves, the community needs to be altered. As situations arise, the community needs to be adjusted. In other words, we try to be proactive with our community. If students care about the environment and each other, learning is more likely to take place.**

In Sue Wyman and Michele Engelsiepen's team-taught kindergarten, students learn everything they need to know to be socially adept for the rest of their lives: how to say "please" and "thank you," how to remain quiet if they don't have something nice to say, and how to be respectful to both adults and their classmates.

More sophisticated social routines are taught by first-grade teacher Jill Yates: (1) learning how to respect classmates' personal space when they are standing in line, sitting on the floor, and working at their desks; (2) interpreting the emotions of others by reading their facial expressions and nonverbal cues, as well as listening to their tones of voice; (3) giving and receiving compliments; and (4) asking appropriate questions that are focused on work and products. For a complete list of classroom social routines, consult Resource A.

Teaching manners and character may seem like somebody else's job, but the WITs who contributed to the book believe that social routines, taught as part of building classroom communities, are essential to learning.

> I pay attention to the social structures in my classroom. I watch my students on the playground. I know who my leaders are, and I focus on winning their loyalty first. I keep my eyes and ears open all the time. If I sense there has been a problem at recess or an issue among some friends, I bring it into the open. I ask about it, listen intently to both sides, and then talk about solutions. I'm a process person, and I engage my students in the process of addressing conflict and seeking reconciliation. The world of school is more than the academic context of the classroom. If we don't recognize that, we're always in competition. For me, it's all in the realm of learning . . . learning how to work with others, how to state your opinion, how to win and maintain friendships. It's worth the time it takes to sort out issues that the children are facing, always with the goal of returning to our work with clean minds and fresh hearts.
>
> —Jill Aspegren

Q and A

 Elaine: Besides modeling, what are some other ways to help ELL (English Language learner) students learn classroom organizational, academic, and social routines quickly?

Jerry Jesness: Even if ELL students are being mainstreamed and even if it is policy to not use the students' native language in the classroom, there should be a time and a place where the native language can be spoken. If there is an ELL pullout or scheduled tutoring time, a speaker of the students' language could explain classroom rules and other essentials then. If not, arrangements could be made during playtime or before or after school. If there are no employees who are able to translate, a parent volunteer could assist. This is essential at the beginning of school and useful until the ELL students have a minimal grasp of basic English communication skills.

What's Ahead?

In Chapter 5, we'll consider the second of the 3Rs—rubrics. This topic is a less familiar one, but it's essential for raising student expectations and holding students accountable for higher achievement. Be prepared for more challenging reading ahead, but don't become discouraged. There are many examples that illustrate the "big idea" of the chapter—students can achieve the standards more readily with rubrics.

Chapter 5

Rubrics That Raise Expectations and Achievement

Sharing a scoring instrument [checklist, rating scale, or rubric] with students from the outset allows them to see the specific criteria on which their work will later be judged.

—Mertler (2003, p. 126)

Y ou no doubt have already jotted down several essential routines (organizational, academic, and social) from Chapter 4 that you want to teach to your students in the first 3 weeks of school. This chapter seeks to help you take the next step in becoming a WIT: learning how to design and teach the use of rubrics to your students.

The chapter has two goals: (1) to clearly explain what a rubric is and how it relates to its close cousins, rating scales and checklists, and (2) to show you how all three of these tools, if well designed and appropriately taught, can help you raise expectations and achievement in your classroom. This chapter cannot make you an instant expert, but you will acquire enough knowledge to choose and construct rubrics that motivate your students to improve their work products.

Raising expectations and achievement entails far more than teaching students the right answers, although all teachers focus on content and background knowledge in their daily lessons. Grading true-false or multiple-choice tests is relatively simple. The answers are either right or wrong. However, WITs have bigger goals for their students, and therein lies the importance of using performance assessments in which students' work products or performances are evaluated along a continuum of excellence, thereby enabling them to see precisely what they must do to be successful.

The term *rubric* is used in two ways in this chapter. The first meaning is the accepted academic definition of the term: *a scoring guide, consisting of specific pre-established performance criteria, used in evaluating student work on performance assessments* (Mertler, 2003, p. 126). The term *scoring* usually modifies *rubric*.

The second meaning of rubric used in this chapter is the one I had in mind when I chose *rubrics* to be the second of the 3Rs: *a generic set of performance-based assessment tools that includes checklists and rating scales useful for conveying behavioral, social, and academic expectations to students.* This broad interpretation is my working definition of the term, the one I intend to convey throughout the book. So if you encounter the term *scoring rubric* while you're reading, think Definition 1. When you see the term rubric, think Definition 2.

When they are well constructed and explicitly taught, scoring rubrics, checklists, and rating scales have the potential to accomplish the following goals:

1. Define in precise and age-appropriate language what you want your students to know, do, or be while they are in your classroom as well as when you send them on to the next level.
2. Communicate those expectations to students in positive and empowering ways through the collaborative development of rubrics.
3. Objectively assess students' progress toward meeting the academic and behavioral goals you have set forth and provide helpful information for modifying your instruction.
4. Provide students with ongoing opportunities to self-assess their own academic, social, and behavioral progress.
5. Assist you in teaching your students not only the what but also the how and why in more explicit, systematic, and supportive ways.

With the advent of standards-based instruction and the expectation that all students will achieve, scoring rubrics are frequently touted as the answer to many of education's most perplexing problems (Goodrich, 1997). But like all educational innovations, it's "buyer beware." Rubrics are like scales or blood pressure monitors. They provide lots of interesting information, but unless one is motivated to change, based on the scores one receives, the information is worthless.

Scales and blood pressure monitors tell you that you're overweight or your blood pressure is too high. Similarly, scoring rubrics for writing can inform both you and your students of their shortcomings as writers, but this information is generally insufficient to help the poorest students write better paragraphs. To improve their writing, students need the same things that folks with high blood pressure need: motivation, instruction, and perhaps even some specialized interventions.

In a fascinating study of the impact of instructional rubrics on eighth graders' writing and their knowledge of the qualities of effective writing, Andrade (2001) found that "simply handing out, reviewing and explaining instructional rubrics can orient students toward the criteria for writing as communicated by the rubric and can help students write to those criteria, but a more intensive intervention may be necessary in order to help all students perform at higher levels consistently" (p. 13). And that is the point of this chapter. WITs don't just hand out, review, and explain instructional rubrics. They use them as teaching tools, very early in the school year, to raise expectations and show students how to meet them.

What Is a Rubric?

Scoring rubrics are designed for one purpose only: evaluating (i.e., assessing, scoring, or grading) academic work products—tasks that students have undertaken. Scoring rubrics offer both teachers and students a specific definition of "quality" with a range of intermediate achievement points along the way for which students can aim as they become more proficient. A quick way to determine if you're looking at a scoring rubric rather than a checklist or rating scale is to apply this test: Can I use this instrument to evaluate and grade a student work product or to assess students' ability to perform a certain task on a summative evaluation? If your answer to that question is *no,* then your instrument is not likely to be a scoring rubric. That doesn't mean that it won't be useful for raising expectations and achievement. It only means it isn't a true scoring rubric. A rubric has two identifying features: (1) a list of critical attributes, dimensions, or criteria on which the *task* will be judged and (2) a range of descriptors or numerical ratings that define the *work product* in detail.

Scoring rubrics can be either holistic or analytic. A *holistic scoring rubric* gives teachers the freedom to quickly evaluate a student product for its *overall* quality, proficiency, or understanding of the specific content and skills. A holistic evaluation can be done in one reading. *Analytic scoring rubrics* are more complex and require judging separate parts of a work product (assignment) and then summing up the scores on the individual parts to obtain a final score. Scoring according to an analytic rubric takes much longer, as teachers must examine the work several times, each time evaluating a different element or dimension of the work.

Judith Cimmiyotti has developed a brief generic, holistic scoring rubric for evaluating her sixth-grade students' proficiency in problem solving—one of the standards tested on the Washington Assessment of Student Learning (WASL). The assigned task involves demonstrating understanding of a problem-solving strategy. The scoring rubric displays a range of four different levels of proficiency. (See Figure 5.1.)

Figure 5.1 Problem-Solving Strategy Rubric

4	3	2	1
Student identifies question and strategy used.	Student identifies question and strategy used.	Student identifies question and strategy used.	Student misidentifies question and strategy used.
Student shows work using the strategy and explains work using pictures, words, or numbers.	Student shows work using the strategy and attempts to explain work using pictures, words, or numbers.	Student attempts work using the strategy and attempts to explain work using pictures, words, or numbers.	Student shows little work using the strategy and does not attempt to explain work using pictures, words, or numbers.
Student records solution using correct units.	Student records solution using correct units.	Student records solution using correct units.	Student records solution without correct units.

SOURCE: Reprinted by permission of Judith Cimmiyotti.

What Is a Checklist?

Checklists are also helpful for communicating and teaching expectations to your students. A checklist is a simple evaluation instrument requiring a forced-choice answer. Some checklists require a check mark or initials to be placed on a line to indicate that a certain procedure or step in a process has been followed. Catherine Clausen's second graders use the following Quality Published Work Checklist (Figure 5.2) to make sure they have fulfilled all of the requirements set forth for posting their work on the Awesome Author's board. This checklist communicates her high expectations to students each time they write and publish.

Some checklists call for yes or no responses to a list of questions. First graders in the classrooms of Michelle Perry, Darlene Carino, and Candace Darling use a variety of checklists to help them assess their work or behavior. The following yes-no checklist (Figure 5.3) is a beginning-of-the-year self-assessment for writing. Note the picture cues that help beginning readers "read" the checklist. Later in the year, the checklist will use words.

Darlene, Michelle, and Candace also use a checklist to help students master their morning routine (see Figure 5.4). It is used as both a self-assessment and a report to parents.

What Is a Rating Scale?

Rating scales are a third way to communicate raised expectations. One example of a rating scale is the evaluation instrument you complete after a professional development session. Participants are asked to assign a number to indicate the degree to which certain qualities, characteristics, traits, or practices were evident in the presentation. Rating scales are often used by teachers to rate homework quality, preparedness for class, and participation levels. Val Bresnahan uses a combination rating scale and checklist to rate each one of her students daily on these three criteria (see Figure 5.5 and its explanation in Figure 5.6). Note that although *she* assigns the rating, her students maintain the grade sheet, using a short checklist on the instrument to evaluate their strengths and weaknesses during the week.

How With-It Teachers Use Rubrics

There are numerous reasons to construct rubrics. However, for purposes of teaching the 3Rs, the most important reason is that writing a rubric compels you to articulate your academic and behavioral expectations for students in succinct and explicit ways. The mantra for this chapter is "If *you're* fuzzy about what you expect, your students will be even fuzzier." The second important reason to develop and

(Text continues on page 102)

Figure 5.2   Quality Published Work Checklist

Quality Published Work Checklist

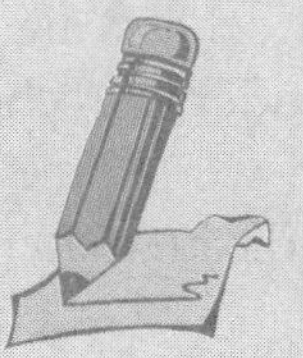

Put a check mark on the line after you have checked your work.

_____ 1. Correct (dictionary) spelling

_____ 2. Your best handwriting

_____ 3. Neat work and quality illustrations

_____ 4. Correct punctuation (ending marks, capitalization, etc.)

_____ 5. Correct heading (name, date, title)

_____ 6. Neat cover and title page (for published book only)

_____ 7. Other important parts of a book (dedication page, about the author page, and table of contents, for published book only)

_____ 8. Organization (page numbers, chapter title, for published book only)

SOURCE: Reprinted by permission of Catherine Clausen.

Figure 5.3   How Does My Writing Rate?

How Does My Writing Rate?

Circle the correct answer to each question.

1. Name _____	Yes	No
2. Finger [image] space	Yes	No
3. Punctuation marks	Yes	No
4. Neat writing on lines	Yes	No
5. Makes sense	Yes	No
6. Correct spelling	Yes	No

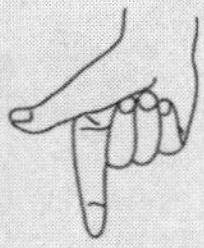

SOURCE: Reprinted by permission of Michelle Perry, Darlene Carino, and Candace Darling.

Figure 5.4   Ready or Not?

Ready or Not?

	Each Day	Most Days	Some Days	No Days
1. Sign up for lunch	4	3	2	1
2. Have sharpened pencils	4	3	2	1
3. Turn in homework folder	4	3	2	1
4. Get morning work	4	3	2	1
5. Write name on papers	4	3	2	1
6. Pick out "just right" books	4	3	2	1
7. Am ready to begin on time	4	3	2	1

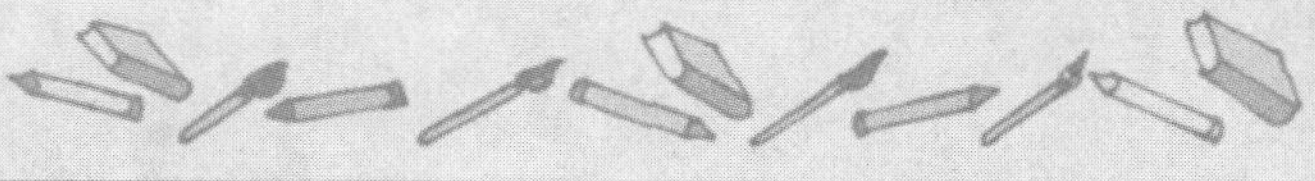

SOURCE: Reprinted by permission of Michelle Perry, Darlene Carino, and Candace Darling.

use rubrics is that once you have put your high expectations on paper, either by yourself or in collaboration with your students, you have made a contract with your students that includes accepting the responsibility for helping them achieve those expectations. If you don't believe your students can learn, they won't.

Scoring rubrics generate the most leverage if written by the teacher who will do the scoring—the individual who knows precisely what each word means and what the subtle differences between *Advanced, Proficient, Developing*, and *Unsatisfactory* are. The second-best scoring rubrics are those developed collaboratively by teachers and students.

Figure 5.5   Small Group Weekly Grade Sheet

Small Group Weekly Grade Sheet

Name: _____   Date: _____

Please see Small Group Weekly Grade Sheet Explanation for how points may be earned.

1	2	3	4	5	6	7	8
DATE	*DAY*	*Homework (5)*	*Class Work (5)*	*Preparedness (5)*	*Participation (5)*	*Total*	*Homework Grade (20)*
	Monday						
	Tuesday						
	Wednesday						
	Thursday						
	Friday						

Total points earned		
Total points possible		
Percentage (%)		Small group average

(Continued)

Figure 5.5 (Continued)

This week I did my best in

Homework

Class work

Preparedness

Participation

I will improve by

_____

I need to improve in

Homework

Class work

Preparedness

Participation

Student Signature

Teacher Signature

Parent Signature

SOURCE: Reprinted by permission of Valerie Bresnahan.

Figure 5.6   **Small Group Weekly Grade Sheet Explanation**

Small Group Weekly Grade Sheet Explanation

A total of 20 points may be earned each day. Points are earned in the following ways:

Area	Points	Explanation
Homework	5	Homework turned in on time with all parts of the assignment attempted
	4	Homework completed but not brought to class. Student has to return to locker to retrieve homework
	3	Homework turned in a day late with all parts attempted
	2	Homework turned in a day late with some parts not attempted
	1	Homework turned in more than a day late with all parts attempted
	0	Homework not turned in or not completed
Classwork	5	Assignment is completed with 95%–100% accuracy
	4	Assignment is completed with 90%–94% accuracy
	3	Assignment is completed with 80%–89% accuracy
	2	Assignment is completed with 70%–79% accuracy
	1	Assignment is completed with 60%–69% accuracy
	0	Assignment is completed with less than 60% accuracy

Preparedness	5	Student is seated in the appropriate desk when the bell rings, with all necessary books, materials, supplies, and homework. Supplies that MUST be ready on the desk at the start of every class are
		    Homework assignment planner
		    Two SHARPENED pencils
		    Dry-erase marker
		    Dry-erase board
		    Blue resource binder, workbook, and notebook

(Continued)

Figure 5.6 (Continued)

Area	Points	Explanation
	0	Student is missing ANY one of the supplies at the start of class, does not have homework, or is not seated when the bell rings
Participation	5	Student actively participated in class with no reminders necessary to stay on task or follow class rules; NO TALK OUTS
	4	Student actively participated in class with one reminder; ONE TALK OUT
	3	Student actively participated in class with two to three reminders
	2	Student participated in class with more than three reminders
	1	Student needed many reminders to stay on task; TWO TALK OUTS
	0	Student needed constant reminders to pay attention or disrupted other students' learning; MORE THAN TWO TALK OUTS

Homework Grade

☐ An additional 20 points per day may be earned for the quality and accuracy of homework assignment.

☐ In addition to receiving a grade for being turned in on time, homework receives a separate grade for the quality and accuracy of the work.

☐ The total possible points earned per homework assignment are 20, regardless of when during the week the assignment is turned in.

☐ Homework MUST be turned in during the week it is assigned.

☐ Homework WILL NOT be accepted after 1:15 PM on the last school day of the week the homework is assigned.

SOURCE: Reprinted by permission of Valerie Bresnahan.

Figure 5.7 Quality Work Rubric

4—Excellent	3—Satisfactory	2—Fair	1—Poor
I did my very best work.	I did a good job.	I can do better.	I did not take my time on my work.
My name is on all my papers.	My name is on all my papers.	My name is missing on some of my papers.	My name is not on my papers.
All of my work is completed neatly.	All of my work is completed.	I forgot to do some parts of my work.	I did not do all of my work.
My handwriting is neat and easy to read.	My handwriting is good.	My handwriting is not as neat as it should be.	My papers are messy and hard to read.
There are very few mistakes (1–3).	I made some mistakes (4–6).	I made more mistakes (7+).	I made a lot of mistakes.

SOURCE: Reprinted by permission of Maggie Wesolowski.

Maggie Wesolowski: Second Grade

At the beginning of the year, Maggie Wesolowski and her second graders spend a lot of time talking about quality work, what its characteristics are, and the importance of taking pride in the work they do. Maggie says, "We go over the holistic scoring rubric together (shown in Figure 5.7), and I show them pretend examples of each qualifier. In the early part of the year, I talk to each child individually about their work so they can see why a particular assignment received a 1, 2, 3, or 4. If they are getting 1s or 2s, we discuss what they need to do to move up to a 3 or 4.

"My students' work folders have a monthly calendar on the front, and each day I put the daily work grade (using the rubric) next to the date. The calendar system is helpful because I can make a note if a student is having trouble with a certain skill. I also write a small H near the date to indicate students required help to complete their work. This information reminds me who needs additional instruction in specific skills. I save the calendars so when I need to report to parents about students' strengths and weaknesses, I have specific information. As an added incentive, each time students accumulate six 4s, they pick a treat from the prize bucket. Any 4s left over at the end of a month are not lost. They're put in the bank to start accumulating again in the next month."

Larry Snyder: Middle School Social Studies

Middle school social studies teacher Larry Snyder specializes in designing both engaging tasks *and* scoring rubrics. These serve to motivate his students to interact with the content of his course and notch up their reading and writing proficiencies to new levels. He loves rubrics, and for good reason. He is able to give complex assignments and yet grade them in a relatively short period of time. When asked to share one or two favorite rubrics with me for possible inclusion in the book, Larry sent more than a dozen. Just looking at some of the titles made me want to do the assignments. The Colony Letter and Map Rubric, shown in Figure 5.8, is designed to evaluate the following task:

> **Assume the role of a colonist who has settled in ONE of the 13 colonies in the early 18th century. In four or more paragraphs of five to seven sentences each, write a letter to a friend in Europe describing the colony in which you have settled. Include the following aspects of life in your colony:**
>
> - **Reasons for colonization, including religion, desire for land, and economic opportunity**
> - **Interactions between Native Americans and European settlers, including agricultural and cultural exchanges, alliances, and conflicts**
> - **Indentured servitude and the introduction of slavery**
> - **Early representative governments and democratic practices that emerged, including town meetings and colonial assemblies**
> - **Include several reasons why your colony may have been a better choice than another colony.**
>
> **Be complete and specific with details and examples. You may use the colonies chart you completed when your fellow classmates presented their brochures [an earlier assignment]. When you have completed the letter, label the 13 colonies correctly on the map. Remember to print the names of the colonies horizontally on the map.**

Larry's scoring rubric has a traditional design: The elements of the assignment are on the vertical axis and the rating scale is on the horizontal axis. Even though the written assignment contains a great deal of information about what Larry wants to see in his students' letters, he lists those critical elements or criteria for the task once again on the vertical axis: (1) reasons, (2) Native American interaction, (3) introduction of slavery, (4) government, (5) reasons supporting the choice of the colony as a place to settle, and (6) the map.

Figure 5.8   Colony Letter and Map Scoring Rubric

Colony Letter and Map Scoring Rubric

	4	3	2	1	0
Reasons	Reasons for colonization are well organized and contain all of the following: religion, desire for land, economic opportunity	Reasons for colonization are organized and contain all of the following: religion, desire for land, economic opportunity	Reasons for colonization are somewhat organized and contain at least two of the following: religion, desire for land, economic opportunity	Organization of information is somewhat confusing and contains two of the following: religion, desire for land, economic opportunity	Information lacks organization or all elements are missing
Native American Interaction	Discussion of interaction between Native Americans and Europeans is well organized and contains all of the following: cultural exchange, agricultural exchange, alliances, and conflicts	Discussion of interaction between Native Americans and Europeans is organized and contains at least three of the following: cultural exchange, agricultural exchange, alliances, and conflicts	Discussion of interaction between Native Americans and Europeans is somewhat organized and contains at least two of the following: agricultural exchange, alliances, and conflicts	Organization of information is somewhat confusing and it contains only one of the following: cultural exchange, agricultural exchange, alliances, and conflicts	Information lacks organization or all elements are missing
Intro of Slavery	Information on indentured servitude is well organized and includes many important facts	Information on indentured servitude is organized and includes several important facts	Information on indentured servitude is somewhat organized and includes several important facts	Information on indentured servitude is somewhat disorganized and includes two or fewer important facts	Information lacks organization or includes no important facts

(Continued)

Figure 5.8 (Continued)

	4	3	2	1	0
Government	Letter includes well-organized information on representative government and democratic practices as well as both of the following: town meetings and colonial assemblies	Letter includes organized information on representative government and democratic practices and at least one of the following: town meetings and colonial assemblies	Letter includes somewhat organized information on representative government and democratic practices and at least one of the following: town meetings and colonial assemblies	Letter's information on representative government and democratic practices is somewhat confusing, but it contains at least one of the following: town meetings and colonial assemblies	Information lacks organization or includes no important facts
Support of Colony	Support for colony is well organized and gives at least three reasons asking for support	Support for colony is organized and gives at least two reasons asking for support	Support for colony is somewhat organized and gives at least one reason asking for support	Support for colony is somewhat confusing and gives only one reason asking for support	Information lacks organization or includes no reasons for support
Map	All 13 colonies are labeled correctly	All but one colony is labeled correctly	All but two colonies are labeled correctly	All but three of the colonies are labeled correctly	More than three colonies are labeled incorrectly

SOURCE: Reprinted by permission of Larry Snyder.

Figure 5.9   Scoring Rubric for Winter Break Newspaper

4—Excellent	3—Satisfactory	2—Fair	1—Poor
Pictures	Three pictures with color	Two pictures with color	Fewer than two pictures, not colored
Sentences	Five sentences about each picture	Four sentences about each picture	Fewer than four sentences about each picture
Capitalization and Punctuation	All capitals and punctuation correct	Most capitals and punctuation correct	Missing capitals and periods
Spelling	All third-grade words spelled correctly	Most third-grade words spelled correctly	Some third-grade words spelled correctly

SOURCE: Reprinted by permission of Kathi Kennedy.

An analytic scoring rubric provides students with detailed information about exactly what their assignment should include to receive a top grade.

Kathi Kennedy: Third Grade

Kathi Kennedy often collaboratively creates scoring rubrics with her third graders. They understand how to construct them and know why they are useful tools. Whenever Kathi makes an assignment, she first models for students how to do what she has assigned. In this case, it's a classroom assignment based on their experiences while on vacation. After she has modeled the assignment, she leads the class in developing a rubric for it.

> **When I create a rubric with my class, I begin by asking, "What would you expect a third grader to do to earn a good score on this project?" Usually someone will throw out a suggestion, we discuss it, and then we vote on whether it should be included in the rubric. I facilitate the discussion, but most of the ideas come directly from them.**

The rubric Kathi's class developed for their newspaper project is shown here, in Figure 5.9.

How With-It Teachers Use Checklists

Checklists are teaching tools that, once created, can be left on your walls during the year to remind students of the expectations. Checklists will help your students reach your expectations even more readily if you systematically model and teach what they look like in actual practice.

Rhonda Carpenter: Fifth Grade

At the beginning of each school year, Rhonda Carpenter and her fifth graders develop a With-it Student Checklist together. The most recent checklist ended up looking like the one shown here, in Figure 5.10.

Of course if you and your students set out to develop a checklist describing a with-it student in your classroom, it will no doubt look different from Rhonda's. However, the impact of a collaborative checklist on student behavior of any kind has less to do with the specific items on the list than with the power of sharing ideas as teacher and students. By the time the final draft appears on your bulletin board, the process has become more important than the product. The end result of this collaboration is that most students will internalize the list and make it their own. Those who don't will need continued teaching and reminders.

In order to engage in a similar collaboration with your students, pay close attention to how Rhonda guides her students to nail down a specific description of what someone who is doing each of these things would look or act like. She can definitely observe the presence or absence of four of the six behaviors. But two of the behaviors are impossible to directly observe. How can a teacher know that a student's ears are listening? Possibly by hearing students repeat or summarize what she said or by seeing them follow some directions that were given. The problem is this: Anyone can *look* like they're listening. In the case of this statement, Rhonda can only look for evidence of hearing. As students reflect on what "listening" looks like, they gain a new understanding of how they should be acting and responding if they want their teacher to know they are listening.

Particularly interesting is the discussion that follows when the students talk about the last item on the checklist.

"I ask students how I, as the teacher, might know that their brains are actually thinking, since I can't see into their brains to know, " Rhonda says. "The students have no problem coming up with answers for me:"

- "You would know our brains were thinking if we participated intelligently in the discussion."
- "You would know our brains were thinking if we asked meaningful questions."
- "You would know our brains were thinking if we were able to answer some of the questions you asked."
- "You would know our brains were thinking if we wrote down something in our Learning Journal right away when you said it was important to remember."

Figure 5.10 **With-It Student Checklist**

With-It Student Checklist

_____ 1. Your eyes are on the teacher.

_____ 2. Your ears are listening.

_____ 3. Your hands are empty.

_____ 4. Your knees are pointed toward the teacher.

_____ 5. Your voice is silent.

_____ 6. Your brain is thinking.

SOURCE: Reprinted by permission of Rhonda Carpenter.

- "You would know our brains were thinking if we turned to our neighbor during Pair and Share and identified three new words we learned from the story we just read."
- "You would know our brains were thinking if we were able to come up with a list of things we have to do differently the next time we write a book report or do our math homework."

Rhonda continues, "One thing that I make clear to my students is that they don't always have to be right to show me their brains are thinking. For example, a statement like, 'I'm not sure about this (whatever the topic is about), but . . . ,' from a student proves to me that their brains are thinking and trying to problem solve."

When Rhonda wants her students to exhibit all six behaviors on the checklist, she says, "Give me a 6 on the Rubric." Rhonda calls this list a rubric, and that's understandable, since _rubric_ is an evaluation and standards term with which her students are very familiar, and her students are very aware of the importance of scoring a 6, so calling this checklist a rubric gives Rhonda a great deal of leverage in terms of student motivation and interest. However, it's virtually impossible to create a scoring rubric for these statements since they ask for a yes-no forced-choice response, there is no task or work product to examine, and there are no descriptors for gradations of attainment.

"I'm very careful not to overuse 'Show Me a 6 on the Rubric,' so when I say it, students know that we're heading into some serious content and they need to get ready to learn."

Figure 5.11   Our Writing Workshop

Our Writing Workshop

Author: _____   Date: _____

1. I shared my work with _____ (child's name).	
2. I edited my work for punctuation (., !, ?), spacing, capitals Ryan_made_a_cake.	
3. I published my work using (circle one)	

SOURCE: Reprinted by permission of Lyssa Sahadevan.

Lyssa Sahadevan: Kindergarten

During the second semester of the school year, Lyssa Sahadevan gathers her students on the rug to talk about the things that good writers do. Together they brainstorm a list of characteristics and develop a three-item checklist (see Figure 5.11). Lyssa says, "The class agreed with me that more than three items would be confusing." The first item they agreed on was sharing their writing with a buddy to (1) see if it makes sense, (2) check for errors, and (3) receive positive comments. Lyssa says, "They liked the statement but wanted to have a space on the checklist to write down the names of their buddies."

The students debated at length about what should be included in Item 2 related to editing. They decided to focus on spacing, punctuation, and capital letters at the beginning of a sentence. They were quite adamant about not including phonetic spelling and sight words since in their words, "These should be done automatically." The students were also quite definite about wanting pictures instead of words in Item 3, and Lyssa gave in.

Lyssa explains why this is her favorite scoring rubric. "We have a county writing rubric for all kindergarten teachers to assess student writing, but this is more meaningful to the students because we created it together."

How With-It Teachers Use Rating Scales

Rating scales can also help students view their work products or behavior in a more discriminating light. There is a powerful difference between telling students to do something because you told them to and pointing to a rating scale describing their level of maturity. With the first approach, you can be drawn into a power struggle with some students. However, referring to a posted maturity scale that students can read and think about more readily produces a positive attitude on the part of students.

Mary Koster: Middle School Math and Science

"I display the Maturity Rating Scale [shown in Figure 5.12] on my bulletin board. It stays up all year, and each student gets a laminated copy. During the first 2 weeks of school, I have the students rate their 'maturity' at the end of each day. Next to the posted maturity scale is a Consequences Poster that reads, 'If you choose not to follow the classroom procedures or expectations, there will be consequences. Consequences will be fair and logical. They will be determined on an individual basis, since each situation is unique and each person is a unique individual. To be fair does not mean giving identical treatment but rather giving

Figure 5.12   Student Maturity Rating Scale

High Maturity Level (Score of 5 or 6)

Student demonstrates a high degree of self-control
- Never talks out in class
- Stays on task
- Remains in seat appropriately
- Doesn't waste time in group learning formats
- Is always respectful of peers, teachers, and supervisors

Student is very self-disciplined
- Does assignments in and out of class without prompting
- Never procrastinates
- Plans ahead

Student is an asset to the class
- Provides leadership
- Volunteers to take part in discussions
- Helps others
- Maintains positive relations with peers

Student has a positive attitude about school
- Is positive and enthusiastic about school
- Sees the connection between grades and work habits
- Always follows class rules and procedures
- Strives for improvement in future performance

Average Maturity Level (Score of 3 or 4)

Student demonstrates some degree of self-control
- Usually does not talk out
- Stays on task most of the time
- Remains in seat appropriately most of the time
- Doesn't waste time in cooperative learning groups
- Is always respectful of peers, teachers, and supervisors

Student is somewhat self-disciplined
- Usually does assignments in and out of class without prompting
- Generally does work on schedule
- Is learning to plan ahead

Contributes to class
- Occasionally takes a leadership role
- Volunteers to take part in discussions
- Helps others
- Maintains positive relations with peers

Has a generally good attitude about school
- Likes school more for the chance to be with peers than anything else
- Often tends to take the short-term, easy ways and fails to see long-term consequences
- Sees the connection between grades and work habits
- Doesn't always follow class rules and procedures
- Usually is disinterested in setting goals for future performance

---

Relative Immaturity (Score of 1 or 2)

Student shows little self-control
- Frequently talks out and needs teacher intervention
- Has a hard time staying on task
- Is often out of seat
- Needs supervision in a group situation
- Shows little respect for peers, teachers, and supervisors

Student shows little self-discipline
- Needs a great deal of prompting to get assignments done
- Frequently misses work
- Generally procrastinates

Student does not contribute to class
- Rarely takes a leadership role
- Participates only when called on or often makes remarks that are disruptive to discussion
- Does not usually help others or tends to distract others
- Engages in negative peer behavior

Student has a poor attitude about school
- Seems to dislike school
- Sees little connection between school and later life
- Shows no respect for the rights of others
- Seldom follows class rules and procedures
- Isn't concerned about future performance

SOURCE: Adapted from the Maturity Self-Assessment Scale by permission of Mary Koster.

each student what is needed. Everyone will be treated with dignity and respect, but not everyone will have the very same consequences. Though there may be times that I will not condone your actions, you are still a valued member of this class, and you will be treated as such.'"

Using a Rubric, Checklist, or Rating Scale to Motivate Student Performance

Deanna Barrett teaches language arts and is the department chair at Aki Kurose Middle School Academy in Seattle. The challenges of raising achievement in a low-performing school where nearly 75% of the students receive free or reduced-price meals have consumed her energies for the past 4 years. When Deanna returned to education after a long career as a travel agent, the educational landscape was dramatically different from the early 1970s when she began her teaching career. Accountability, results, and the WASL were the buzzwords. Her sentiments about state tests at that point were not particularly positive. However, neither was the performance of students at Aki Kurose. In 2000–2001, the percentage of students achieving proficiency in writing was 23.5, in reading, 11.4, and in math, 4.2.

As a writing teacher, Deanna was sent for WASL training almost immediately. It was then that she had an opportunity to score some tests and become familiar with the standards. It changed her outlook completely. She says, "I knew that our students could become more effective writers if only they were taught. I also knew that I could take what I had learned in the session, and we could develop a writing rubric to focus our instruction. Our students had no idea what the basics of writing even were."

The efforts of Deanna and her colleagues paid off. By 2001–2002, 43.5% of the seventh graders were at the proficient level. The trend was upward, but it wasn't moving fast enough to satisfy Deanna. She noticed that many students didn't even try when they took tests. They skipped items, gave up when the clock showed they had ample time left to work, and failed to employ even the most basic test-taking strategies. Even when they knew the content, they seemed to lack confidence and would not try even the simplest questions. Deanna and the school leadership team hypothesized that if a rubric worked for raising writing achievement, perhaps one focused on test performance attributes might work similarly. To that end they developed My Best Performance Rubric to be used as an instructional tool with students. The instrument is designed like a rubric, with four categories of achievement, but includes elements of a checklist as well (see Figure 5.13).

Figure 5.13   My Best Performance Rubric

My Best Performance Rubric	☆ Exceeds Standards ☆	Meets Standards ☆	Approaching the Standard–Needs Improvement	Standards Not Met
Preparedness	I am quiet and in my seat on time, with my pens, pencils, notebook, planner, and any other supplies I need.			
Respectful Attitude	I am polite to my classmates and adults and respectful of their right to work without disruption.			
Confidence and a Positive Attitude	I *always* show that I believe in myself by being serious and focused and by taking pride in doing my very best. I know that confidence will positively impact my work.	I *consistently* show that I believe in myself by being serious and focused and by taking pride in my work. I know that confidence will positively impact my work.	I *sometimes* show that I believe in myself by being serious and focused. Sometimes I get discouraged, and it becomes hard for me to be proud of my work.	I *do not* take my work or achievement seriously. I often get discouraged and *do not* show that I am confident.
Time Management	I use *all* of the time I am given to work on my task and check my work. I keep my attention focused on doing my very best.	I use the *majority* of the time I am given to work on my task and check my work. I consistently keep my focus on doing my very best.	I *sometimes* use only a portion of the time I am given to work on my task and check my work. I am frequently unfocused and inattentive.	I *do not* stay focused on doing my best. I use only the minimum amount of time I am given to work attentively on my task. I rarely check my work.
Reading the Questions Carefully (Being Sure About What I'm Being Asked to Do!)	I use *all* of these strategies to follow the instructions correctly: I underline key words of the instructions. I number the steps of the instructions. I restate the question in my answer.	I use at *least two* of these strategies to follow the instructions correctly: I underline key words of the instructions. I number the steps of the instructions. I restate the question in my answer.	I *sometimes* rush through reading the instructions and am in a hurry to answer the questions. I *sometimes* do not use many of the strategies that are needed to help make me successful.	I *do not* read the instructions or I carelessly rush through reading the instructions. I *do not* use any set strategies effectively.
Perseverance and Determination	I *always* push myself to continue working on the task, even when difficulties arise or a solution is not immediately clear.	I *consistently* try to continue working, even when the task is difficult or a solution is not immediately clear.	*Sometimes* I get discouraged and give up. The task seems to take too long, and *sometimes* I decide not to continue to try.	I often become frustrated and tired. I do not feel like I can do well on my task and *do not continue* to try my best.

Figure 5.13 (Continued)

My Best Performance Rubric	☆ Exceeds Standards ☆	Meets Standards ☆	Approaching the Standard–Needs Improvement	Standards Not Met
Making an Attempt on Every Task	I *always* pay attention to places where the instructions say things like "show all your work" "describe or show" "give two examples"	I *consistently* pay attention to places where the instructions say things like "show all your work" "describe or show" "give two examples"	I *sometimes* pay attention to places where the instructions say things like "show all your work" "describe or show" "give two examples"	When I turn in my assignments, I *do not* check to see that I've answered everything completely.
Resourcefulness	When I am confused or unsure of how to do something, I brainstorm all of the different ways I might solve the problem. Then I try several approaches until I feel comfortable with my answer.	When I am confused or unsure of how to do something, I think about how to solve the problem using strategies I know. I *consistently* use a strategy I feel comfortable with.	When I am confused or unsure about how to do something, I *sometimes* get frustrated and give up. Every now and then, I try to answer the question or solve the problem using a strategy that I think will help. As a result, I often leave answers blank or give incomplete responses.	I *do not* think of any strategies that will help me solve the problem or answer the question. I frequently get frustrated and give up. As a result, I often leave answers blank or give partial responses.
Using Resources and Tools to Check My Work	I use *all* of the resources and tools that I am allowed to use to make my work stronger. *(calculator, thesaurus, dictionary, graphic organizers)* I use my finger or a pencil to scan my work to be sure I'm not leaving blanks where there should be an answer!	I *consistently* use all of the resources and tools that I am allowed to use to make my work stronger. *(calculator, thesaurus, dictionary, graphic organizers)* I use my finger or a pencil to scan my work to be sure I'm not leaving blanks where there should be an answer!	I *sometimes* use the resources and tools that I am allowed to use to make my work stronger. My original draft or response rarely shows that it's been improved. I *sometimes* use my finger or a pencil to scan my work to be sure I'm not leaving blanks where there should be an answer!	I *do not* use the resources and tools that I am allowed to use to make my work stronger. My work does not show that I've improved upon the original draft or response. I *do not* scan to be sure that I'm not leaving any blanks where there should be an answer.

SOURCE: Copyright © 2004 by Aki Kurose Middle School Academy. Reprinted by permission.

Taking tests requires a confident mind-set, a strategic approach, and a deep desire to do your best. In addition to improving their instructional strategies in all content areas, the faculty at Aki Kurose now begins each school year by teaching their students that giving up before you start is not an option at Aki Kurose.

What's Ahead?

Chapter 6 will help you to get a handle on the third and final R—rules. In addition, you'll find helpful information about the controversial topic of using rewards with students. WITs weigh in with a variety of approaches that will help you firm up your rules and rewards and then teach them in an organized way to your students.

Chapter 6

Rules and Rewards That Build Character and Motivation

Although it is widely acknowledged as important, the

teaching of rules in clear and unambiguous terms is not

easily accomplished. The general practice is for teachers

merely to recite the rules by telling them to students.

This practice is based on the assumption that students

already know how to behave and that the teaching of

what's already known is simply not necessary; in fact, it

may appear redundant and in some cases silly.
—Kameenui & Darch (1995, p. 70)

There's always a bit of excitement in the air when a new semester begins. As Jean Piazza's high schoolers file into her classroom, they're anticipating a different kind of class, one in which they'll learn a variety of strategies to help them tackle reading and writing assignments with more confidence. But before they've even settled into the seats they have chosen, Jean tells them they aren't actually enrolled in Strategic English after all: They're going to take an extended vacation together.

"I compare our class to going on a tour," Jean explains. "I use this analogy throughout the course."

Jean doesn't go over the syllabus with her students; she shows them the course map. Then she further piques their curiosity by telling them that when necessary, they will take side trips and make rest stops, similar to those they experience on a car trip.

"Occasionally if something catches our fancy," Jean tells her students, "we may just depart from our scheduled itinerary for a day and explore an intriguing question that we agree needs answering." The class always makes a rest stop when they complete a unit. "This is the time we check to be sure everyone is still with us," Jean explains. "We don't want to leave anyone behind when the bus pulls out—when we move on to the next unit."

The students keep notebooks (their photo albums) and collect work samples (souvenirs of their trip) throughout the semester. According to Jean, the "trip" analogy helps her students take ownership of the course. They maintain some control over the itinerary and can call for side trips or rest stops whenever they need one. Along with their teacher, they make the rules in their classroom.

The analogies and models used by WITs to enlist their students' support of and compliance with their behavioral expectations are informed by approaches that emphasize dignity (Curwin & Mendler, 1999), caring (Noddings, 1992), cooperative learning (Johnson et al., 1994), learning communities like tribes (Gibbs, 2001), responsive schools (Cobb, 1992), and assertiveness (Canter, 2001).

Many WITs follow no specific program or philosophy but, like kindergarten teacher Barbara LaMastus, subscribe to simple but elegant concepts like character and responsibility as foundations for learning. Barbara doesn't wait long to tell her students that in her classroom, they are no longer ordinary children. They are now Tyson Tigers, students of character and achievement. To remind them of the obligations that accompany this honor, they recite their class motto and school cheer daily.

Although their metaphors may differ—tigers, tourists, or tribes—WITs all have the same lesson plans for the first day of school: to teach their students the rules that will make their classroom a special place to live and learn. Before the rules can be taught, however, they have to be chosen or collaboratively developed with the students.

The Challenge of Choosing the Third R: Rules (and Rewards)

Settling on the routines and rubrics you want to use, as we did in Chapters 4 and 5, is child's play compared to choosing the rules (and rewards, if desired) that will "govern" your classroom. The typical classroom management textbook makes it sound quite simple and straightforward:

1. Make classroom rules consistent with school rules.
2. Involve students in making the rules to the degree that you are comfortable and to the degree that the students' age levels and sophistication permit.
3. Identify appropriate behaviors and translate them into positively stated classroom rules.
4. Focus on important behavior.
5. Keep the number of rules to a minimum (3–6).
6. Keep the wording of each rule simple and short.
7. Have rules address behaviors that can be observed.
8. Identify rewards when students follow the rules and consequences when they break them. (Burden, 2000, p. 95)

These eight guidelines are good ones to follow, but they don't tell you what to do when 3 of your 20 students are oblivious to the concepts of respect and responsibility that are the cornerstones of your behavior plan. The experts rarely mention the challenges of teaching in a place where there are no school rules to keep order in the hallways and little administrative support. If developing rules consisted only of drawing up a short list and posting it on every bulletin board, there would be no behavior problems in schools. However, as you have probably already surmised, the underlying secret to a smoothly running classroom lies not merely in *having* rules but in *teaching* your rules (or concepts and principles) to your students and then *consistently* upholding them in your daily practice.

Regrettably, there are some students who are at risk academically and also behaviorally. In far too many schools, those students are in the majority. They haven't yet learned how to be respectful and responsible. You cannot just tell them to be models of decorum. You must explain, model, give specific behavioral examples and nonexamples, guide their daily practice, and affirm their ability to be students of character. You must then continue to remind and reinforce, sometimes for much longer than you think should be necessary. Don't ever assume. To be an assumptive teacher when it comes to academics means that many students will fail to master the standards and outcomes. To be an assumptive teacher when it comes to your students' behavior, however, means that you will not only fail to become a WIT, you may even lose your job.

Here are just a few of the questions that must be addressed before you can face your students on the first day:

- Will you adopt a popular discipline model or design an eclectic behavior plan that combines the strengths of several different models?
- How many rules do you need?

- Will your rules be conceptual (respect and responsibility) or behavioral (no talking when the teacher is talking)?
- Will you decide what the rules are, or will you develop them collaboratively with your students?
- Will you develop a list of consequences that is faithfully followed or a flexible plan that deals with problems on an individual basis?
- Will you have a behavior incentive program from the first day, or will you wait and see?
- Will you include rewards in your plan, and if so, what kind? Will they be planned or spontaneous?

The WITs who contributed to this book can help you explore these issues. They don't have all the answers, but they do offer some options for your consideration. You will discover that there are multiple ways to create productive and positive classroom environments. WITs use what works for them. The challenge for you is to find a model (or models) that meshes with your personality and teaching style but is flexible enough to handle students who fall outside the norm.

Q and A

Q Elaine: What do you do when you have a pervasive behavior problem that is undermining your class morale (e.g., stealing, bullying, or teasing)?

A Michelle O'Laughlin (E): I have a class meeting. I teach the rules for class meetings at the beginning of the year, and we review them periodically as needed. We use this same format for one-on-one problem solving, teaching students to use the class meeting procedures for mediating issues themselves and relying less on adult intervention. I actually had a businessman borrow our rules to use in his staff meetings.

Class Meeting Rules

- Sit in a circle.
- Make eye contact.
- When discussing the issue, move toward solution, rather than restating the problem over and over.
- Say, "I like you, and I don't like it when you _____ because it makes me feel ___."

- Listeners are silent. No interruptions.
- Ganging up is not acceptable. Don't nod heads. It is like ganging up.
- No put-downs are allowed. One put-down requires two put-ups (positive, affirming statements). Talk kindly.
- Maintain confidentiality. What is said here stays here.
- Arguing is not tolerated.
- Show respect for others' feelings.
- Be clear in conveying your message.

The Basic Approaches to Discipline

There are four basic approaches to dealing with students' behavior (or misbehavior):

1. The *behavior modification approach* in which you shape or modify student behavior by consistently and systematically rewarding (reinforcing) appropriate student behavior and removing rewards for inappropriate behavior (some call it punishing)
2. The *interpersonal relationship approach* in which you seek to develop trust and close relationships with students, using these relationships as a motivator for positive behavior (McLoughlin, 2005)
3. The *cooperative group process approach* in which you use group dynamics and rapport to foster unity and cooperation to accomplish academic tasks and achieve behavioral expectations
4. The *authority approach* in which you seek to establish your position as the person-in-charge through a definitive statement of rules as well as consequences for failing to comply with these rules (adapted from Ryan & Cooper, 1995, p. 60)

Q and A

Elaine: How can teachers deal with students who come to kindergarten (or any grade) without the basic social skills needed for learning (e.g., waiting for a turn to speak or act, understanding and following directions, and actively listening)?

Paula Larson (E): Teachers must believe that 5-year-olds (or any age student) can sit and wait for their turns, listen to others, and keep their bodies still for a full 20 to 30 minutes. I keep my expectations extremely high to have the results I do. Teachers must remember that if students are not attending, they are not processing the information and skills being taught. It is impossible to talk and listen at the same time, so I am really tough on my students. I nail them the first time they start squirming. But I also shower them with praise when they get it right.

I teach three nonnegotiable and consistently enforced rules to my students:

1. *When I am talking, you are not.* I ask my students to repeat that sentence with me often until they reach the point of automaticity. When I say, "When I am talking, you are . . .," they answer, "*not.*"

2. *Sitting tall.* Most of my instruction takes place while students are sitting on the carpet. Rather than listing all of the things I want students to do while they're on the carpet, I teach them exactly what I mean by the phrase *sitting tall:* It means folded legs, hands in lap, mouths closed, eyes on me, and leave your shoe laces alone. Once I have modeled, we practice, and once they have mastered sitting tall, all I need to say at the beginning of a lesson or as a reminder is, "Sitting tall."

3. *Quiet hands.* I explain to my students that they can only answer a question if I call on them, and in order for me to call on them, I must see what I call *quiet hands.* Quiet hands are hands that are raised without students talking at the same time. I explain and model, and we practice how that works until they have it. I cannot and will not call on someone who does not have a quiet hand. In the beginning, my students say what they want to say the minute they put their hands in the air. I stop them. I remind them. Then I call on a student who is doing the right thing. I make positive comments about that student doing the right thing. And then the very next person I always call on is the student who was talking out of turn earlier. I praise that student profusely for using a quiet hand.

This process takes some time in the beginning of the year but far less time than you might expect, if you are consistent. I often say this during a question-and-answer time: "With a quiet hand, who can tell me what the setting of this story is?" Then I have communicated the expectation at the beginning, rather than taking time from the lesson.

Here are some examples of how WITs have adopted, adapted, and combined these various approaches to create plans that work for them.

Shannon Coombs: First and Second Grade Combination Class

Shannon Coombs believes in the power of building interpersonal relationships, often affirming students for just being themselves. She hands out plenty of accolades for excellent work and behavior. However, she realizes that some students, for a variety of reasons, fail to respond to this approach and need an alternative. Here's an example of behavior modification at work in her classroom:

> **I am a firm believer in intrinsic motivation, but I have one student with a difficult home life and serious health problems who failed to respond positively to anything I did. In order to jump-start some positive classroom (and recess) behavior, the principal and I initiated a behavior management program in which he has the opportunity to earn stars every half hour. He earns a star on his chart by doing his work, paying attention in class, and not being disruptive. When he accumulates three stars, he earns the privilege of going to the principal's office to report on his progress. He may read a story to her, talk to her about his day, and so on. He also gets a piece of candy from her when he visits, but we will be fading that out of the plan soon. Our hope is that this plan coupled with some positive one-on-one attention will be enough to motivate him to follow our rules.**

[Note: Many educators are replacing sugary, nonnutritious candy with nonfood incentives like stickers and tokens that can be cashed in for small prizes. For ideas, consult the WIT's List in Resource A.]

Jill Aspegren: Fourth Grade

Jill Aspegren uses her own version of the interpersonal approach to deal with student misbehavior. She never uses discipline charts, checks on the board, regular rewards, or punishments. She describes her approach to managing student behavior in this way:

> **I just don't think rewards go the distance in real life. Nobody stops you on the highway and gives you a candy bar for driving the speed limit. You obey the speed limit as a member of the community or you take the risk of getting a ticket.**

If you do take the risk, you might get a ticket and you might not. You might receive a huge fine or you might be given a warning. I am very clear about my expectations for students' behavior, but I deal with almost all of my discipline issues on an individual basis. I expect my students to talk things over with me if I approach them about a behavioral concern. I expect the truth from them, and I do the best I can to make decisions that move us toward the greater goal. For example, if a student doesn't finish the homework and has a reasonable explanation for its lateness, I accept that, agree on when it will be finished, and move on. If a different student doesn't finish the homework, but I sense a case of laziness and too much television, I talk with the student about my concerns and suggest some possible interventions or punishments.

> We believe that a reward can be as simple as a smile, a thumbs-up, or a pat on the back. We teach our students that they need to feel rewarded by knowing that they simply did their best. However, we do feel that everyone, including adults, needs recognition and "prizes" to help keep them motivated to do their best.
> —Darlene Carino, Candace Darling, and Michelle Perry (E)

Kelly Paul: Fourth Grade

Kelly Paul uses a combination of the cooperative group process and behavior modification to keep her class behaving and achieving:

I know that some educators believe rewards are detrimental, and I'm sure, used to the extreme, they can be. But I have found that when used in a balanced way, they encourage students to work cohesively toward a common goal and can be a motivating force for some children. After all, even as adults, we enjoy rewards. I use a point system in which teams can earn points throughout the day for virtually anything—a job well done, all team members having their homework done, or everyone earning over a 90 on a quiz. I have popsicle sticks color coded with points in denominations of 50, 100, 1,000, 5,000, 10,000, and 100,000. Each day, sticks are added to or subtracted from the team can (which is color coded with the color assigned to the team).

Rules and Rewards That Build Character and Motivation

Susan Graham: High School Spanish

Susan Graham teaches high schoolers in a challenging urban environment. Her goal is to have all of her students speaking Spanish by the end of the school year, and accomplishing that goal requires every minute of her allocated instructional time. Although her sense of humor and "soft" side are very evident in the colorful PowerPoint presentations she has developed to teach her rules (the popular cartoon character Suzy the Duck, from Suzy's Zoo, shows up on each slide waving at the students), she nonetheless communicates her expectations and consequences directly and explicitly. She assumes nothing.

> Try not to get into a power struggle with students or become exasperated about the things they fail to do or do wrong. For example, when students ask questions because they haven't read the directions on the board, I simply point to the board. I try to begin my requests to students with "please" or "I need to have you..." While this last phrase seems a little awkward when you first start using it, a request for students' help is more likely to be followed than a direct order.
>
> —Susan Graham (S)

The behavior and attitude she teaches most explicitly is respect, using multiple nonexamples to make sure her students are very clear about the concept. The first slide of her rules presentation contains this statement: "Disrespect is not an option in this classroom." She goes on to list and model the specific behaviors that she considers to be disrespectful and defines them during her lesson: (1) swearing, (2) raising your voice, (3) mumbling under your breath, (4) sighing, (5) "tsking," and (6) making any other types of mouth-clicking noises. She explains to students that although these responses may not be disrespectful in their neighborhood or relationships with peers or family members, they are definitely not acceptable at school or in the workplace. Susan explains, "When my students see my huffing, tsking, and eye rolling, they laugh, but they also quickly realize how inappropriate those behaviors are in my classroom. I explain that there are different rules for different games, and school is a different game from the neighborhood."

Here is the range of consequences in Susan's classroom:

1. A look [I know what you're trying to get away with, and I'm giving you a silent warning now.]
2. A Post-it note on the student's desk noting the problem [This is your second warning. Please stop talking when I am talking.]
3. A private conference with the teacher [Will you please stay after class for a few moments? I need to talk with you about your behavior.]
4. A note or a call to your home [I'm going to be calling your dad tonight to tell him about your disrespectful behavior in Spanish class.]
5. A referral to security [Susan picks up her phone and asks for security to come and pick up a student from her classroom for disrespectful behavior.]

She also displays the following statement in her PowerPoint: "If you speak to me or treat me disrespectfully, expect to leave the classroom." She goes on to say, by way of an additional reminder, "I very rarely bother the deans. I take care of my own problems; so when I do write a referral, I get very quick results."

Susan Biltucci: Fifth Grade

If you are looking for a behavior plan template, look no farther. Susan Biltucci's plan shown, in Figure 6.1, is a good place to start. She states two general rules and then explains each of them in greater detail, specifying exactly what respect and responsibility mean in her classroom. She spells out the consequences, leaving some leeway for instances when she may want to bend the rules to fit a special circumstance. She then describes the goodies that will be forthcoming to students each Friday if they follow these rules.

Nettie Griffin: Kindergarten

Nettie Griffin and her kindergartners brainstorm a list of possible rules on the first day of school. Using that list, she works with her students to develop a final set that she then spells out more specifically. The majority of Nettie's students have attended 2 years of preschool, and the concepts of rules and behavior plans are familiar ones to them and their families. See Figure 6.2, Kindergarten Classroom Rules. The rules become part of what Nettie calls the Stoplight Behavior Plan, shown in Figure 6.3. Her plan fits in with a schoolwide set of rules. The plan is sent home on the second day of school, along with a contract for parents to sign after they have discussed the rules with their children. Students who are unable to follow the rules receive a Behavior Slip (shown in Figure 6.4) to take home as a reminder to do better the following day.

What Works and What Doesn't?

Mr. Ames and Mr. Jones (pseudonyms for teachers I have known) have the same eighth-grade students for different periods each day. Mr. Ames teaches Language Arts during seventh period, and Mr. Jones has the group for American History during fourth period. The students are attentive, hardworking, and respectful in Mr. Jones's classroom. Mr. Ames experiences another side of their personalities.

(Text continues on page 135)

Figure 6.1 Susan's Behavior Plan

What Are the Rules?

1. Respect yourself, others, and property.

2. Take responsibility for your choices and actions.

What Do the Rules Mean?

1. Respect yourself, others, and property.

   - Follow directions the first time they are given.

   - Keep hands, feet, and objects to yourself.

   - Receive permission before speaking.

   - Remain in the designated area.

   - Do not use bad language, tease, or make unkind, disrespectful, or inappropriate remarks to others.

2. Take responsibility for your choices and actions.

   - When you have made a good choice, praise yourself and continue making good choices.

   - If you made an unwise choice or acted in an inappropriate manner, accept that it was not a good choice, do what is appropriate to amend the unacceptable choice, like apologize, and then learn from it to improve your behavior.

What Are the Consequences?

   - Warning

   - Time-out, a letter or call home to parents, loss of privilege, or other action deemed appropriate by the teacher

   - Discipline report presented to the principal for further action

What Are the Rewards?

Students who exhibit positive behavior will receive Friday Free Time, where they can use board games, spend time at the computer, read, and draw.

Students who earn Friday Free Time have the privilege of going to my classroom Web page and accessing a site with a variety of links to online learning games. Students may also access this Web page when their homework is done and they are ahead of their requirements for Accelerated Reader. My classroom Web page is located at http:www.geocities.com/Athen/ Bridge/4917.

SOURCE: Reprinted by permission of Susan Biltucci.

Figure 6.2   Kindergarten Classroom Rules

Kindergarten Classroom Rules

1. Follow directions the *first* time they are given.

2. Treat all people with respect. (Use kind words; no teasing or put-downs.)

3. Keep hands, feet, and objects to yourself.

4. Respect and care for all school property.

5. Use an indoor voice when speaking: no yelling or screaming.

6. Walk in the room and hall at all times.

*These rules correspond with the schoolwide rules listed on the discipline slip.

Please review this classroom plan with your child, sign, and return the form by next Friday. Please do not hesitate to call me if you have any questions about this plan.

I have read the classroom discipline plan and discussed it with my child,

_____

(Write your child's name)

_____

Parent/Guardian Signature

SOURCE: Reprinted by permission of Nettie Griffin.

Figure 6.3   Stoplight Behavior Plan

Stoplight Behavior Plan

Dear Parents,

Your child deserves the most positive educational climate possible for his or her growth. In order for this to happen daily, we will be using the Stoplight Behavior Plan. This plan provides clear expectations for behavior in which the students fully understand the consequences of their actions. It also provides a way to reward students who display good behavior consistently. The Stoplight Behavior Plan allows us not only to redirect negative behavior, but to also reinforce and reward positive behavior. The plan and our classroom rules are outlined below.
Each day, all of the children's names start out on the green light.

1. If a child chooses to break a rule, a verbal reminder is given. Their name remains on the green light.

2. The second time a rule is broken, the child moves his or her name to the *yellow light* to remind them to slow down and think about what they are doing.

3. If a child continues to choose not to follow the classroom rules, the child moves his or her name to the *red light* to let them know they need to STOP and think about the rules. They also need to fill out a "ticket" that holds the child accountable for their behavior.

4. The fourth time a child breaks a rule, the child's name is off the stoplight and a discipline slip is sent home.

To encourage children to follow rules, I will support appropriate behavior with verbal recognition, positive notes or awards, and phone calls home.

If a child has continuous difficulty in following classroom rules, an individual behavior plan will be set up.

SOURCE: Reprinted by permission of Nettie Griffin.

Figure 6.4   Student Behavior Form

Name _____

Rules I Broke Today

Date _____

_____

I need to    and think about the class rules.

_____

I need to    and think about what I am doing.

_____

I am having a GREAT day by following the rules!

I am going to try to have a better day. _____

Signature _____

SOURCE: Reprinted by permission of Nettie Griffin.

The teachers are new on the job. Mr. Ames obviously missed class the day that discipline was covered in his undergraduate training. He needs some solid advice, and soon, regarding how to choose, teach, and enforce a set of rules in his classroom. Unfortunately, he's already made all of the classic mistakes:

- He posted a list of vague and wordy rules, reading them aloud once to his students.
- He didn't take the time to teach his rules so that students would know precisely what he expected and understand the reasons behind his rules.
- He doesn't have a plan for what to do when students act inappropriately, and so he ignores their misbehavior for as long as he can.
- When he finally pays attention to misbehavior, he overreacts, humiliating students in front of their classmates. Once he's lost his temper, students go back to misbehaving, and he goes back to ignoring them.

Mr. Ames needs counsel from a WIT—high school English teacher Marjorie Wood. The rules in Marjorie's class are explicit. Three of the six rules emphasize academic pursuits, and they are all stated positively:

- Follow rules and guidelines in student handbook.
- Follow teacher directions readily.
- Cooperate with others and respect their property.
- Speak at appropriate times using acceptable language.
- Come to class prepared with essential materials.
- Work during all work times.

Marjorie teaches these rules each semester, using a PowerPoint presentation that spells out her expectations in plain language. She also posts the rules in her classroom and refers to them as necessary. When new students enroll, she takes time for a whole-class discussion, asking her current students to explain each rule and provide reasons for it. She reviews and reteaches the rules at the end of each marking period, a time when students are evaluating their progress. She guides them to examine areas of their behavior that may be keeping them from getting top-notch grades.

If they produce, Marjorie's students get rewards. Some of the incentives are clearly intrinsic: self-satisfaction, better grades, and improved reading and writing skills to apply in their content classes. She spends time selling her students on the benefits of her strategic English class and then delivers the goods by helping them become academically successful. She knows that many behavior problems stem from students' inabilities to understand or do the class work, and she teaches to mastery for every student. There are also extrinsic rewards in Marjorie's class: positive notes or telephone calls home; free time to read, draw, or go to the library; and extra credit points. Then, because she knows students love surprises, she brings bagels and juice to keep their energy levels high during tests. She also periodically gives them time to choose a computerized learning game, like PowerPoint Jeopardy, as a reward for working extra hard. Marjorie rarely, if ever, has behavior problems with her students. They are too busy learning.

Q and A

Lindsay Wiley (E): What is an appropriate consequence for breaking a rule such as *No name-calling*? I want to teach students the value of being respectful to others, but just giving them a detention or forcing them to make an apology to someone seems rather meaningless.

Judith Cimmiyotti (E): I use a combination of my "Discipline Circle" (referred to in Chapter 1) and a "Think Zone" to handle all of my behavior problems. Let me explain. I work within two circles during the day. The *first* circle is my invisible teaching circle at the front of the room, around my overhead LCD machine. The *second* circle is the discipline circle, usually just outside the classroom door. I teach the meaning of these two circles to my students during the first 3 weeks of school. I believe that clearly differentiating between these areas allows students to feel secure about where and how they will be disciplined.

To handle situations like the one you mentioned in your question, I move to my discipline circle before I say or do anything. Once there, I briefly conference with students and offer them opportunities to eliminate the inappropriate behavior immediately. Offenders get only one more warning after that and then I send them to the Think Zone (a quiet desk at the back of the room facing a wall) to complete a reflection sheet. I don't say a word. I walk directly to a student's desk and place a Time Out for Reflection Sheet on it (see Figure 6.5). Students know (because I taught the process at the beginning of the year and review it periodically) they must immediately remove themselves from the group, go to the Think Zone to complete the reflection sheet, and then return to the group after they have regained control of their emotions and completed their paperwork.

Figure 6.5   Time Out for Reflection

Time Out for Reflection

Name _____

Date _____

Answer the following questions and return the Reflection Sheet to your teacher.

1. What did the behavior look like?

2. What should the behavior look like?

3. What are three actions you will take to achieve the desired behavior?

4. Circle the one action you will focus on as you return to your seat.

SOURCE: Reprinted by permission of Judith Cimmiyotti.

With-It Teachers' Roundtable

RULES AND REWARDS

Elaine: What are the important rules in your classroom?

Jenny Hoedeman (E): Our rules are simple and straightforward. Take care of yourself. Take care of others. Take care of the environment. We then do a lot of brainstorming about what these rules look like. Then everything can be brought back to these questions: Are you taking care of others when you push ahead in line? Are you taking care of the environment when you throw your wrapper on the floor?

Elaine: How do you decide on the rules and consequences for your classroom?

Carol Howell (E): Our rules are determined collaboratively. They are established on Day 1 and followed consistently throughout the year. The major consequence of misbehavior or not completing work to expectations is not being able to participate in "choosing" at the end of the day. For most children, the privilege of interacting with interesting materials and peers in a relaxed atmosphere at the end of the day is a great incentive for positive and productive behavior. I avoid extrinsic, tangible rewards (stickers, candy, etc.) because I think they are ineffective in the long run. Choosing, in itself, serves as a daily reward. Of course, compliments and sincere praise are given regularly, and we celebrate successes often.

Elaine: How do you teach the rules to your students?

Jill Yates (E): I assume nothing and teach everything. I have found that too many assumptions about what *quiet, independent,* and *sharing* mean to students leads to problems. At the beginning of the year, I go out of my way to find model behaviors to reward. This allows me to point out specific examples of what I expect and will praise, while giving other students concrete examples of what to work toward. In first grade, most students have an extreme desire to please and be recognized. Every year, the first "color change" on our behavior chart is extremely emotional. By focusing on positive behaviors, most negative behaviors are eliminated right away, but it takes a lot of conscious energy on my part to lay this foundation for the year.

Barbara LaMastus (E): Sometimes we act out scenarios, and students point out the rule that applies to the situation. We discuss problems as they occur, making learning experiences out of them in a nonjudgmental way.

Consistency is the most important component of any set of expectations. Be there—watching, giving a little visual clue like a little smile along with a head leaning to one side and a bit of a raised eyebrow. It says, "I know you know that what you are doing is not appropriate." I slip in many friendly, silent reminders to students to be their best selves.

Elaine: How about rewards and incentives? Do you believe in them?

Jill Aspegren (E): I consistently use spontaneous rewards over expected ones. I remember buying doughnuts on the way to school once just because I was so pleased with all the hard work we were doing. I might give students the "afternoon off" and let them read and play quietly after we have finished a difficult task or unit of work. I want my students to work hard without the lure of a treat because for me that's a life lesson.

Bobbie Oosterbaan (E): Students can easily become jaded with extrinsic rewards, and on a teacher's salary, I cannot afford to give out expensive prizes. Even inexpensive ones can become burdensome. But I have found that privileges are something students never tire of receiving. For example, at the end of the year, when the office needs to have registration packets returned, most students are not at all motivated to return them until I offer them a reward they adore. I allow students to take off their shoes starting on the day they bring the packet back, and they can keep them off until Friday when everyone needs to have the packets in. The students quickly figure out that the earlier they bring them in, the more days they can go stocking-footed in the classroom.

Paula Hoffman (S): The essential reward for students in my classroom is their mastery of my class content and the feelings of self-worth and respect that come from that. It's actually a great reward for me as well. Don't teachers need rewards and reinforcement for their efforts too?

Val Bresnahan (S): After over 25 years of public school teaching, I have come up with the simplest and perhaps the most ridiculous reward system I've ever used. But it really works. For a correct response or appropriate behavior, I tell the students to give themselves points on their point card—a 1" × 2" inch piece of brightly colored card stock. I might decide that certain activities are worth more points: "This is worth 10 points if you can get this answer." When they have accumulated 100 points on their cards, they receive a piece of Jolly Rancher candy (a big hit at my school) and put the card into the point jar. If the class can make it through one 45-minute class period with fewer than three behavior warnings, then one card is drawn from the point jar. The winner receives a chocolate candy bar. This simple system is a powerful motivator for sixth-grade students. The difference between students' attending behaviors with and without the point cards is amazing. Those students who do not need this type of reinforcement to maintain their attention usually wean themselves off it.

However, those that need it continue to be motivated by it. Please do not tell Alfie Kohn about this!

Angela Mariano (E): I use SCAMOs (sharing and caring about myself and others). The SCAMO concept isn't original with me, but over the years I've completely adapted it to my classroom. There are several ways to earn SCAMOs: Execute the morning routine quickly and quietly, turn in your homework assignment, have a clean desk check, execute the pack-up routine quietly and quickly, achieve a 90% or 100% on AR (Accelerated Reader) tests, finish all of your class work, *and* demonstrate caring for others. Ways to show caring for others include stacking chairs for classmates if they go home sick, picking up trash without being asked, lending a pencil or other materials to a neighbor, or saying something encouraging to a classmate.

A SCAMO is a yellow ticket, like the ones used at carnivals. Students put their initials on the tickets and keep them in safe places. A WAMOS (wasting all my organizational skills) is, as you might guess, a way to lose a SCAMO. I keep track of each WAMOS on a clipboard containing my class roster. It has five columns for the days of the week, where I mark a tally for each WAMOS next to students' names. I also give the clipboard to special area teachers (e.g., music and art) so they can use the system when my students are with them. Students receive a WAMOS for talking in line, not paying attention, not following directions, getting out of their seats without permission, and being disrespectful. On Friday, the kids take out their SCAMOs and count them up. Every WAMOS costs them a SCAMO. So if a child had 10 SCAMOs and 4 WAMOS, they would lose 4 SCAMOs, and only have 6 left. They can spend their SCAMOs like money at my class store. Many students even choose to save SCAMOs from week to week so they can get better prizes. The merchandise is inexpensive but the kids love it. I have pencil grips, bookmarks, erasers, stickers, and candy. For 25 SCAMOs, they can buy a no-homework pass. For 30 SCAMOs, they can purchase a lunch date with me and even invite a friend. You wouldn't believe how many kids save for this privilege (and it's free for me).

Elaine: What about intangible rewards?

Jill Yates (E): I use both tangible and intangible rewards. I give students a lot of teacher recognition with both private and publicly shared comments. I highlight opportunities for class celebrations—asking students to gather and listen to someone share a new learning, discovery, or high-quality product. However, I also hand out tangible items, such as stickers, stars, notes home, and warm fuzzy coupons.

Yvette Wallace (E): My rewards to students come in the form of recognition for good work products. When they do exceptional work, I ask permission to share their work with the class. I compliment students on specific aspects of their work. This helps to mold the work of others as well. In addition, I might be so excited about their work that I will ask permission to share it with other teachers or the principal. This is a great source of pride for them. I also make surprise phone calls. Students know that if I plan to call their homes about something they have done, they will always know about it beforehand *unless* it is a complimentary phone call. Those calls are surprise phone calls. I always let students know ahead of time about calls related to behavioral or academic concerns, so they have an opportunity to tell their parents when they get home. The surprise phone calls don't take much time, but they go a very long way, especially at the beginning of the year.

Elaine: What about food?

Theresa Panziera (E): No food is ever given as rewards in my classroom. I do hand out praise like candy. My students love it, and I enjoy giving it. However, I should point out that I am not the only one praising students. They all praise each other in my classroom.

Check out the WIT's List in Resource A for more than 70 rewards and reinforcers. In addition, there is a section of edible rewards that are either low-sugar or contain no sugar at all.

Q and A

Rhonda Carpenter (E): What would be the natural consequence for students who don't follow classroom procedures for keeping their voices down?

Sara Wiles (E): When my students simply can't remember to keep their voices under control, they "lose them." For example, if we are working on a group activity that requires communication, my students have been taught how to use *inside* voices. If the noise level gets too loud, I simply say, "Voice check." If I have to check students' voices three times, then they lose their voices and are unable to talk for the remainder of that activity.

What's Ahead?

If you can't wait to begin planning for the first 3 weeks of the school year or new semester, get ready. Chapter 7 describes step-by-step how to develop a personalized 3 + 3 = 33 plan.

Chapter 7

How to Develop a 3+3 = 33 Plan

Where there is harmony in the classroom environment,

There is order among the students.

When there is order among the students,

There is learning in their minds.

—Paraphrase of a Chinese proverb (McEwan)

The time has come to develop your own personalized 3 + 3 = 33 plan. Your next school year (or second semester) could be the best one you have ever experienced. Whether you are a first-time teacher or an experienced veteran, a 3 + 3 = 33 plan will not only help you survive the first 3 weeks, it will also ensure that you and your student s thrive during the remaining 33 weeks. This chapter will lead you through a seven-step process to accomplish that goal, one step at a time. You'll have one last opportunity to hear from many of the WITs who contributed to this book. Susan Graham is the featured secondary teacher and Yvette Wallace is the featured elementary teacher. They explain many aspects of their 3 + 3 = 33 plans in detail for you.

If you have time to reread pertinent sections of the book before you develop your plan, the investment will be worthwhile. If you were just hired and are due in your classroom tomorrow, cancel all family obligations and social engagements for the next 3 weeks. You will need every evening to read, plan, and stay one step ahead of your students. Follow these seven steps:

1. Get organized.
2. Complete the WIT Questionnaire Short Form (Form 7.1) and answer the Reflective Questions in Form 7.2. Then write a brief, reflective essay titled The Kind of Teacher I Want to Be.

> Teach your students to be organized, and always be one step ahead of them. Anticipate obstacles before they occur and always have a backup plan. Do it right the first time.
>
> —Darlene Carino, Candace Darling, and Michelle Perry (E)

3. Plan your classroom space and seating plan or plans.
4. Design your walls and bulletin boards.
5. Choose the key routines, rubrics, and rules you want to teach in the first 3 weeks and task analyze each one.
6. Develop a one-page lesson plan for each routine, rubric, and rule you selected in Step 5.
7. Draft a detailed, minute-by-minute plan for every day of the first 3 weeks of school.

Step 1: Get Organized

Before you put your personal 3 + 3 = 33 plan down on paper, assess your own organizational abilities. If you struggle with getting or staying organized, can't seem to find anything when you need it, but don't want to throw anything away either, it's time to turn over a new leaf. If you want your students to keep neat desks, have clear minds, and turn in organized homework, you must set an example. In order to develop your 3 + 3 = 33 plan, you need to get organized. That takes supplies. You may already have them, but if not, go shopping immediately at an office supply store. You may be thinking to yourself that you have tried this approach before to no avail. Don't despair. This year will be different. Now you will know what to do with the supplies you buy. Your first decision prior to purchasing supplies is to determine whether you prefer a notebook or a file crate for organizing your 3 + 3 = 33 materials. If you choose a notebook, read the following paragraph. If you prefer a crate, skip this paragraph and read the next one.

The Notebook Option

Buy a 3" three-ring notebook, 12 three-hole-punched tabbed dividers (make sure they are the kind into which you can slip small labels), and 12 three-hole-punched envelopes in which to organize and store the materials you will collect during the school year. Buy a label maker and make a professional-looking label for the spine of your notebook: *The First Three Weeks.* Now that you have the label maker, put labels on drawers, cabinets, files, and other notebooks in your classroom. You will be amazed at what a little bit of organization does for your morale. Also buy a ream of three-hole-punched paper on which to make all of your photocopies (e.g., articles, items from the book, ideas from workshops you attend). Otherwise you will always have loose sheets spilling out of your binder. This is not only a bad example to your students, but you'll continue to be just as disorganized as you were before you bought the notebook.

The File Crate Option

If you don't like the idea of a notebook, buy a plastic file crate designed for hanging files. I prefer an enclosed plastic tub with a cover rather than a milk crate. Dirt, junk, and bits of food always seem to find their way into milk crates. You can purchase smaller filing boxes that use regular manila folders, but I find they only create more disorganization since they are always sliding down and getting lost. Purchase a box of hanging files. You can buy inexpensive "ugly" green ones, but for just a few pennies more per file, you can have beautiful colors. If you don't like being organized to begin with, splurge on the brightly colored files. According to the research in Chapter 2, the colors will grab your attention and remind you of their importance. Also buy a label-making machine and make a label for your crate. The advantage of the crate system over the notebook system is that you won't have to buy three-hole paper or open and shut a binder every time you want to file something away. You can simply drop material into hanging files. The files can also be removed and carried around. Getting organized is a process of experimentation. Just because one system doesn't work for you doesn't mean you're a hopeless case. It only means that you need to find another system.

Setting Up Your Notebook Dividers or Hanging Files

Make labels for each of the numbered italicized topics listed below and slip them into the plastic tabs of the dividers or the hanging files. The dividers and hanging files will come with small pieces of white cardboard that fit inside the tabs, but to use them, you'll have to handwrite your labels. I prefer making a list of labels in a nice easy-to-read font on the computer and then cutting them out and slipping them into the tabs, using the cardboard as a backing for the paper label. These labels are much neater and easier to read than handwritten ones. Since you will be using your 3 + 3 = 33 materials for as long as you teach, the time you invest in preparing your tabs will be worth it.

1. *Space and Seating.* Put drafts of your seating plans, sketches of possible room arrangements, and photocopies of blank seating plans behind this divider.
2. *Boards and Walls.* Take photos of your bulletin boards from year to year as a guide to volunteers and students who may be helping you put up bulletin boards in subsequent years. Also make notes of stores and Web sites where you want to purchase materials.
3. *Academic Routines.* Include photocopied articles and workshop handouts related to the teaching moves, models, and various academic routines you want to use in this section. Make a copy of Table 3.1, Teaching Moves, to include in this section, for easy reference.

4. *WIT's Tips.* This is the section in which you will place information about Signals, Noise Breakers, Time-Savers, and Attention Getters. Photocopy the WIT's List in Resource A and reread it with a highlighter or sticky arrows in hand. Mark the ideas you want to include when you complete the WIT Questionnaire in Step 2. Jot down ideas you've seen other teachers use effectively, as well as techniques that have worked well for you in the past. Refer to this section if you're having a management problem. You will often find a solution here.

5. *Organizational Routines.* Make notes of the routines you use and how you will change them in another year. Always write your ideas down immediately. Otherwise you will forget them and make the same mistakes the following year.

6. *Social Routines.* Be sure to check out Resource A, which contains a variety of social routines for K–12.

7. *Rubrics.* Put samples and ideas for evaluation instruments you want to use or modify in this section. Make photocopies of the rubrics from Chapter 5 that you want to adapt for your own classroom.

8. *Rules and Rewards.* Add materials you collect from colleagues and teacher Web sites that might prove helpful.

9. *Lesson Plans.* Put all of your completed lesson plans for the first 3 weeks in this section, as well as photocopies of blank lesson plan forms for easy access.

10. *Miscellaneous.* This section is for items that don't readily fit into any of the other categories. When you accumulate five or six items on a new topic, create a new section or file.

11. *Questionnaires.* Put your completed WIT Questionnaire, your answers to the reflective questions, and your Reflective Essay in this section.

> **Classroom management and preparedness are crucial to the success of teachers. Too many teachers plan on a day-to-day basis. I prepare a one-year general plan to ensure a spiraling of my curriculum. I also keep notes regarding what works and what doesn't, to use in planning for the next year.**
> —Sue VanderNaald-Johnson (S)

> **Being organized is the key to an efficient, productive classroom. Everything, from the materials we use to our stored supplies and manipulatives, is labeled and organized. If you know exactly where things are, you have more time for teaching.**
> —Candace Darling, Darlene Carino, and Michelle Perry

Advice From Susan Graham on Getting Organized

"I make a separate notebook (with about six pockets) that is specifically for the first 3 weeks. It contains everything I need—seating charts, rules, and a welcome letter, plus all of the worksheets, lists, and so on that need to be photocopied for class activities. I also have all of my lesson plans prepared for the first 3 weeks, with one day per sheet, since the first days include so many short activities. I do all of my photocopying for the fall before I leave for summer vacation. Then when school begins, I only have to prepare my seating charts. I also make notes on my lesson plan sheets from the prior year so that during the summer I can revise my previous lesson plans."

Step 2: Answer Questions and Write a Reflective Essay

Step 2 involves answering two sets of questions in preparation for writing a brief reflective essay. Form 7.1 contains a short version of the questionnaire used to gather information from the WITs. Answering these questions will help you figure out what is already working for you (what you want to keep on doing) and encourage you to choose additional routines, rubrics, and rules to add to your repertoire. If you come to a question you can't answer, review the applicable chapter again. The questions are numbered to correspond to the chapters in the book. Don't forget to browse through the WIT's List in Resource A. This resource contains a dozen different lists and menus packed with ready-to-use ideas from WITs. When you have finished these tasks, you will have completed the hands-on half of Step 2.

Form 7.2 contains the "thinking" part of Step 2—seven reflective questions to help you clarify the beliefs and values that will shape your approach to teaching the 3Rs. Once you have answered the reflective questions, write a short essay titled The Kind of Teacher I Want to Be. Knowing what you believe and then putting those beliefs in writing are essential steps to becoming a WIT.

Step 3: Arrange Your Space and Choose a Seating Plan

Arranging Space

Although you don't need to consult a feng shui specialist before you arrange your classroom, do follow Val Bresnahan's advice from Chapter 1 and spend time envisioning yourself and your students using the space. If the room has too much furniture, explore moving some of it elsewhere. Please consult with your principal before hiring a moving van, however. Once you have arranged the furniture to your satisfaction, do a walk-through to check for traffic flow and safety.

> Classroom space is very much like "time" in a classroom. There is never enough. Therefore students need to know that every inch of it has a purpose. The room can't just "look good." It has to work for everyone.
> —Joanne French (E)

Form 7.1   WIT Questionnaire, Short Form

The following questions correspond to the "big ideas" found in Chapters 1 through 6. Definitions are provided to refresh your memory regarding the specific meaning of terms. Write down the specific routines, rubrics, and rules you already use that you want to keep (if you are currently teaching), as well as additional ideas from the chapters that you would like to add to your 3 + 3 = 33 plan. An asterisked question indicates the presence of lists and menus in the WIT's List (Resource A).

1a. *Classroom Arrangement:* The way in which desks, chairs, tables, and other furniture are arranged to maximize learning (e.g., the creation of territorial and functional spaces in the classroom)

    What is working for you that you want to include in your 3 + 3 = 33 plan?

    What approaches and ideas from Chapter 1 do you want to include in your plan?

1b. *Classroom Seating:* The ways in which students are seated in your classroom (e.g., team pods for cooperative learning, rows for independent work, study carrels for students who need quiet places, etc.)

    What seating arrangements are working for you that you plan to include in your 3 + 3 = 33 plan?

    What new approaches from Chapter 1 do you plan to implement?

2. *Classroom Decor:* The walls of the classroom and how they are used to extend and enhance learning (e.g., displaying student work or posting a reminder of teaching moves on the back wall)

    Jot down a list of the specific items you currently have posted on your walls that you want to continue using.

What new items do you want to add to your walls and bulletin boards?

3a. *Teaching Moves:* Generic teaching actions (i.e., the things teachers do and say in the course of instruction—facilitating, explaining, modeling, and coaching)

Which teaching moves do you currently use with great success?

What additional teaching moves, of the 16 described in Chapter 3, do you plan to practice and add to your repertoire?

3b. *Teaching Models:* Patterns of instruction that are recognizable and consistent, often associated with certain individuals or schools of thought (e.g., cooperative learning and direct instruction)

Which of the teaching models do you currently use with success?

What additional teaching models would you like to add to your repertoire?

3c. *Signals:* Actions, gestures, sounds, or signs used as a means of communication (e.g., raised hand to signal "stop talking and return to your seat")

What are the signals you currently use with success that you wish to keep in your 3 + 3 = 33 plan?

What additional signals do you plan to add to your 3 + 3 = 33 plan?

(Continued)

Form 7.1 (Continued)

3d. *Noise Breakers:* Techniques, signals, and strategies that reduce noise levels in your classroom (e.g., use of a deci-bell to let students know they need to lower their voices, the consequence of losing their voices for getting too many warnings about loud talking)

What are the noise breakers you currently use with success that you wish to keep in your $3 + 3 = 33$ plan?

What additional noise breakers do you plan to add to your 3Rs plan?

3e. *Time-Savers:* Specific practices that increase the amount of time available for instruction and independent practice (e.g., using brief time blocks for review and practice)

What are the most effective practices you use to minimize time wasting in your classroom?

What additional time-savers do you plan to add to your repertoire?

3f. *Attention Getters:* Things you do and say to get and keep students' attention (e.g., moving closer to a student, using a student's name in an example, picking up the pace of instruction)

What are the most effective (positive) things you do to get students' attention that you wish to retain for your $3 + 3 = 33$ plan?

What additional attending moves would you like to practice and add to your repertoire?

4a. *Organizational Routines:* Classroom procedures that keep students and "stuff" organized and moving efficiently, with little wasted time (e.g., procedures for lining up, passing in homework, or what students do when they enter the room in the morning)

What organizational routines that you currently use will you retain for your $3 + 3 = 33$ plan?

What organizational routines do you need to add to your 3 + 3 = 33 plan?

4b. *Academic Routines:* Procedures you follow to facilitate teaching and learning (e.g., procedures for sharing ideas with partners, checking homework, checking for understanding)

What are the essential academic routines in your classroom that you wish to retain for your 3 + 3 = 33 plan?

What additional academic routines do you plan to add to your 3 + 3 = 33 plan?

4c. *Social Routines:* Behavioral patterns that keep interpersonal communications and relations in the classroom on a positive and productive plane (e.g., procedures for giving and receiving compliments, greeting the teacher and classmates daily, listening to someone else's viewpoint)

What are the essential social routines in your classroom that you wish to keep for your 3 + 3 = 33 plan?

What additional social routines do you plan to add to your 3 + 3 = 33 plan?

5. *Rubrics:* A generic set of performance-based assessment tools that includes checklists and rating scales useful for conveying behavioral, social, and academic expectations to students

What rubrics do you currently use that you want to keep?

What additional rubrics do you need to create, either for specific projects you regularly assign in your grade level or content area or collaboratively with your students?

(Continued)

Form 7.1 (Continued)

6a. *Rules:* Authoritative principles set forth to guide behavior in the classroom (e.g., "Students are expected to be responsible and respectful at all times")

What rules do you currently use that you want to keep?

What additional rules do you want to incorporate into your student behavior plan?

6b. *Rewards:* Benefits obtained as a result of an action taken or a job done (e.g., a silent cheer, pat on the back, privilege, tangible prize of some kind)

What rewards or reward system do you currently use that you want to keep?

What other types of rewards or approaches to giving rewards to your students do you want to implement?

Copyright © 2006 by Corwin Press. All rights reserved. Reprinted from *How to Survive and Thrive in the First Three Weeks of School,* by Elaine K. McEwan. Thousand Oaks, CA: Corwin Press, www.corwinpress.com. Reproduction authorized only for the local school site or nonprofit organization that has purchased this book.

Advice From Yvette Wallace on Arranging Space

"In addition to table groups (4–6 desks pushed together), I have two tables, one for meeting with small groups and a second for a volunteer to work with a group. These spaces are also utilized by any student during work time when they need more space or a change of scenery for whatever reason they decide. After I have decided on the placement of desks and other furniture in a new room, I pull out the chairs (where they would be normally when second graders are seated and working) and try to walk through the room. If it doesn't work with the seats out, it's not going to work. I allow plenty of space near the entrance of the room, where students will hang backpacks, and near student mailboxes.

Form 7.2   **Reflective Questions**

1. What do I want my classroom to look like?

2. How do I want my classroom to sound?

3. How do I want my students to feel in my classroom?

4. How do I want my students to treat me as a person?

5. How do I want my students to treat each other as human beings?

6. What kind of information or values do I want to communicate to students about the worth of work, perseverance, and learning from one's mistakes?

7. How do I want my students to remember me when the last day of school finally ends and I am no longer a part of their daily lives?

SOURCE: Adapted from Kameenui & Darch (1995, pp. 66–67).

This makes the clean-up traffic at the end of the day more manageable. I use two rug areas, the main one near the calendar for class discussions, read-alouds, and similar activities. There is another slightly smaller space in the front of the room where most students can sit on the rug, and students with seats nearby can see from their seats, for student presentations and demonstrations, when the students need to be closer. The rug areas, table spaces, and the library space are all places where individuals, pairs, or groups can meet to work on centers, read, or write collaboratively."

Choosing a Seating Plan

The next thing to do is to choose a seating plan. Review the decision-making questions in Chapter 1 to help you determine the best plan for you. Several generic templates are included here (Figures 7.1–7.4) to help you visualize how different seating plans will mesh with the teaching models and instructional activities you plan to use.

Figure 7.1 Horizontal Rows Seating Plan

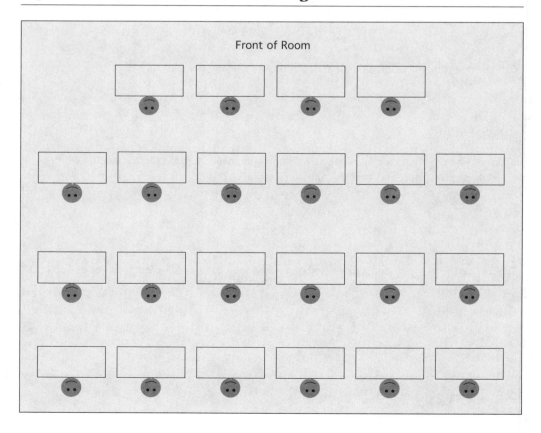

Figure 7.2   Pairs Seating Plan

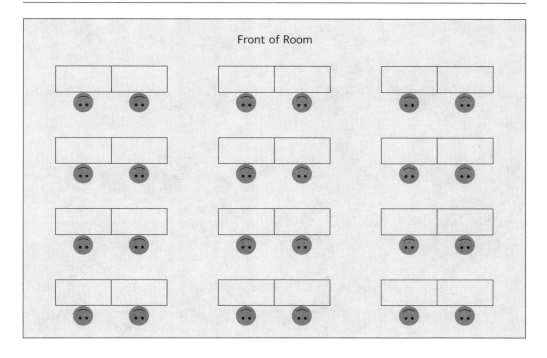

Figure 7.3   U-Shape Seating Plan

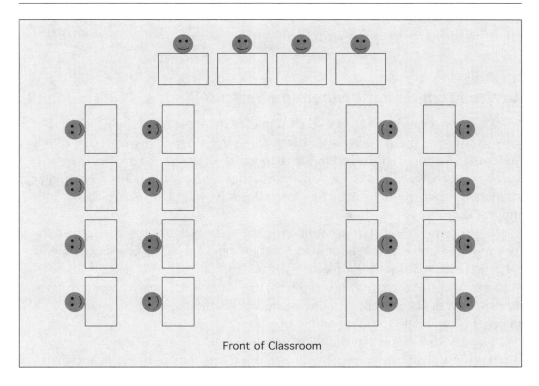

Figure 7.4   Table Groups Seating Plan

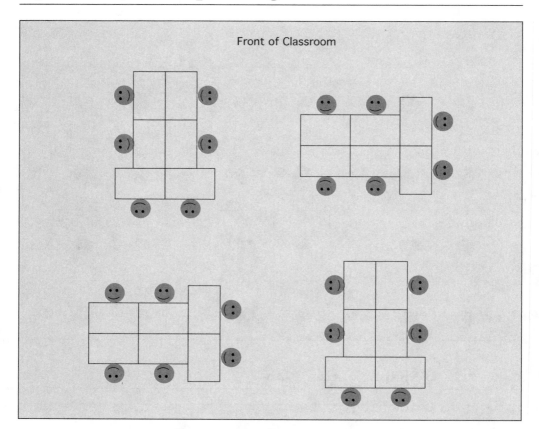

Advice From Susan Graham on Seating Plans

"I've tried a variety of ways to communicate the location of their assigned seats to students on the first day, but it seemed that no matter what I did, the students still wandered around trying to locate their assigned seats or, even worse, were crowded in a big group around the overhead. Of course, elementary teachers can put students' names on their desks, but in high school, that's impossible.

"It was only when I started numbering the seats and giving students a chart showing the numbered desks containing their names that the first day suddenly got much easier. Students didn't have to locate their seats with respect to the windows or count the rows and columns to figure out where they were supposed to sit. This simple routine made an enormous difference in how quickly I could begin teaching on the first day.

"I tape colorful calendar numbers from the teachers' store onto the desks. I then put numbers and names on the seating charts for each section and make copies of the seating charts for each student on the first day of school. When I greet them at the door on the first day, students get the seating chart [Figure 7.5], my welcome letter [Figure 7.6], and their bell work [Figure 7.7].

"The oversize numbers on the desks make it easy for students to find their seats, and all of my students are in their seats and working on their first assignment when the bell rings. Also, since they have their own copies of the seating chart, they can begin to learn the names of their classmates right away.

"You can see from my seating chart that I have pairs of desks facing forward, auditorium style. With this arrangement, the room feels bigger, and I have wide aisles. Since we do many quick pair activities (e.g., Tell your partner one thing you remember from your reading), all students automatically have a partner. For more extended pair activities, I ask the students to turn their desks so they're facing their partners. This arrangement helps on-task behavior for practice conversation activities or quizzing partners. I also ask students to circle their desks for some class games and activities."

Advice From Yvette Wallace on Seating Plans

"I cluster students in groups of four to six, with their desks facing one another. I use information from last year's teachers to set up my initial seating plan, placing struggling students next to more capable or compassionate ones.
I place students with behavioral concerns apart from one another and students who are likely to need more help from me on the edge of the room where I will be better able to meet with them frequently and unobtrusively. I also take into account student comfort, trying to make sure each boy or girl has another student of their gender *and* a student from their previous class at their table team.

"Students are grouped this way to encourage discussion. From the first few days of school, they are asked to discuss with a neighbor, come up with an answer or suggestion as a table group, work together to come up with a team name, and so on. Teams also work together to clean specific areas of the room at cleanup time. The arrangement underlines our idea of teamwork."

Step 4: Design Your Walls

Designing your walls and bulletin boards is the easiest of the seven steps, especially with the advent of collaborative bulletin boards. Follow the advice given in Chapter 2. Keep it simple. Invest in reusable backgrounds for your bulletin boards, put up headings that highlight what will be appearing soon, and then put your students to work on the first day creating posters, individual

(Text continues on page 161)

Figure 7.5   Susan's Seating Chart

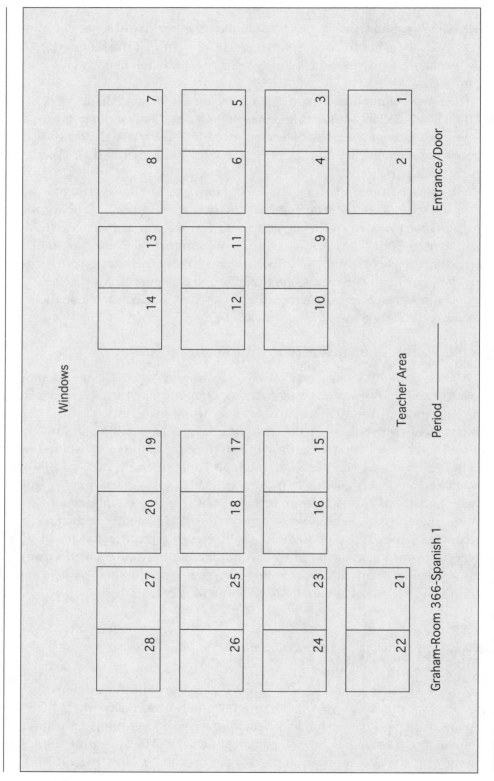

SOURCE: Reprinted by permission of Susan Graham.

Figure 7.6 **Susan's Welcome Letter**

¡Bienvenidos a la clase de español!

My name is Miss Graham (Señorita Graham). I am 40 years old and I live in Romeoville. I grew up in Darien, Illinois, which is a southwest suburb. I graduated from Illinois State University in 1986 with a degree in Spanish Education with a minor in French. I have been teaching at Joliet Central for the past 19 years. I received my master's degree in Teaching Languages from the University of Southern Mississippi in 1997. I like to go to the movies and out to eat with my friends. I also really enjoy spending time at home reading or with my family. I have two brothers, two nephews, and one niece. I love being an aunt. My nephews and niece visit me often, and we play, read, make cookies, and watch movies. We also go bowling, swimming, and miniature golfing.

I love teaching Spanish. I'm looking forward to a great new school year. I'll try to challenge you as well as help you to enjoy the process of learning Spanish by providing meaningful class activities using a variety of traditional and creative methods. We will address all the parts of learning a language: reading, writing, speaking, listening, spelling, grammar, and culture.

By now you have found your assigned seat. I will assign new seats each quarter, so you'll get to sit in different parts of the room and work with a variety of your classmates. I'll be explaining the basic rules and procedures as we go along so that class runs as smoothly as possible. And we will begin speaking Spanish today! I hope you're ready to get started.

Please use your textbook to complete the simple activity on the back of this letter. This is your first bell work assignment. You will have bell work everyday. I will explain more about bell work as soon as we begin class. When you are finished with your bell work, please just sit quietly and wait for class to begin.

Thank you.

SOURCE: Reprinted by permission of Susan Graham.

Figure 7.7   Susan's Bell Work for First Day

El Alfabeto

Pp. 10–11 in your textbook

What is the first letter of the Spanish word for the following things?

1. Magnet? _____

2. Carrot? _____

3. Snow? _____

4. Bear? _____

5. Umbrella? _____

6. Airplane? _____

7. Flower? _____

8. Pencil? _____

9. Scissors? _____

10. Clock? _____

11. Money? _____

12. Suitcase? _____

13. Cheese? _____

14. Yogurt? _____

15. Boot? _____

16. Glasses? _____

17. Egg? _____

18. Unicorn? _____

19. Ladder? _____

20. Pig? _____

SOURCE: Reprinted by permission of Susan Graham.

Figure 7.8   Task Analysis for Going-Home Routine

1. Get papers from the mailbox.

2. Put papers on desk.

3. Get coats, backpacks, and lunchboxes.

4. Return to desks.

5. Put on coats.

6. Sit down.

7. Listen for any messages.

8. Wait for the teacher to pass out papers.

9. Pack papers in backpack.

10. Line up and leave when the teacher says good-bye to individual students by name: "Good night, Amy. I'll see you tomorrow."

SOURCE: Reprinted by permission of Sandi Seckel.

shields, or bumper stickers that will make your walls work for you. The experts in classroom management suggest that you keep your decor low key: "Don't spend a lot of time decorating your room. You will have many other more important things to do to get ready for the beginning of school. . . . Don't overdecorate. Wall space that is cluttered with detail can distract students and make a room seem smaller. Hanging mobiles and decorations from the ceiling can also be overdone. Your room will seem small enough when your twenty-five to thirty students are in it" (Evertson, Emmer, Clements, & Worsham, 1994, pp. 4–5).

Step 5: Choose and Analyze Your Routines, Rubrics, and Rules

Hopefully you have been collecting the routines, rubrics, and rules that you want to add to your repertoire. Put those together with the 3Rs you already use, and you're on your way. Once you have compiled your final list, task analyze your 3Rs: List the steps involved in following each routine, rubric, or rule. For example, Figure 7.8 displays Sandi Seckel's (E) task analysis of her end-of-day routine.

At first glance, a task analysis looks like nothing more than a to-do list for going home. But don't let its simplicity fool you. Each of these ten actions requires some type of explanation, direction giving, modeling, and practicing. Here are just a few of the questions that will undoubtedly pop into your students' minds when attempting this routine if you haven't taught it explicitly, systematically, and supportively: Where is the mailbox? Why do you call it a mailbox? Why doesn't it look like a mailbox? What kinds of papers will be in it? What types of messages will the teacher give to me? How will I remember all of them? What if I can't read the messages? What kinds of papers will the teacher pass out? What is passing out? What will I do with the papers once I get them? Where do I line up? Can I be first?

When teaching rules, words like *respect, responsibility, fairness, inappropriate*, and *misbehavior* need very specific definitions, examples, and nonexamples before students will be on *your* wavelength. Even words like *swearing, fighting*, and *name-calling* need to be

> Our students [first graders] perform better academically and behaviorally when there are no changes in our daily routine. So unless there is a special circumstance, our day never varies.
>
> —Michelle Perry, Candace Darling, and Darlene Carino (E)

defined in detail. Is fighting hitting someone anywhere at anytime, or is fighting clenching a fist and punching someone in the face? What about pushing and shoving? Do they constitute fighting? Depends on which student (or teacher) you ask for a definition. Is rolling your eyes and smirking disrespect or merely indigestion? Only you can tell your students the answer to that question and demonstrate exactly what disrespect looks like. If you have some favorite buzzwords that you often use, give your students explicit definitions, explanations, examples, and nonexamples of what they mean to you.

The 3Rs are like magic in classrooms. When they have been well taught and mastered by students, teaching appears to be an almost effortless undertaking. Everything runs smoothly—almost all of the time. Yvette Wallace's routines cover almost every imaginable eventuality in her classroom. There are of course the usual routines for calendar and bathroom that nearly every primary teacher employs, but Yvette also has routines for volunteers, parents, privacy, and visitors. She leaves nothing to chance in her classroom.

Advice From Yvette Wallace About Organizational Routines

"The Calendar Routine. This routine has been the most effective since I have turned it completely over to my students. Students are assigned different jobs, beginning with Calendar King or Queen, who tells the complete date; has a volunteer predict the number, color, and shape of the next date in the calendar pattern; and counts in ordinal numbers up to the date. Next comes the Pattern Counter. This helper keeps a running tally of days in school by adding a numeral to the hundreds pocket chart, then leading students in skip counting to today's number in a funny voice. After that comes the Money Manager. The Money Manager selects coins to total the number of days we've been in school. Finally, the Weather Monitor checks the temperature and chooses two descriptive weather terms that best apply to the day (cloudy, rainy, sunny, partly cloudy, windy, etc.).

"Numbering Students. Each student is assigned a numeral alphabetically at the beginning of the year. We use the numerals in many different ways.

- Students write their names, numbers, and the date at the top of each paper. Their numerals are on their mailboxes. This system allows me to collect papers in numerical order, correct them in order, and enter them in order into the grade book. After I enter papers into my grade book, the papers are then "mailed" to student mailboxes in the same order, thus saving time shuffling papers back and forth.
- Students always line up in numerical order when we leave the room (not when returning from a special class or recess, etc.). The student whose number matches the date is the line leader for that day. The student who is at the end of the line is always in charge of turning off the lights as we leave. This way, each student has a chance to be at the front of the line (usually no numeral falls on a weekend month after month). Near the end of the month, when our class numbers go to, say, 25, and the date is the 28th, I'll declare another number (one that was on a weekend that month) to be the front of the line for that day.
- Student numbers are also useful for getting into different groups (odds, evens, one-digit numbers, or two-digit numbers).

"Lost and Found. Our classroom lost-and-found has made our cleanup time go more smoothly and helps students recover lost items, such as barrettes, markers, and so on. It is simply a small plastic tub. Students put found objects in, and once every 2 weeks or so, students empty it out, placing unclaimed pencils, markers, and glue sticks in the classroom bins and holding up personal items, such as lanyards or polished rocks, in front of the class to find the owner.

"The Sub Job. The most coveted classroom job in my room is the Sub. One student per week takes over any classroom job for someone who is absent. The students are very careful about paying attention to when they need to sub for someone. This routine eliminates the need for me to pick someone else every time a helper is absent.

"The Bathroom Routine. When my students ask to go to the bathroom, I usually say, "Yes, but, can you wait . . . for me to finish explaining the assignment or for another student to return?" My other response is, "Can you wait or is it an emergency?" This means the kids know that I am unlikely to say no. But if I think they are playing or going to the bathroom too much, I say so. If they need to hear the next point in the lesson first, I say so. This means students know they can go when they need to but do not abuse the privilege.

"The Bathroom Signal. Students use a raised pointer finger to indicate that they would like to be excused to go to the restroom. This saves us many interruptions

during whole-class lessons, small-group lessons, or individual conferences. Students who are requesting to go to the restroom place themselves at a respectful distance (far enough away to ensure privacy for the small group or individual) and raise their pointer fingers. I can respond with a nod without even breaking stride in my teaching or interrupting the students with whom I'm working."

For other field-tested organizational routines from Yvette, see Figure 7.9.

Step 6: Develop Lesson Plans

All of the hard work you have invested in Steps 1–5 will be wasted if you don't get Step 6 absolutely right. Yvette has devised a simple way to organize and teach the 3Rs that will work at any grade level.

Advice From Yvette Wallace About Teaching Routines

"I use a set of procedure cards that I have developed to teach the routines, rules, and expectations in my classroom. Each 3" × 5" card has a procedural question written on the front and an answer to the question written on the back. [Figure 7.10 contains samples of four of Yvette's cards. A list of procedure questions and answers that can be converted into cards is shown in Figure 7.11.]

"I use these cards in several ways throughout the school year. First, I use the cards to *plan.* During the week before school starts, I sort the cards into three piles: Need to Know First Day, Need to Know First Week, and Need to Know First Few Weeks. At the same time, I also make any needed changes to the existing cards and add any procedures (routines, rubrics, and rules) that I developed or changed during the past school year.

"The second use for these cards is *instructional.* I use the cards to teach my opening lessons to a new class. As I explain and model each routine, I put that card in a pile where the class can see it and let them know that when we have learned enough of the procedures, we'll play a game together.

"The third use for the cards is for *review.* At the end of the first week, I use the previously introduced cards to play quiz-style games during transition times and just before we go home in the afternoon. I also plan a block of time to play Jeopardy with the cards.

"The last use of the cards is to *orient* new students, student teachers, or long-term substitutes of procedures in the classroom."

Lesson Plans to Teach the Routines

Yvette is skillful enough to teach her 3Rs from 3" × 5" cards, but if you are brand new to teaching or have never systematically taught the 3Rs in your classroom, you

Figure 7.9 Yvette's Organizational Routines

Privacy Routine

From the first week of school, we discuss how everyone is different and may learn differently or at a different pace. We also discuss the importance of a student's learning team (teachers, student, and parents). In addition we talk about the concept of *personal space*. Students are taught through example and role-play how to keep a respectful distance between the teacher and an individual student having a discussion. From then on, I need only ask for "privacy" when speaking with a student, and the others know to step back a few feet. Students know how important these discussions are to each student's growth. Students are also encouraged when they have a problem with a classmate to try talking to the person in a private space (usually the back corner of the room).

Classroom Visitors

I talk with students about what to do when visitors come to our classroom. We talk about why different visitors are there and how to make them feel welcome but not embarrass them. So if we are expecting someone to speak to us (the principal, the counselor, a student group), we go about our business, and when they arrive, each student cleans up and goes to the designated space (seat or rug). On their way, they touch another student on the shoulder to make them aware of the visitor's arrival. This eliminates students calling out "They're here," rushing around, or wasting time waiting for someone to arrive. For other visitors, students know to continue working because the visitor either came to see how well we work together or came to speak to someone privately (usually me). Once we discuss this and talk about how embarrassing it would be to walk into a room and have people shout that you were there or start pointing, students internalize this routine very well.

Dismissal Routine

When students are dismissed, they give me an "H" before leaving (a hug, high five, or handshake). This personal goodbye is a wonderful opportunity for me to do one of the following: (1) whisper congratulations on a specific good job that day, (2) remind them of something they need to remember, (3) tell them something I've noticed about their work that day, and (4) become aware that a student is leaving the classroom.

Library Organization

The library is organized by topic. Each book has a computer label with the topic printed and an accompanying icon on the back. All books with the same label are stored in a tub with a matching label. Students can then find and return books easily.

Parent Volunteer Organization System

Each math group and reading group has a magazine file near the entrance to my room. In that file are the plans and materials needed for the next few lessons with that group. Parent volunteers need only to get the box for the group they are working with and get started. Just outside the entrance to my room, I have a table set up for volunteer projects. The table is divided into three sections: Urgent (projects that need to be done first), To Do (projects that can be done but are not immediately necessary), and Completed (where parents leave completed projects).

Parent Communication System

I have a parent communication binder that helps me to keep track of contact information for parents as well as record when we've talked or e-mailed. This information is neatly kept all in one space. The binder has a communication log for each student on the left facing page and the Family Communication Survey (filled out by parents the first week of school) on the right facing page. The survey lists phone numbers, e-mail addresses, good and bad times to contact families, names of parents, and other information I need at my fingertips when I am making a call. The Communication Log is a place to record (briefly) conversations and dates of contact.

SOURCE: Reprinted by permission of Yvette Wallace.

Figure 7.10

What should I do if I finish my morning work early?	**Read silently in a book that's just right for me.**
How do I get permission to go to the bathroom?	**Make eye contact with the teacher. Hold up two fingers and wait for the teacher to nod OK.**
What is the signal for entering the building after recess?	**The teacher will raise her right hand and hold it high. Then she will motion to us with her hand to walk into the building in front of her.**

SOURCE: Reprinted by permission of Yvette Wallace.

may feel more comfortable using a traditional lesson plan format. Here are two templates to guide you (see Forms 7.3 & 7.4). An actual mini-lesson for teaching a routine using Form 7.4 was included in Chapter 3 (Darla's Mini-Lesson). Note that the third column in both templates is titled Teacher's Script.

That is where you write down the words you will speak during your lesson. Experienced teachers who have taught a routine for years can skip this step. However, when you are onstage in front of students for the first time, don't wing it. In the beginning, overplan. If neither of these templates appeals to you, adapt them or design your own. However, be sure to include the following essential teaching moves in every lesson: explaining, giving directions, modeling, and guiding practice.

Step 7: Write a Detailed Lesson Plan for the First Day of School

You are now ready to develop a detailed plan for the first day of school. If you're an elementary teacher, see Figures 7.12 and 7.13. If you teach at the secondary level, Susan Graham offers some planning advice for class periods and blocks.

Advice From Susan Graham on Teaching Routines, Rubrics, and Rules on the First Day

"I tell students at the beginning of the year that I will explain all of my routines (particularly the academic ones) very carefully the first time we do

(Text continues on page 170)

Figure 7.11   Yvette's Procedure Questions and Answers

Q: Tell what you know about kind and safe behavior when traveling in the hallways of our school.

A: Walk quietly in my own space. Stay in line with the class. Walk directly to where I am going.

Q: Write on the board what should be at the top of every one of your papers. Tell us why.

A: Name and class number. These help the teacher identify and organize papers.

Q: Tell or show where your Morning Work goes when it is finished.

A: Turn-in basket.

Q: Tell what you know about three ways to respect another person's space in our classroom.

A: (1) Respect a person's desk space, including the teacher's. Do not go into that space. (2) Respect a person's personal property, such as backpacks, bags, and supplies. (3) Respect a person's physical space. Don't crowd them.

Q: Explain what the line leader's responsibilities are when holding the door open. Then tell what the line leader should do when everyone has gone through the door.

A: Hold the door from the front, not from behind. Do not touch the students who are going through the door. When finished, walk quickly to catch up with the line and regain your position in the front.

Q: Tell the different ways you can share a problem with the teacher.

A: Write in my Response Journal, ask for a private conversation, write a note, or draw a picture.

Q: Explain one positive consequence of following the rules in our classroom.

A: Answers will vary and could include these: I will get a Good News Note, a compliment, a phone call at home, a note written to my parents, team points, and I will have more friends.

Q: Tell when we normally get drinks in our room.

A: After each special activity, like art or music, and recess, or anytime I need one when it is not "teaching time."

Q: Give an example of how to be kind when reminding a friend to follow the rules.

A: Remind them, help them, or show them. These work better than tattling, threatening, or yelling.

Q: Tell or show the best way to manage yourself in line.

A: Face front, voice off, stay in my own space.

Q: Talk about the rules for chapter books in our room.

A: One chapter book from our class library may be in my desk at a time. If I decide I don't like the chapter book I chose, I may trade it. Make a bookmark from scratch paper to keep my place. Don't fold over the edge of the page.

Q: Give directions on how to get to the office from our classroom.

A: Out the pod door and up the stairs. The office is at the end of the hall on the left. (I have a card for each important place in the building: recess area, gym, library, buddy classroom, music room, cafeteria, etc.)

Q: Explain or show how to keep our library organized.

A: Labels on the backs of the books match labels on the matching tub.

Q: Tell at least two important things to remember when there is a fire drill.

A: MOST IMPORTANT: (1) Stay calm. (2) Get to a safe place. (I use these two rules for ANY emergency.) (3) Walk quickly and quietly. (4) Listen for instructions.

SOURCE: Reprinted by permission of Yvette Wallace.

Form 7.3   **Modeling Lesson Plan 1 for Teaching Routines, Rubrics, and Rules (3Rs)**

Step	Description	Teacher Script
Anticipatory Set	Teacher activates background knowledge and experiences of students in order to build connection to the routine, rubric, or rule (3R) being taught.	
I Do, You Watch	Teacher models how to do what the students will be expected to do as an outcome of the lesson.	
I Do, You Help	Teacher models once again with the help of selected students.	
You Do, I Help	All students perform the 3R under the guidance of the teacher.	
You Do, I Watch	All students complete the 3R independently while still under the teacher's supervision.	
Closure: Summarizing Statement	Teacher summarizes the purpose and possible applications of the 3R and gives a homework assignment, if applicable.	

SOURCE: Adapted from Shannon Coombs' Modeling Lesson Design based on the work of Madeline Hunter. Reprinted with permission.

Form 7.4 Modeling Lesson Plan 2 for Teaching Routines, Rules, and Rubrics (3Rs)

Lesson Step	Action	Teacher's Script
Anticipatory Set	Teacher states the goal or outcome of the routine, rubric, or rule (3R).	
Teacher Models Nonexamples	Teacher models or role-plays why the 3R is important by showing what it *doesn't* look like.	
Teacher Models Examples	Teacher models or role-plays what the 3R *does* look like.	
One Student Models	As student models, teacher gives compliments and points out to everyone the critical attributes of the 3R.	
Two Students Model	As two students model, teacher affirms what they are doing and again highlights the critical attributes of the 3R.	
Small Group Models	As the small group models the 3R for the class, the teacher again praises and notes the critical attributes of the 3R.	

(Continued)

Form 7.4 (Continued)

Lesson Step	Action	Teacher's Script
Whole Class Practices	The whole class practices the 3R under the teacher's supervision.	
Feedback	Teacher gives enthusiastic, positive, and specific feedback to teach or correct students' performance. If some students don't follow the procedure correctly, teacher assumes that more practice is needed.	
Practice	Teacher repeats the above steps (all or part) each time the 3R is used until it is mastered. Teacher repeats the steps occasionally throughout the year, to review, for new students, and for consistency. If appropriate, students execute the 3R while the teacher times them.	
Reflections	Teacher chooses an appropriate whole-group discussion time to reflect with students about the 3R and reminds them of the reason for it.	

SOURCE: Adapted from Darla Ryser's Mini-Lesson. Reprinted with permission.

them so they can master the routines. After introducing myself (see letter earlier in the chapter) and my rules (see description in Chapter 6) using two different PowerPoint presentations, I teach the basic routine we follow in every class period—bell work, song, lesson, and work time [see Figures 7.14–7.16]—and then follow up my teaching with review activities later on in the week and at the beginning of the second week of school.

"The first time we use a new routine, I explain it slowly and carefully, and then I re-explain and remind students of it when we do similar activities in the future. I don't teach all of my routines on the first day. I gradually teach them

Figure 7.12   **Plan for the Morning of the First Day of School**

---

*Students should place all supplies in desks temporarily, as they will be checked in on the second day.

8:30–8:45	Show Off Your Character (activity sheet). This is used to set the tone for the morning. It's simple, needs no explanation, and is placed on students' desks because no morning work routine has been taught.
8:45–9:00	Introduction to Daily Morning Routine (Students must be taught a systematic routine showing how to enter the classroom, sign up for lunch, where to get morning work, where to place it when finished, how and when pencils should be sharpened, and the rules for using the bathroom. I do it, we do it, you do it is the lesson format.)
9:00–9:30	Transition to the rug by echo singing the following words to the tune of Frère Jacques.

> I am walking,
>
> I am walking.
>
> To the rug.
>
> To the rug.
>
> I'll sit in a circle.
>
> I'll sit in a circle.
>
> Quietly. Quietly!

	Introduce Morning Meeting (Introduce and model greeting and share components of Morning Meeting using the I do it, we do it, you do it lesson format.)
9:30–9:50	Read the story *I Am Too Absolutely Small for School* by Lauren Child. Both the students and teacher make connections to how they felt prior to coming to school today.
9:50–10:00	Go on a Bear Hunt with Dr. Jean's CD.
10:00–10:30	Put on your Explorer hats. We're taking a tour of the room.
10:30–11:00	Brainstorm the Rules and Consequences. Allow students to be an active part of the rules-making process. How do WE want our classroom to run? What should be done if a rule is broken? The end result should be three or four rules (e.g., Treat others the way you want to be treated). When discussing consequences, introduce the behavior stoplight and student buses (part of behavior plan).

SOURCE: Reprinted by permission of Michelle Perry, Candace Darling, and Darlene Carino.

Figure 7.13 **Plan for the Afternoon of the First Day of School**

Time	Activity
11:00–11:05	Math-er-cise: Using a variety of exercise movements, practice counting to 20.
11:05–11:15	Model the routine for lining up to go to lunch.
11:21–12:06	Lunch/Recess
12:06–12:15	Quiet rest time (play soft background music).
12:15–12:45	Read the story *Wild About Books* by Judy Sierra and Marc Brown. Introduce how to make a book selection based on the "Goldilocks Theory" (not too easy, not too hard, but just right). Model how to choose two appropriate books for students' daily reading folder, which students fill each morning with new books This folder is kept on their desks all year. This provides students who always finish their work early with something meaningful to do. Introduce BEAR Center (Be Excited About Reading).
12:45–1:10	Introduce the word of the month (Responsibility). Have students draw a picture showing how they can be responsible at school. Also take students' pictures during this activity for use later on a bulletin board.
1:12–1:42	SPECIAL (Music or Art). Remind students of hallway travel rules.
1:50–2:15	Calendar math
2:25	Dismissal Routine

SOURCE: Reprinted by permission of Michelle Perry, Candace Darling, and Darlene Carino.

over a period of 3 weeks, one or two each day. One of the first academic routines I teach is a memory-enhancing vocabulary exercise in which students draw pictures for the words and a smaller picture as a pronunciation prompt (see Figures 7.17–7.18). [Note: Further explanation of this activity is found in Chapter 4 in the Academic Routines section.]

"I also hand out my syllabus [see Figure 7.19] for the entire school year on the first day of school and go over it with students so they can begin to understand how it will be possible for them to learn a foreign language. Many students are nervous at the prospect. Some aren't sure that they will be able to master all of the vocabulary. Having the entire year mapped out this way helps them to see that we will take it one step at a time, and I will be there to help them each step of the way.

"As students leave my classroom on the first day, I give them several things to take home to their parents. I strongly believe in parental involvement, and I work hard to engage the parents of my students in every way I can. I give students a welcoming letter for their parents [Figure 7.20] and an invitation to write a brief description of their child for me [Figure 7.21]. Not everyone does it, of course,

(Text continues on page 181)

Figure 7.14   **Daily Routine for Español Uno**

Bell Work

Quiet time to transition into Spanish with a short, easy activity

- Check the board as soon as you enter the classroom
- Pick up materials from the basket (if necessary).
- Begin immediately.
- Wait quietly for class to begin once you've finished.

Song

Active time to move into Spanish with some rhythm and happy music

- Usually one song per week
- Monday–Thursday: Activity with part of song
- Friday: Sing along with the slides

Lesson

Active time to learn and practice Spanish

- Presentation of new material
- Practice activities
- Correct homework
- Ask questions
- Group or pair practice
- Games and activities

Work Time

Quiet time for individual work to practice and reinforce material

- Work on your own so YOU know what you're doing
- Ask questions of classmates or teacher when you need help.

SOURCE: Reprinted by permission of Susan Graham.

Figure 7.15   Daily Routine Review for Español Uno

Please fill in the rectangles with either *Quiet time* or *Active time*.
Then fill in three important points about each part of our daily routine.

Bell Work

To transition into Spanish with a short, easy activity

_____

_____

_____

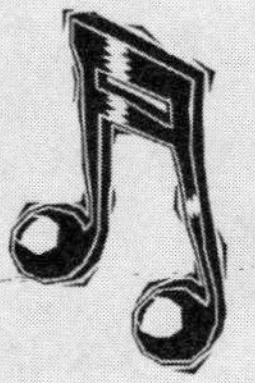

Song

To move into Spanish with some rhythm and happy music

_____

_____

_____

Lesson

To learn and practice Spanish

_____

_____

_____

Work Time

For individual work to practice and reinforce material

_____

_____

_____

SOURCE: Reprinted by permission of Susan Graham.

Figure 7.16   Give One, Get One

1. Please write something we've done so far this year in each of the parts of our daily routine.

2. Talk to at least three other people to remind you of other activities in each part of our daily routine.

3. Stand in a circle around the room when you've filled in your sheet.

Give One: Bell Work	Get One: Bell Work
1. _____	1.
	2.
	3.

Give One: Song	Get One: Song
1. _____	1.
	2.
	3.

Give One: Lesson	Get One: Lesson
1. _____	1.
	2.
	3.

Give One: Work Time	Get One: Work Time
1. _____	1.
	2.
	3.

SOURCE: Reprinted by permission of Susan Graham.

Figure 7.17   Sample Picture Vocabulary

Sample Picture Vocabulary

libro	sacapuntas
ventana	lápiz/lápices
pluma	bandera
reloj	mesa
pizarra	puerta

SOURCE: Reprinted by permission of Susan Graham.

Figure 7.18 **Vocabulary Template**

Vocabulary Template

1. Please draw a picture of any 10 vocabulary words for practice.
2. Then draw a small picture in the box that helps you remember what the word sounds like.

SOURCE: Reprinted by permission of Susan Graham.

Figure 7.19 Syllabus

Español Uno   Señorita Graham

First Semester		Second Semester	
Week of	Topic(s)	Week of	Topic(s)
22–Aug	School, numbers 1–20	4–Jan	Basic Spanish Noun Bingo
29–Aug	Days, alphabet, greetings	9–Jan	2–2 Vocabulary–school schedules, lunch food
5–Sep	1–1 Vocabulary–people, conversation	16–Jan	Question words, fruits and vegetables
12–Sep	1–1 Grammar–subject pronouns, *ser* (verb)	23–Jan	*Ir* and *estar* (irregular verbs)
19–Sep	1–2 Vocabulary–clothes, colors	30–Jan	2–3 Vocabulary recreation
26–Sep	Say Hola to Spanish (story and vocabulary)	6–Feb	2–3 Grammar–*er* and *ir* (verbs)
3–Oct	1–2 Vocabulary–adjectives	13–Feb	*El Rey Leon* (En Español)
10–Oct	1–2 Grammar–articles, adjectives, plurals	20–Feb	Big Vocabulary Review
17–Oct	1–3 Vocabulary–family	27–Feb	Big Vocabulary Review
24–Oct	Day of the Dead (Mexican Culture)	6–Mar	Say Hola to Spanish Again (story and vocabulary)
31–Oct	1–3 months and *tener* (verb)	13–Mar	Big Verb Review
7–Nov	2–1 Vocabulary–school	20–Mar	Big Verb Review and *Shrek* (En Español)
14–Nov	2–1 Grammar–*ar* verbs, review subjects	27–Mar	SPRING BREAK
21–Nov	*Tarzan* (En Español)	3–Apr	3–1 Vocabulary–feelings, emotions
28–Nov	Numbers 1–100 and telling time	10–Apr	3–2 Vocabulary–sports
5–Dec	*Frosty* (En Español)	17–Apr	3–2 Grammar–stem changing verbs
12–Dec	Review for exams	24–Apr	PSAE testing week and *Toy Story* (En Español)
19–Dec	Exam Week	1–May	3–3 Vocabulary–weather, seasons
Quiz Every Week		8–May	Review for finals
		15–May	*Buscando a Nemo* (En Español)
		22–May	· Exam Week

SOURCE: Reprinted by permission of Susan Graham.

Figure 7.20 Parent Welcome Letter

¡Bienvenidos a la clase de español!

Queridos Padres y Familias,

My name is Susan Graham (Señorita Graham). I am your child's Spanish One teacher. I have been teaching at Joliet Central since 1986. I love teaching. I use a variety of methods to help students learn easily and enjoy the process of learning Spanish. I also have some simple ways for families to feel involved. I hope you decide to participate in one or more of these activities. Believe it or not, high school students still enjoy and benefit from family involvement.

Family Activities

- *Video.* I have a short video to introduce myself, show you our classroom, and share my expectations. Students will be bringing the video home during the first few weeks of school. Please ask about it.

- *Open House.* The school's Open House is early in the fall. Please consider attending. I'd love to meet you.

- *E-mail list.* I send occasional updates about our class activities using a confidential e-mail list.

- *One million words or less.* I look forward to these essays from parents. It's wonderful to learn about the students through the eyes of those who love them.

I look forward to a great school year.

Sincerely,

Señorita Graham

SOURCE: Reprinted by permission of Susan Graham.

Figure 7.21   One Million Words or Less

Name of student: _____

E-mail addresses of parents or family members (optional):

_____   _____

_____   _____

One Million Words or Less

Please help me to get to know my new students by telling me about your child in "one million words or less." These will be kept confidential. Feel free to use the back of this sheet or to use additional or other paper. Thank you! Gracias.

_____

_____

_____

_____

_____

_____

_____

_____

_____

_____

_____

_____

_____

_____

_____

SOURCE: Reprinted by permission of Susan Graham.

but there is enough participation every year for me to consider this a very worthwhile exercise. I believe my parent routines are a very important part of my responsibility as a teacher. Some students also receive an introductory video to show to their parents. I have several copies of the video, and I rotate them through the entire class during the first 3 weeks."

What's Ahead?

If you have developed a personalized plan to teach routines, rubrics, and rules to your students in the first 3 weeks of school as described in this chapter and do implement that plan as modeled by the WITs you have met throughout the book, here's what you can anticipate during the remaining 33 weeks of the school year (according to the research summarized in the Introduction):

- Increased (not decreased) time for teaching
- Increased (not decreased) time on task by your students
- More academically successful students (rather than fewer)
- More positive (rather than negative) students
- Fewer (rather than increased) discipline problems and referrals
- More independent and self-reliant students (rather than dependent and helpless ones)
- Higher (rather than lower) student achievement
- More positive (rather than negative) attitudes from students
- A high (rather than low) degree of parental support
- Less (rather than more) stress and increased (rather than decreased) levels of job satisfaction

The premise of 3 + 3 = 33 is that the more consistently you teach your students the 3Rs (routines, rubrics, and rules) of your classroom in the first 3 weeks, the more productive the rest of the school year (33 weeks) will be. Instead of merely surviving the school year, you and your students will thrive. *You* will accomplish more because your students will be prepared to learn. *You* will have fewer discipline problems because your students will have mastered the rules. *You* will have more energy because your students will be carrying their share of the workload. Your principal will adore you. Parents will send you thank-you notes. Your colleagues will secretly envy you. But most important, your students will become high-achieving, self-reliant, independent, lifelong learners.

Resource A

With-It Teacher's List

Attention Getters for Off-Task Students

Move Closer

If students are off task during a lesson, stand close to the offenders for a minute or two. Later, ask them to stay in at recess or after class to talk about respectful behavior during instruction (Panziera).

Make Eye Contact

Make eye contact with students. If appropriate, give them a little wink to let them know you've caught them daydreaming.

Be Gentle

If appropriate, gently touch the student on the shoulder or tap your finger slightly on the student's desk or book to focus attention, whisper a reminder in a student's ear, or ask if help is needed.

Be Direct

Some students may need to have very direct instruction regarding precisely what your hand and eye signals mean. In that case, tell them that when you look at them and make eye contact or tap on their desks, you are telling them to pay attention to you or to stop doing something inappropriate (Wiley).

Stop and Wait

Wait patiently to go on until the students in question stop talking.

Pop the Question

Direct a question to the particular section of the room where the student is seated or to a student near the disengaged student.

Give Them a Deadline

Call attention to the time remaining and challenge all students to complete 10 more problems or answer one more question, and then set a timer.

Place a Note

Place a sticky note reminder on the desk of the student who is off task (Graham, S.).

Catch Them Being Good

Casually pass out warm fuzzy coupons or "I Got Caught Being Good" stickers, and suddenly everyone (including the student who's off task) will sit up straight and pay attention (Yates).

Give Them "The Look"

Give students the "evil eye," "the hairy eyeball," or "the look." These labels generally refer to a stern look (similar to the one your mother gave you that conveyed total disgust and disappointment with your inability to do what was right). If you don't overdo it, "the look" works wonders.

Wait

One of the most effective signals to quiet down off-task students is to stand in front of the class with a very annoyed look on your face. This tends to quiet them down relatively quickly. The other signal that usually gets results is "the stare." If students are not following rules or directions, just staring at them will usually turn them around once they have noticed you (Leighty).

Use Names

Use the name of students who aren't paying attention in a math problem for the class to solve (Reichenbach), or call them to the front of the room to help you with the lesson (Sahadevan).

Change Locations

Invite the students who are off task to move to a more comfortable, less distracting location and gently reengage them in their work (Gardner).

Keep 'Em Guessing

- Put students' names on popsicle sticks that have one end colored red and one end colored green. During a lesson, draw the stick from the cup and call on that person to answer. Put the stick back in the cup after you call on the student. Students won't know if they are going to be called again because you put the stick back in. You will know which sticks to pick because you put the green end into the cup after you have called on a person. The red end sticking up indicates that you have called on that person already (Koster).
- Before the first day of school, prepare a set of cards with each student's name on one card. About the size of ½ an index card, these serve as a way to call on students without showing preference. Shuffle them on Monday and then use them throughout the week in the order they fall. They are also useful for substitutes (Hoedeman, K.).

Keep 'Em Moving

Ask questions that require movement in the response. For example: "Raise your hand if . . ." or "Write your answer in the air" or "Show with your hand what a ____ would look like" (Koster).

Watch the Clock

Stare silently at the clock until students are ready to listen. Silence, humor, and dramatic gestures are always more effective than angry lectures (VanderNaald-Johnson).

Attention Getters for Whole-Group Instruction

Use Proximity

Proximity is the number one attention getter for teachers. Never sit down unless you're working with a small group of students. Keep moving. Never teach from just one spot. The closer you move to students, the more likely their attention will improve (Pope, M.).

Show and Tell

Provide both written and verbal directions so students will know exactly what is expected and won't have to waste time asking for directions a second time.

Break It Up

Chunk tasks into shorter segments and set a timer to keep the pace perky.

Vary Your Voice

Change the tone or volume of your voice. Nothing loses students faster than a monotone.

Use Group Dynamics

Develop lessons that rely less on you to engage students and more on the dynamics of group members to engage each other (Leighty).

Mix It Up

Use props to generate interest. Wear a costume or a clever hat to get your message across. Tape or video the anticipatory set of your lesson or a set of very important directions or recruit a student or teacher to go on camera. Present your rules as if you were a network news anchor.

Stack Your Blocks

Expect your students to "Stack Their Blocks" (hands on desks, sitting straight and tall, feet on the floor, and eyes on the teacher) during direct instruction (Carino, Darling, and Perry, with inspiration from Jean Rogers, an occupational therapist with whom they work).

Fair Warning 1

Give verbal cues, such as, "When I finish giving my directions, I'm going to use my name cards (a deck of cards with students' names) or name can (a container with popsicle sticks that have all of the students' names on them) to choose someone to repeat the directions for us" (Carpenter).

Fair Warning 2

Lean over and tell students privately that you will be calling on them shortly.

Keep It Moving

Use a perky instructional pace and call on lots of students in a very short period of time to keep them attentive.

Get Moving

If students appear off task or sleepy, do 30 seconds of stretching exercises.

Shift Gears

When you notice students beginning to fade, be ready to interject a think-pair-share (Kagan, 1993) or partner reading activity to reenergize your class (Robertson).

Use Peer Pressure

Assign the table captains of small cooperative groups the responsibility for making sure that everyone at their table is attending and on task. Often students will respond to requests from peers quite gracefully, especially if the captains have been taught how to offer corrective feedback (Howell).

Say SLANT

Teach the SLANT strategy (University of Kansas, 2005). SLANT stands for

- *S*it up
- *L*ean forward
- *A*ctivate your thinking
- *N*ote (take notes)
- *T*rack the talker

Once your students have mastered the prompt, just say SLANT and it will bring them back on task (Amacher).

Identify Target Students

Develop a list of Target Students who need extra help in understanding directions and getting started with independent work. Once you have finished giving directions to the whole group, move immediately to these targeted students to check on their understanding of the assignment. Don't wait for them to ask.

Give Brain Breaks

Give students Brain Breaks in between lessons if you see they are getting antsy. Brain breaks can be little physical challenges, like trying to turn their right legs in a clockwise circle while they make the number 6 in the air with their right hands. Display an optical illusion on the screen to tax a different part of the brain (Koster).

Ask, "Could It Be Me?"

If several students are not paying attention, reevaluate what you are doing. Is there something you could be doing to make a lesson or activity more interesting or relevant? If so, do it.

Bulletin Board List

Class Rules

Daily Assignments

Daily Procedures

Lesson Objective

State, District, or School Standards or Outcomes

Lesson Objective

Charts Under Construction by the Class

Job Charts

Daily Calendar

Commercial Calendars With Content Photos (American History Calendar, Famous Artists Calendar, Calendars in Foreign Languages)

Writing Traits Chart

Reading Traits Chart

Students' Hopes and Dreams

Posters: Student Created, Teacher Created, Collaborative, Motivational

Rubrics: State Department of Education, District, Teacher, Collaborative

Primary Word Wall

Intermediate-Secondary Word Wall

Photos: Field Trips, Special Events, Students

Procedure Charts

Breakfast and Lunch Menus

Schedules for Special Teachers

Schedules for Block Periods

Student Work: Art, Writing, Projects

Student Writing Samples

Mission Statements: Class, Teacher, School

Class Awards

Exit and Reentry Accountability Log (Trips to Library, Bathroom)

Classroom Theme Displays

Character Words

Inspirational and Motivational Quotations

Formulas

Maps

Charts

Lexicons

Concepts

Procedures for Drills and
    Emergencies: Fire, Tornado,
    Hurricane, Lockdown, Earthquake

Letter Charts

Sound-Spelling Correspondence
    Charts

Star, Student of the Week or Month

Thermometer, Graphs to Measure
    Class Goals

Days of the Week

Months of the Year

Color Words

Sight Words

Number Words

Book Selection Clues

Reading Skills Charts

Sound and Letter Cards

Graphic Organizers

Brainstormed List of Writing Topics

Juicy Words Charts

KWL-Plus Charts

News Clippings (Current Events)

News Clippings (School Events and
    Students in the News)

Fluency Graph (Classroom Goal)

Attendance and Lunch Counts

Cooperative Learning Aids:
    Prompts, Rules, Procedures

Daily Assignments

Long-Range Assignments

Student Book
    Reviews and Poetry

Places We've Been

Things We've Done

Proofreading Checklist

Schedule of Upcoming Events

Planning Calendar for Long-Range
    Assignments

Task Completion Chart

Reading Incentive Posters and Book
    Jackets

Biographical Posters

Compass Points

Periodic Table

Ways to Check for Understanding

- Students respond chorally; teacher notes the percentage of students who respond correctly and addresses those who don't.
- Students indicate their choices for the correct answer to a question from one of two or more possible answers by holding up prepared color-coded cards.
- Students display one of two response cards: Yes or No.

- Students display nonverbal signals, such as thumbs up or thumbs down, or arms crossed or arms uncrossed, to indicate their choice of true or false regarding the correctness of a statement.
- Students fold pieces of plain paper into fourths, using each of the eight sections (using both front and back of paper) to write responses and then hold them up for the teacher to see.
- Students pair with a partner and quietly explain a concept or process to each other while the teacher circulates and listens. Numbered Heads is a version of pairing in which students are permanently numbered One or Two, and the teacher gives a direction such as, "Ones tell Twos the main idea of this paragraph, or Twos tell Ones what you think will happen next in the story" (Graham, A.).
- Students write a question about the concept under discussion and ask a partner, and then all students turn in those questions that could not be answered so the teacher can address them.
- Students keep a journal or learning log in which they write entries on each lesson in a particular unit.
- Students write their answers to questions or problems on whiteboards and hold them up for the teacher to see.
- Students place a sticky arrow or flag on the part of the story that answers the question.

Homework Helpers for Upper-Grade and Secondary Teachers

Oops Board

Classroom management is pivotal, and the more specific it is, the better. I use a system I call an Oops Board on which I post a note to students reminding them of any missing assignments. Each day begins with this routine. On it might be the entry "Sp.–1/24." When the student completes the spelling assignment from 1/24, I put a line under this entry to tell me this assignment is completed. This gives me accurate feedback for report cards and homework completion (VanderNaald-Johnson).

Number Your Homework

I assign a special number to each child on the first day of school. When they complete homework, they must write their special number in the upper right-hand corner of the page. When they hand in the homework, they are to put their page in chronological order with the class papers. It makes it easy to see who has handed in their work and who has not. I remind them many times on how to do this during the first few weeks of school (Biltucci).

It's Due When It's Due

Homework is due at the beginning of the period. If it is turned in later during the class or during the day, it is 10% off. If it is turned in after that day, it is 50% off. These rules are written on my syllabus, and I go over this at the beginning of the year (Bender).

Absent Students

Assign a student in the classroom or someone on the absent student's team to pick up a "We Missed You at School Today" folder from the basket on your desk and put all of the work papers, returned homework papers, and so forth in the folder. The folder could be taken home by the absent student's sibling, a buddy in the class, or just be placed on their desk until they return to class.

The Paper Chase

Purchase a stackable wire desk tray for each class period. Put five manila folders, one for each day of the week, in each wire tray. Put the extra assignments for each class in the proper manila folder, so a student who was absent on Tuesday can go to the file, look in Tuesday's folder, and get the missing work. At the end of the week, collect all of the week's assignments and put them in a hanging file folder. Each week has its own hanging file, labeled with the date. Students who missed a day last week, or who lost a paper, can go to the hanging file and get their assignment. This process takes some extra teaching and reminding, but by the end of the first semester, most students are able to get their own missing assignments without assistance (Wood).

Hoedeman's Homework Helpers

1. Put a To Do item on the Morning Checklist reminding students to put their homework out on their desks as soon as they sit down. Walk around with a checklist and give credit to those who have completed the assignment.
2. Check homework with the whole class, calling on different individuals to give the answers, discussing and answering students' questions as you go.
3. Give a homework quiz. Hand out a piece of paper and ask students to fold it into four rectangles two times, thus forming eight boxes. Ask students to put selected problems from their homework in three to

eight of the boxes formed. Also draw the piece of paper on the board with the rectangles marked and place the numbers of the homework problems in each box. Of course, students are not permitted to have their textbooks out during this time. They can only use their completed homework assignment. They copy the problem, their work, and their answer in the specified boxes. These sheets are labeled to correspond with the assignment (e.g., Homework Quiz 11). Collect and score them.

4. Collect one assignment each week. It's called "surprise collect" because students never know which day it might happen. Check the whole assignment, give them a grade, and include comments. This practice keeps students doing their homework.

5. Pass out a transparency or two to each group along with overhead pens. Ask someone in each group to prepare one or two of the homework problems to present on the overhead. This is a good exercise in public speaking and "teaching."

6. Divide the whiteboard into big squares, put a problem number in each one, pass out the dry-erase markers, and ask individuals to come up to the board to work the problems. Be sure to thank those students who make mistakes because we all learn something from them!

7. Ask students to highlight four selected answers on their homework; collect and check only those four.

8. Check the assignment together and make a list on the board of what has been learned from the mistakes that were made. This encourages those who get one wrong to figure out why so they can raise their hand and contribute an idea. Here's a sample list that might be generated by students.

> **Copy the problem correctly.**
>
> **Simplify all answers!**
>
> **Divide carefully when changing improper fractions to mixed numbers.**
>
> **Be sure to "flip" the divisor.**
>
> **Label your answer.**

9. For a change of scenery, give everyone a clipboard and ask them to take their checking pens and get with a partner anywhere in the room and compare their answers, making notes about where they disagree. Then get together as a whole group and discuss any questions.

10. Give students clipboards on which to put their homework and have them sit on the floor while you project a transparency with answers on a convenient spot on the wall. Just moving to a new place can help concentration (Hoedeman, K.)

Noise Breakers

Being Careful Drivers

When students are walking in the hallways, use the "driving" metaphor. Students are not permitted to honk (talk in the halls), peel out (squeak their shoes), speed (run in the halls), or scrape bumpers or guardrails (touch each other or the walls) (Perry, Carino, and Darling with inspiration from Cheryl Stack).

Gab Fest

Set aside 10 minutes before school starts and during recess as a chat time. Once a week allow students to come in during lunch and chat with you or each other. Use buddy talk or partner sharing during lessons, which allows for socialization (Wiley and Anstatt).

Post a Sign

Make a set of laminated signs that say "No noise," "Respond only when asked," and "Class discussion okay." Post them on your whiteboard as appropriate. For example, during silent reading, use the "No noise" sign (Wiley).

Change Locations

Permit students to move from their desks to a table in the room or a spot on the carpet if it helps them to focus on their work.

Silent Signal

To avoid wildly waving hands when asking questions of the whole group, tell students to use another signal when they know and want to volunteer the answer (e.g., putting their hands on top of their heads, laying a finger aside their noses, or crossing their arms).

Time Out for Pencils

Use a "pencil time-out" area, and if students are tapping their pencils, put their pencils in time out (Wiley).

Time Out for Hands

If too many students are shuffling papers or creating noise with their hands, ask everyone to put their hands on their head for a moment to quiet them down (Wiley).

Losing Voices

When the noise level is too high, say, "Voice check." After three voice checks, students "lose their voices" and cannot talk for the rest of the activity (Wiles).

No Twosies

Expect students to walk in alphabetical order in the hallways. No "twosies" (walking side by side) or "invisible elephants" (gaps in the line) are permitted (Graham, A.).

Last One Out

If you have assigned someone in your classroom the job of turning off the lights and closing the door when you exit the classroom, put that person in charge of turning off one light when he or she feels students are getting too loud (Ryser).

Erase One Letter

Write STOP on the board. If it becomes too loud, erase one letter. If all letters are erased, stop immediately and assign mundane independent work rather than the group work previously being enjoyed so boisterously (Paul). Write the word RECESS on the board and erase one letter at a time until the room is quiet. If the whole word disappears, so does recess (Zaccaria).

Use a "Deci-Bell" to Lower the Decibels

Purchase a small bell and call it your "deci-bell." Do a mini-lesson on decibels and what they are. Find out the decibel levels of different sounds, like jackhammers, jet planes, elevator music, and whispers. Explain that you will tap (or ring) the bell if your students are too loud. "Three taps and you're out" means the students must work in total silence and independence" (Koster).

Turn Off the Pencil Sharpener

No pencil sharpening during instruction (large or small group).

Nonverbal Language

Teach and use American Sign Language signals for the following often used words: *yes, no, bathroom, wait,* and *stop.* Students can seek help and get responses from you without verbally interrupting a lesson, read-aloud, or conversation with another student (Oosterbaan). Or teach your students to use one finger to ask to use the bathroom and two fingers to request academic help.

Body Language

Teach basic body language awareness to your students so they will be able to "read" their friends, thus reducing the likelihood of problems between individual students (Oosterbaan).

The Golfer's Clap

Use silent signals like the Golfer's Clap (noiseless clapping that doesn't distract), thumbs up, or a pat on the back to show approval.

Silent Hallways

Teach students quiet ways to communicate with friends they see passing in the hallway (e.g., a silent wave, blowing kisses, pretending to hug, or using sign language to spell "Hi") (Carino, Darling, and Perry).

Think Ahead

Before asking a question, always preface it with "Can anyone raise a hand and tell me . . . ?"

Preface a question or request with the words "I'm looking for someone quiet to . . ."

Mozart or Bach

Play classical music quietly as a calming noise buster. If students can't hear the music, then their voices are too loud.

It's Your Turn

Teach students to tap one another on the shoulder quietly to signal "It's your turn." This is helpful when students are taking turns on the computer, someone is testing individual students, or remedial teachers are changing groups (Carino, Darling, and Perry).

Electric Stoplight

Purchase an electric stoplight that can be set to a variety of different decibel levels depending on how much noise you permit during different periods of the day. When the noise level remains within a certain range, the light stays green. If the students begin to get too loud, a yellow light flashes. If the students do not lower their voices, a red light flashes, meaning they must get silent immediately (Aronson).

Just Imagine

When your students walk down the hallway, ask them to imagine they are walking in space or under the sea. To do so, they need to wear space helmets or diving masks. This necessitates holding their hands over their mouths. Of course, no sound can escape when they are wearing masks (teacher included). As the year progresses, students may wear invisible masks, but if any sound leaks out, students must find a new mask (Oosterbaan).

Stop Along the Way

If your students have a difficult time remaining quiet during a very long walk from one end of the building to the other, identify stopping points along the way. Say to the line leader, "Take us to office." Then say, "Now, we're ready to head for the library" (Kennedy).

Another Way to Say . . .

Teach kindergarten students to put both hands on top of their heads to signal when they are finished with an assignment rather than shouting out, "I'm done!" (Wyman and Engelsiepen).

Quiet Game: Version 1

One student (of the teacher's choice) sits in a rocking chair in front of the room and calls on someone who is "sitting tall" (see Chapter 6 for a description) to trade places in the chair. The student in the chair must find someone who is doing exactly the right thing. Students can have only one turn, and they must make a decision quickly. Play this game many times with the teacher watching and reminding. Use the game when an adult comes to the room and needs to speak with you or if you need to deal with an emergency. The scenario for playing the game when an adult steps into the room sounds like this: "Maria, start the Quiet Game in my chair. Remember to look for people sitting tall." Then the teacher is free for no more than 5 minutes. This game keeps both students and teacher calm and focused, ready to resume whatever they were doing before the interruption (Larson).

Quiet Game: Version 2

Use this version when you line up for dismissal. When it is time to line up, the children are asked to play the Quiet Game. Count 1, 2, 3, and they zip their lips and lock their hands. Post a class list at the front of the classroom in large enough print for students to read. Point to one name on the list, and that child lines up. If that student is quiet, the children are winning. If the student is noisy, the teacher is winning. Play this game at other times, too, such as pack-up time or any time that the noise level is too loud (Wyman and Engelsiepen).

Quiet Game: Version 3

Play the Quiet Game as a table challenge and keep score. Check a table, and if it is quiet, the table earns a point. The table with the most points wins! This game has many different versions depending on what's going on. It is a very simple game, but the children just love it, making it an effective classroom routine (Wyman and Engelsiepen).

Quiet Game: Version 4

Play this version of the Quiet Game once the students begin the independent work portion of an assignment. The idea is to see who can go the longest without talking. Introduce the Quiet Game by writing a request on the board or mouthing the words (a virtual whisper). Then explain that all questions have to be written down or mouthed. Play this game for only 15 to 20 minutes at a time. Students who finish without talking out loud sometimes get a small treat, but students enjoy this game so much that the rewards are not needed after a while. To play this game in buddy pairs, the buddies ask their questions via their whiteboards (Shires and Scott Rose).

The X Factor

Put a big red X on the overhead. This symbol communicates that there is to be absolute silence during a specified time period (Carpenter).

Measure Your Voices

Ask students to use their 6-inch or 12-inch voices, which means anyone sitting more than 6 or 12 inches away from them shouldn't be able to hear them (Williams).

Invite Your Animals to School

Invite your personal favorite stuffed animals to your classroom. These special guests visit tables only where students are working quietly. Of course, your stuffed animals must have names and personalities so that your students feel very privileged to have them seated at their tables (Oosterbaan).

Talk Like the Animals

Use the pets in your classroom to help students understand that language and communication involve more than words. Teach them to communicate wordlessly, like the animals do (Oosterbaan).

Signals That Silence Students

Wind Chimes

Hang an attractive wind chime in your classroom and touch it to signal the need for absolute quiet (Siringo).

Raised Hand

Many schools adopt a buildingwide raised hand signal (Wong & Wong, 1998). Teachers raise their hands, and as soon as students notice the raised hand, they stop talking and raise *their* hands. A surefire secret to the success of this attention getter is to refrain from talking until you have achieved absolute silence. Avoid the temptation to begin talking too quickly in an attempt to drown out the talkers. You will succeed only in encouraging them to drown out your voice.

Lights Out and Listen

Turn out the lights to signal a transition to the next activity. If the students are in tune with the daily schedule posted on the board, they will immediately begin to clean up and prepare for the next activity (Pilkington).

Echo Chorus

Say: "One, two, three, eyes on me." The class echoes back, "One, two, eyes on you." Reciting this phrase is students' cue to *stop* whatever they are doing, *look* at the teacher, and *listen* for further instruction. Expect 100% participation and wait. You will receive it (Cimmiyotti).

Echo Clapping, Snapping, Stomping, Waving, or Clicking

Begin a clapping (or some other kind of pattern) and teach your class to echo that same pattern back. This is a nonverbal signal for the class to *stop, look, and listen* to the teacher for further instructions (Wallace).

Give Me Five: Version 1

Hold up your hand with five fingers displayed. This requires students to focus on what they see as well as what they hear. Usually several students will stop talking and immediately attend when they see that your hand is in the air. As soon as you see at least five students quietly looking at your hand, begin to lower your fingers until only your index finger is displayed. At this point the room should be absolutely silent.

Give Me Five: Version 2

Say: "Give me five." Then put up one finger as you recite each step: (1) eyes on speaker, (2) lips closed, (3) ears listening, (4) sitting up straight, and (5) hands and feet quiet. When you complete the counting, you will have five fingers showing and a quiet class (Wesolowski).

Give Me Five: Version 3

Say: "Give me five." Then wait for students to (1) stop talking, (2) look at you, (3) sit up straight, (4) listen, and (5) keep their hands and feet still. If this routine is well taught at the beginning of the year and not overused, it is perfect for those times when you absolutely need to get all students' attention for a very important announcement (Zaccaria).

Musical Attention Getter 1

Play a scale slowly on a toy xylophone. By the time you reach the last note, expect your students to be ready and attentive. This signal not only keeps you calm but also saves your voice (Wallace).

Musical Attention Getter 2

Burst into song. Your musical attention getter could be an actual song, your own words sung to a familiar tune, or a call-and-response duet. If you're studying state capitals, which students are required to master, do a call-and-response by singing the state and expecting students to sing the capital. This signal serves a dual purpose: getting the students' attention and reinforcing a curricular objective (Wallace).

Sign Language

Use your hand to make an "s" in sign language (a closed fist). This is a nonverbal (and very quiet) way of telling students to be silent because you have something important to say (Dunn).

Rainstick

Use a rainstick to let your students know that you crave peace, silence, and calm in your classroom immediately. A rainstick is a hollow bamboo shoot that is filled with rice or seeds. When the rainstick is slowly turned upside down, the rice or seeds fall to the other end and make a sound resembling falling rain. When the rainstick is turned and the calming sound begins, students stop immediately and give their attention to the teacher (Seckel).

Time-Savers for Every Teacher

Time Your Transitions

Use a timer to time transitions and create competitions between groups or between boys and girls to decrease transition time (Wiley). Or set a timer to convey a sense of urgency to students who procrastinate or dawdle. Provide 10-minute, 5-minute, and 1-minute warnings regarding the end of a work period.

Protect Teaching Time

Negotiate with the principal to ban the intercom during teaching time.

Teach the 3Rs

Teach your routines, rubrics, and rules to mastery.

Have a Plan

Have a plan for every day that includes what you expect you and your students to be doing every minute of the day.

Announce a Lesson in Progress

Put a "Lesson in Progress" sign on your door. This is especially helpful if you have colleagues who interrupt lessons.

Stick to the Agenda

Give students an agenda (a to-do list) every day. It can be written on the board or chart paper, typed on a single sheet of paper, or even worn as a sign around your neck when you initially teach the agenda routine. In early childhood and ELL classes, use picture prompts to accompany your words. Put beginning and ending times or time allotments on the various items.

Establish the Daily Planner Habit

Prominently display assignments that students are expected to complete in class or as homework. Teach students how to copy assignments into a daily planner, beginning at the second-grade level.

Give Spoken and Written Instructions

Make your directions clear, short, and as straightforward as possible. For students who are more visual learners, also prepare a set of written directions.

Value Time

- Be on time for class.
- Have a minute-by-minute plan for important lessons.
- Insist that your students be on time for class.
- Have all of your materials prepared.
- Always begin on time.
- Post a schedule (with times listed) on the board every day, to keep everyone on track.
- Appoint a timekeeper to keep you on schedule.

Prevent Idle Minds

Never permit students to remain idle. Teach routines for what students should do if they finish their work or if they are momentarily sidelined because they don't understand the directions. Your first priority as a teacher is to make sure all students are productively engaged. This goal takes precedence over any administrivia tasks (e.g., taking attendance or gathering a lunch count). Find more efficient ways to accomplish these tasks while you find the students who aren't working and help them begin working (Graham, S.).

Specify a Place for Everything

Teach students where to put notes from home, assignments, homework, money, permission slips, and so on.

Use Parents

Use parent volunteers to complete easy but time-consuming tasks so that your time can be devoted to planning lessons, grading papers, or previewing curriculum materials. Even in middle and high school, use volunteers to photocopy materials, listen to struggling students read aloud, do fluency-building exercises, or put up and take down bulletin boards.

Summarize for Maximum Retention

Summarize the key concepts (big ideas, essential questions, or what's important) at the end of every lesson or class period.

Time-Savers for Elementary Teachers

Protected Teaching Time

Convince your principal to create a master schedule that protects uninterrupted blocks of time for reading and math instruction.

Bathroom and Drinks

- Make sure student bathroom and drink breaks are taken at transition times and not in the middle of lessons. If students must line up and wait for a turn to use the bathroom and to get drinks, use that time to practice math facts, sounds, states and capitals, or any other information that needs to be automatic and accurate.
- Use the time following lunch or recess, when everyone needs to get a drink and go to the bathroom, for the completion of independent work. Students can easily move in and out of the classroom individually, and less time is wasted.
- Rather then giving a group bathroom break, send students to the bathroom one at a time during an activity that students don't want to miss (computers, art, movement activities).

Teaching in the Halls

Special teachers who pick students up from classrooms should have a review routine they use when walking down the hallway with students. Never just walk. Walk and review.

Sponge Activities

- Use transition times for review and practice. Review during lining up. Practice during packing up (Sahadevan).
- Review math and reading skills while waiting—before an assembly, in the classroom while waiting to be called on the intercom, in the hallways while waiting for a music, art, or computer class.

- While waiting in the hallways for lunch or specials, practice math or other facts quietly. Teacher softly says "What's 5 × 7?" and the students show the answer with their hands. Play the "I am thinking of" game. Teacher says, "I am thinking of a reason for the American Revolution that starts with a "T" (taxation).

Eating on the Run

- Give students a brief direction to follow before they can pick their snacks. For example, go to the board and write an addition problem that equals one of the sums. You write 5 on the board and they write 2 + 3.
- Recruit students who finish their snack quickly to help you put up student work on the bulletin board.
- Combine having a snack and silent reading (Paul).

Time-Savers for Secondary Teachers

Do You Have What You Need?

Hang a reminder sign on your classroom door containing a list of materials needed in your class for that day.

Using "Neon" to Get Their Attention

For a change of pace, instead of putting bell-work assignments on the board, give students a brightly colored single sheet of paper containing the assignment and space to write their answers. This offers a motivating change of pace (Graham, S.).

Absent Students

- Keep a list of the week's assignments posted at the front of the room so students who have been absent can easily obtain them.
- Give students a copy of the week's agenda and assignments on Monday. When students are absent because of extracurricular activities, they will have their assignments and know what went on in class.

Protecting Teaching Time

Permit no interruptions during explanations (unless there is bleeding or vomiting that needs your attention).

Taking Attendance in Fifteen Seconds or Less

Alphabetize your students' names. Assign each one a number. As soon as class begins, ask students to count off. If students 1–7 are present but 8 doesn't answer, then 9 says, "8 is absent; 9," and the count continues. Give a student attendance monitor a sheet with the list of numbers printed on it and ask that individual to circle the absent students' numbers. That individual can keep the sheet, and as tardy students arrive, he or she can put an X through the circled number to indicate that the student was tardy. Attendance can be taken in less than 15 seconds, even in larger classes (Bresnahan).

Organizational Routines for Elementary Teachers

Beginning of day

Transition time

Independent work assignments, agenda, to-do list

Roll taking

Where do I sit and do I ever get to sit anywhere else

Storage of supplies, clothing, and snacks

Ordering hot lunch or milk

Washing hands

What to do if you forget your lunch or milk money

What to do if you forget your lunch

Going out for recess

Snack time behavior (getting ready and cleaning up)

How and when to sharpen pencils

How and where to get an already sharpened pencil

What to do when you've finished all your work

What to do when you don't understand the directions

What to do when you need to talk to the teacher who is busy

When you can and can't be out of your seat

When you can and can't talk to your neighbor

Going to the bathroom

What to do when you feel sick

How, when, and where you can get a drink

Where to put homework

Where to put money

Where to put notes from home

What to do with your take-home folder when you get home

Where to find various things in the classroom

How to obtain supplies when you run out

How to figure out which center to go to first

How to figure out what to do in a center

How to walk down the hall

How to line up

How to move from the rug to tables or desks

How to move from tables or desks to the rug

How to sit on the rug

How to organize your desk

How to clean out your desk

How to care for and store supplies

How to get new supplies

Tornado, earthquake, hurricane, fire, disaster, and lockdown drills

Talking in class: when it is permitted, when it is not, how quiet in-class talking must be

How to move to and from the large group circle

How and where to sit for specific groups (e.g., reading, computers, writer's workshop)

How to sit and act in assemblies

How and where to line up outside before school

How and where to line up after recess

The class signal for entering the building

The class signal for dismissal

The class signal for absolute silence while I take care of this emergency or interruption

The class signal for absolute silence and get ready to transition

The class signal for attending during instruction

The class signal for "wise up and pay attention or you'll be in trouble"

How and when classroom computers can be used

Morning Meeting or Sharing Circle

Getting lunch supplies and refills for in-class eating

Rainy- and snowy-day recess

How and when to wash your hands

How to exit the room

How to return to the room (after an assembly, art, music, PE, etc.)

Assignment of class jobs

Job description of each class job

Where the classroom first-aid supplies are

End of day

Handing in papers

Putting a heading on papers

Checking homework

Snack time

What to do when the phone rings

What to do when visitors are observing the classroom

What to do in the hallway when they see friends or teachers

What to do when adults need to speak with the teacher during a lesson

Organizational Routines for Secondary Teachers

Beginning of class, period, or block

Bringing materials to class

What a due date is and where it can be found

How to break long-term assignments into manageable tasks

Assignment notebook or daily planner: how to enter assignments

How to use an assignment notebook on a daily basis

How missing homework assignments are handled

Homework buddy program

Homework Hotline

Returning homework timelines

How and where assignments are posted

Agenda or to-do list posting

Long-term assignments

Communication with parents

How to set up notebooks and keep up to date

Passing and collecting papers to grade

Distributing materials to cooperative groups

Trading papers for grading

Class jobs

How to act during a class discussion

Talking during class (when and when not appropriate)

Note taking

How to act when the teacher is talking and teaching

What to do when the intercom interrupts a lesson

What to do when your pencil breaks and you don't have a replacement

Fire, tornado, hurricane, earthquake, bomb threat, lockdown, and disaster drills

What to do when you finish your work early

What to do when you have a question

What to do when you need to go to the restroom

How to enter the classroom

What to do when you first enter the classroom

Where to find a previous assignment

How to transition from one type of activity to another quickly and quietly

What to do when you want your teacher's attention

How to set up homework assignments

How grades are derived

Where to put your homework

Where to put money and permission slips

Where to put notes from home

What to do if you want to sharpen a pencil

Where to find assignments if you've been absent

What to do when you are tardy

Leaving the classroom

Asking questions

How to let the teacher know when you don't understand

Responding to teacher's request for attention

Changing groups

Keeping your notebook

Emergency alerts

How to ask for help or a conference

Progress reports

When students can be out of their seats

What kinds of student participation are acceptable (call-outs, interruptions, raising hand)

Walking to an assembly

Behavior in assemblies

Coming back to class after an assembly

Going as a class to the library

Leaving the class for any reason

End-of-class routine

Rewards (Tangible But Not Edible)

Ink stamps or notes on student work

Notes to students or parents in assignment books or daily planners

Having time in an art center to create awards for themselves and classmates

Raffle tickets, to be turned in once a week for a raffle (different things every week)

Compliments, verbal praise

Helping the custodian or secretary

Sitting at the teacher's desk for a day

Being allowed to pass out snacks for recess

Being allowed to run errands for the teacher

Phone call or note home

No-homework pass

Bringing something in for show-and-tell

A grab bag of inexpensive "trinkets"

A "mystery pack" (notepad, folder, sports cards)

Watching a video

Two minutes of chat time at the end of class

Writing on the chalkboard

Playing music and letting students draw

Letting students draw while you read aloud

Not having to wear shoes in the classroom

Extra recess (computer, art, game)

Sitting by friends

Decorating the classroom and helping with a bulletin board

Sitting at the teacher's desk for a period of time

Using markers and art supplies

Visiting the library alone (if that is not normally an option)

Writing on the chalkboard with colored chalk

Read outdoors

Wearing bedroom slippers in class

Playing a computer game

Reading to a younger class

Making deliveries to the office

Listening to music while working

Playing a favorite game or work a puzzle

Computer games and Internet access

Earning play money for privileges or purchases in the class store

Being a helper in another classroom

Eating lunch with the teacher or principal

Dancing to favorite music in the classroom

Choosing special activities at the end of the day

Listening with a headset to a book or music on CD

Having a teacher perform special skills (i.e., singing, shooting free throws)

Having a teacher read a special book to the class

Selecting a paperback book

Entering a drawing for donated prizes

Taking a trip to the treasure box (no food items)

Getting stickers, pencils, and other school supplies

Video store or movie coupon

Set of flash cards from the computer

Free time on Internet

Extra play time

Having your picture taken for the "Almost Angels" bulletin board

Helping the teacher

BUG (Being Unusually Good) slips, raffle tickets (which amount to a chance for raffle for candy on Fridays), pencils, school supplies, verbal recognition, or homework passes

Chances for a drawing (baseball game, bowling, swimming party)

Having a KISS (holding the cloth Hershey Kiss Bear)

Certificates

Stickers

Choosing to play an educational game

Playing Homeworkopoly (copy the game board at http://www.teachnet .clm/homeworkopoly)

Rewards (Intangible)

Cheers from classmates (e.g., the Rocket Ship: clap hands and push skyward)

Group pat on the back (all students pat themselves on the back)

Giving yourself a pat on the back while saying "I am getting smarter every day"

Having a partner or neighbor turn to a student and say, "You are awesome"

A round of applause or golfer's round of applause (silent)

Rewards (Low-Sugar or No-Sugar Treats)

Carrot sticks

Celery boats

Crackers

Fish crackers

Apple slices

Cheese sticks

Peanut butter & whatever

Vegetables with dip

Bananas

Orange slices

Apples

Graham crackers

Oatmeal cookies

Animal crackers

Dinosaur graham crackers

Teddy Bear graham crackers

Raisin cookies

Peanut butter cookies

Watermelon

Cantaloupe

Honeydew melon

Dried fruits

Fruit kabobs

Pretzels

Trail mixes

Yogurt

Nut bread

Pumpkin bread

Zucchini bread

Cheese crackers

Nuts

Peanuts

Granola

Popcorn

Grapes

Bread sticks

Cheese & crackers

Raisins

Finger sandwiches (Litz)

Social Routines

How to ask someone to be your partner

How to greet a partner when you first meet them

How to work with a partner

How to work with a small group

How to work with the whole group

How to help or tutor someone else

How to listen to peers

How to listen to the teacher

When to participate in a discussion without "stepping on anyone's words"

How to help someone

How to discuss and share homework

How to ask someone for help

How to say "no" to someone nicely

How to participate in a Morning Meeting

How to give your opinion

How to disagree with someone nicely

Giving a compliment

Accepting a compliment

Learning how to read the body language of others

Learning how to read the body language of the teacher

Introducing two people who don't know each other

Starting a conversation

Listening to a conversation

Keeping a conversation going

Waiting your turn, interrupting in a conversation

Sharing

Compromising

Handling being teased

Saying "no"

Joining a group or activity that is already in progress

Asserting one's own opinions, even those contrary to those of peers or teacher

Handling peer pressure

Apologizing

Playing a group game or participating in a group activity

Handling being left out or verbally rejected

Handling someone asking you to do something you don't know how to do

Suggesting an activity or idea to the group

Seeking help (or a favor) from a peer

Asking a question

Saying "thank you"

Keeping a secret

Disagreeing

Resource B

With-It Teacher Questionnaire

Please provide the following demographic information.

Name:

Home Address:

Home Phone Number:

School Phone Number:

Preferred E-Mail Address:

Grade Levels and Subjects Taught:

Current Assignment:

Name of School:

School Address:

Introduction

Following are a dozen categories of classroom characteristics and practices that impact your success as a teacher. With-it teachers know that all students need explicit, systematic, supportive instruction regarding these practices in order to become highly effective students who eventually become independent, lifelong learners.

With-it teachers teach their students routines, rules, prompts, and scripts that maximize the time available for learning. They use time-savers and noise busters to create environments that are calm and focused. They use bulletin boards and seating arrangements to support their instruction. They share prompts and scripts that enable students to become confident learners. Their instructional methodologies are varied and suit the content objective.

Directions for Completing the Questionnaire

There are 12 bold-faced categories. I have provided a definition and at least one example for each category. Briefly reflect on the three questions you will find in each category: What are the essential practices in your classroom? How and when do you teach them to your students? What questions do you have about this category that you would like to see answered in a book for teachers?

The minute you think of specific practices, ideas, and "tricks" in a specific category, jot down your answers. Please don't worry about the conventions of spelling, grammar, or the like. I will take your ideas and polish them (and then give you credit). Let your ideas flow.

Please don't worry about whether an idea fits in one category or another. This is not a test. Just get your ideas in writing. If you can't think of anything in a specific category, skip it. It's not necessary to answer every question in every category.

1. Classroom Decor: *The walls of the classroom and how they are used to extend and enhance learning* (e.g., posting class rules on the side wall; posting procedures for teacher on the back wall)

What works for you?

How do you teach (convey) the purpose of your classroom decor to students?

What questions do you have about classroom decor that you would like to see answered in a book for teachers?

2. Classroom Seating: *The ways in which desks, chairs, tables, and other furniture are arranged to maximize learning* (e.g., team pods for cooperative grouping, rows for independent work, study carrels for students who need quiet places)

What works for you?

How do you teach (convey) the purpose of your seating arrangement to students?

What questions do you have about seating arrangements that you would like to see answered in a book for teachers?

3. Routines: *A sequence of steps to be followed; the way we do things around here; the order in which we do things around here.* Routines can be organizational, academic, or social.

3a. *Academic Routines*

What are the essential academic routines in your classroom?

How do you teach (convey) your academic routines to students?

What questions do you have about academic routines that you would like to see answered in a book for teachers?

3b. *Nonacademic Routines*

What are the essential nonacademic routines in your classroom?

How do you teach (convey) these nonacademic routines to students?

What questions do you have about nonacademic routines that you would like to see answered in a book for teachers?

3c. *Organizational Routines* (e.g., procedure for passing in homework assignments)

What are the essential organizational routines in your classroom?

How do you teach (convey) these organizational routines to students?

What questions do you have about organizational routines that you would like to see answered in a book for teachers?

3d. *Social Routines*

What are the essential social routines in your classroom?

How do you teach (convey) these social routines to students?

What questions do you have about social routines that you would like to see answered in a book for teachers?

4. **Signal:** *An action, gesture, or sign used as a means of communication* (e.g., raised hand to signal "stop talking and return to your seat")

What are the essential signals in your classroom?

How do you teach (convey) these signals to students?

What questions do you have about signals that you would like to see answered in a book for teachers?

5. Prompt: *A set of words, statements, or questions to help someone remember how to execute a script* (e.g., who, what, where, when); *an acronym to help someone remember how to execute a script* (e.g., SQ3R)

What are the essential prompts in your classroom?

How do you teach (convey) these prompts to students?

What questions do you have about prompts that you would like to see answered in a book for teachers?

6. Script: *A schematic structure that predicts what will (or should) happen next, containing the sequence of actions one goes through when carrying out a stereotypical script; usually involves cognitive processing and decision making* (e.g., a set of steps to follow in writing an essay or book report)

What are the essential scripts in your classroom?

How do you teach (convey) scripts to students?

What questions do you have about scripts that you would like to see answered in a book for teachers?

7. Rule: *An authoritative principle set forth to guide behavior or action; rule following often requires cognitive processing, decision making, and planning*

What are the essential rules in your classroom?

How do you teach (convey) the meaning and purpose of these rules to students?

What questions do you have about rules that you would like to see answered in a book for teachers?

8. Reward: *A benefit obtained as a result of an action taken or a job done* (e.g., special cheers for a job well done—firecracker, sprinkler [teacher and students wave their arms back and forth and make noises like sprinkling water], and the like)

What are the essential rewards in your classroom?

How do you teach (convey) the meaning and purpose of these rewards to students?

What questions do you have about rewards that you would like to see answered in a book for teachers?

9. Instructional Methodology: *A specific approach that increases the likelihood that your students will understand and remember* (e.g., cooperative learning, choral responding, thinking aloud, modeling)

What are the essential instructional methodologies in your classroom?

How do you teach (convey) the procedures, expectations, and characteristics of these methodologies to students?

What questions do you have about instructional methodologies that you would like to see answered in a book for teachers?

10. Attending Moves: *Things you do to get and keep students' attention* (e.g., moving closer to a student; using a student's name in an example)

What are the essential attending moves in your classroom? What are the most effective ways you use to get students' attention when their attention wanders, either individually or as a group?

How do you teach (convey) these moves to students?

What questions do you have about attending moves that you would like to see answered in a book for teachers?

11. Time-Savers: *Specific practices that increase the amount of time available for instruction and independent practice* (e.g., using brief time blocks for review and practice)

What are the essential time-savers in your classroom?

How do you teach (convey) these time-savers to students?

What questions do you have about time-savers that you would like to see answered in a book for teachers?

12. Noise Busters: *Specific practices that reduce extraneous noise in a classroom* (e.g., using silent signals, using whispers)

What are the essential noise busters in your classroom?

How do you teach (convey) these noise busters to students?

What questions do you have about noise busters that you would like to see answered in a book for teachers?

Copyright © 2006 by Corwin Press. All rights reserved. Reprinted from *How to Survive and Thrive in the First Three Weeks of School,* by Elaine K. McEwan. Thousand Oaks, CA: Corwin Press, www.corwinpress.com. Reproduction authorized only for the local school site or nonprofit organization that has purchased this book.

Resource C

Respondents

Kathy Amacher
Middle School Special Education
    Language Arts and Math
Wheaton, IL

Laurie Anstatt
Second Grade
Ewing, NJ

Lisa Aronson
Second-Grade Resource Inclusion
Madison, CT

Jill Aspegren
Fourth Grade
San José, Costa Rica

Rose Bender
High School Social Studies
Ewing, NJ

Deb Bible
Primary Literacy Teacher
Carpentersville, IL

Susan Biltucci
Fifth Grade
Ilion, NY

Melissa Bock
Second Grade
Fishers, IN

Valerie Bresnahan
Middle School Language Arts and
    Special Education
Wheaton, IL

Darlene Carino
First Grade
Ilion, NY

Rhonda Carpenter
Fifth Grade
Beaverton, OR

Phyllis Hawkins Chesnutt
Middle School English
Ooltewah, TN

Judith Cimmiyotti
Sixth Grade
Kirkland, WA

Catherine Clausen
Second Grade
Beaverton, OR

Shannon Coombs
First and Second Grades Combined
Fernley, NV

Candace Darling
First Grade
Ilion, NY

JoAnne Deshon
Third Grade
Newark, DE

Jennifer Dunn
Second Grade
Birmingham, AL

Julie Elting
Third Grade
Madison, CT

Michele Engelsiepen
Kindergarten Team Teacher
Milford, DE

Nancy Finch
Fifth-Grade Inclusion
Madison, CT

Joanne French
Primary Reading Intervention
    Specialist
Ilion, NY

Christine Gabriele
Second- and Fourth-Grade Special
    Education
Madison, CT

Cindi Gardner
Multiage First and Second
    Grades
Madison, CT

Sharyn Genschmer
Fourth Grade
Orlando, FL

Anna Graham
Fourth Grade
Powder Springs, GA

Susan Graham
High School Spanish
Joliet, IL

Nettie Griffin
Kindergarten
Oak Brook, IL

Jenny Hoedeman
Second Grade
Philadelphia, PA

Kathleen Hoedeman
Middle School Math and Science
Upper St. Clair, PA

Paula Hoffman
High School Special Education
Grand Ledge, MI

Carol Howell
Multiage First and Second Grades
Portland, OR

Laramie Hudson
Fourth Grade
Spring Valley, CA

Jerry Jesness
Middle School ELL and Spanish
League City, TX

Heather Juntunen
Fifth Grade
Rolla, ND

Kathi Kennedy
Third Grade
Beaverton, OR

Mary Koster
Middle School Math and Science
Middletown, DE

Barbara LaMastus
Kindergarten
Springdale, AR

Darren Lander
Middle School Math and Bible
Plumsteadville, PA

Paula Larson
Kindergarten
Rockford, IL

Ellen Laubenstein
Third Grade
Ilion, NY

Thomas Leighty
High School Social Studies
Dover, DE

Olga Rodriguez Litz
Kindergarten
Granite Falls, WA

Teresa Losh
Middle School Reading
Ooltewah, TN

Kristen MacKay
K–12 Computer Science
Manilla, Phillipines

Angela Mariano
Third Grade
Orlando, FL

Ann McKelvey
K–5 Music
New Palestine, IN

Vince Meo
Fifth Grade
New Palestine, IN

Mariann Meyer
Second Grade
New Palestine, IN

Lori Mutert
First Grade
Birmingham, AL

Kelly Neumeister
First Grade
New Palestine, IN

Michelle O'Laughlin
Third Grade
Evergreen, CO

Bobbie Oosterbaan
Kindergarten
Oro Valley, AZ

Daniza Palmateer
High School
    Resource English
Holland, MI

Karen Palmateer
High School Special
    Education Reading
Holland, MI

Theresa Panziera
Third Grade
Silver Springs, NV

Kelly Paul
Fourth-Grade Library
    Learning Center
Ilion, NY

Michelle Perry
First Grade
Ilion, NY

Frankie Peterson
Second Grade
Silver Springs, NV

Jean Piazza
High School English
Cody, WY

Jay Pilkington
Middle School Social Studies
Omaha, NE

Sue Plaut
Middle School Reading
Ellicott City, MD

Diane Pope
High School Math
Fulton, MO

Marty Pope
High School Math and
    Communication Arts
Platte City, MO

Nancy Raihall
First-Grade Readiness
Lincoln, DE

Allan Reichenbach,
High School Math
Ewing, NJ

Bridget Rigg-Anderson
Fourth Grade
Fallon, NV

Carol Robertson
High School Science
Fulton, MO

Darla Ryser
Second Grade
Kent, WA

Lyssa T. Sahadevan
Kindergarten
Mobile, AL

Sandi Seckel
Second Grade
Columbus, NE

Stacy Shires
Second Grade
Granite Falls, WA

Sherry Simpson
Reading Specialist
Spring Valley, CA

Gemma Siringo
Fourth Grade
Ilion, NY

Larry Snyder
Middle School Social Studies
Canton, OH

Jean Stewart
Multiage First and Second Grades
Madison, CT

Phyllis Swiney
High School Special Education
Fulton, MO

Dan Szymkowiak
High School Mathematics
Mundelein, IL

Dennis Szymkowiak
High School English
Mundelein, IL

Lori Taylor
Third Grade
Jackson, MS

Ong Thao-Her
Fifth Grade
Powder Springs, GA

Sue VanderNaald-Johnson
Middle School Language Arts
Wheaton, IL

Tara Vitale
First Grade
Madison, CT

Yvette Wallace
Second Grade
Beaverton, OR

Maggie Wesolowski
Second Grade
Ilion, NY

Teffany White
K–5 Special Education
Ilion, NY

Liz Wiebking
Middle School Science
Wheaton, IL

Sara Wiles
Fourth Grade
Beaverton, OR

Lindsay Wiley
Fourth Grade
Spring Valley, CA

Dave Wilkie
Third Grade
Newark, DE

Jennifer Williams
Third Grade
Birmingham, AL

Susan Willingham
Second Grade
Powder Springs, GA

Marjorie Wood
High School Resource English
Muskegon, MI

Wendy Woods
Third Grade
Birmingham, AL

Sue Wyman
Kindergarten Team Teacher
Milford, DE

Jill Yates
First Grade
Granite Falls, WA

Susan Zaccaria
Fifth- and Sixth-Grade Science
Ilion, NY

References

Alexander, R., Rose, J., & Woodhead, C. (1992). *Curriculum organization and classroom practice in primary schools: A discussion paper.* London: Department of Education and Science.

Anderson, L. M., Evertson, C. M., & Emmer, E. T. (April, 1979). *Dimensions in classroom management derived from recent research.* Paper presented at the annual meeting of the American Educational Research Association, San Francisco.

Andrade, H. G. (2001). The effects of instructional rubrics on learning to write. *Current Issues in Education, 4*(4) [Online]. Retrieved May 17, 2005, from http://cie.ed.asu .edu/volume4/number4/

Axelrod, S., Hall, R. V., & Tamms, A. (1979). Comparison of two common seating arrangements. *Academic Therapy, 15,* 29–36.

Borich, G. D. (2000). *Effective teaching methods* (4th ed.). Upper Saddle River, NJ: Merrill.

Brophy, J. (1999). *Teaching.* Brussels: International Academy of Education.

Bullough, R. V. (1989). *First-year teacher: A case study.* New York: Teachers College Press.

Burden, P. R. (2000). *Powerful classroom management strategies: Motivating students to learn.* Thousand Oaks, CA: Corwin.

Bureau of Labor Statistics, U.S. Department of Labor. (2005). Teachers—preschool, kindergarten, elementary, middle, and secondary. *Occupational Outlook Handbook, 2004–05 Edition;* Retrieved October 20, 2005, from http://www.bls.gov/oco/ocos069 .htm

Canter, L. (2001). *Assertive discipline: Positive behavior management for today's classroom* (3rd ed.). Los Angeles: Canter & Associates.

Cobb, C. W. (1992). *Responsive schools: Renewed communities.* Oakland, CA: ICS.

Cohen, S., & Trostle, S. L. (1990). Young children's preferences for school-related physical-environmental setting characteristics. *Environment and Behavior, 22*(6), 753–766.

Cormier, R. (1974). *The chocolate war.* New York: Random House.

Curwin, R. L., & Mendler, A. N. (1999). *Discipline with dignity.* Alexandria, VA: Association for Curriculum and Supervision Development.

Downey, C. J., Steffy, B. E., English, F. E., Frase, L. E., & Poston, W. K. (2004). *The three-minute classroom walk-through: Changing school supervisory practice one teacher at a time.* Thousand Oaks, CA: Corwin.

Duckett, E., Park, D., Clark, D., McCarthy, M., Lotto, L., Gregory, L., Herling, J., & Burlson, D. (1980). *Why do some schools succeed? The Phi Delta Kappa study of exceptional elementary schools.* Bloomington, IN: Phi Delta Kappa.

Emmer, E. T., & Evertson, C. M. (1980, March). *Effective management at the beginning of the school year in junior high classes* (R & D Report No. 6107). Austin: University of Texas, R & D Center for Teacher Education.

Emmer, E. T., & Evertson, C. M. (1981). Synthesis of research on classroom management. *Educational Leadership, 38*(4), 342–347.

Emmer, E. T., Evertson, C. M., & Anderson, L. (1979). *Effective classroom management at the beginning of the school year.* Austin: University of Texas, R & D Center for Teacher Education.

Emmer, E. T., Evertson, C. M., & Anderson, L. (1980). Effective classroom management at the beginning of the school year. *Elementary School Journal, 80*(5), 219–231.

Evertson, C. M. (1982). Differences in instructional activities in higher and lower achieving junior high English and math classes. *Elementary School Journal, 82*(4), 329–351.

Evertson, C. M., Emmer, E. T., Clements, B., & Worsham, M. E. (1994). *Classroom management for elementary teachers.* Needham Heights, MA: Allyn & Bacon.

Florida State University. (2005). ESOL/bilingual terminology (Web Mediated Course Assistant). *ESOL strategies for content area teachers.* Retrieved October 20, 2005, http//fsu.edu/

Gibbs, J. (2001). *Tribes: A new way of learning and being together.* Windsor, CA: Centersource Systems LLC.

Goodrich, H. (1997). Understanding rubrics. *Educational Leadership, 54*(4), 14–17.

Gump, P. (1987). School and classroom environments. In I. Altman & J. F. Wohlwill (Eds.), *Handbook of environmental psychology,* pp. 131–174. New York: Plenum.

Hack, D. (2005, February 3). Goal of Patriots' mastermind: Win big game before it begins. *New York Times.* Retrieved October 20, 2005, from http:www.nytimes.com

Hastings, N., & Schwieso, J. (1995). Tasks and tables: The effects of seating arrangements on task engagement in primary schools. *Educational Research, 37*(3), 279–291.

Hastings, N., Schwieso, J., & Wheldall, K. (1996). A place for learning. In P. Croll & N. Hastings (Eds.), *Effective primary teaching: Research-based strategies.* London: David Fulton.

Hoyt, L. (2002). *Make it real: Strategies for success with informational text.* Portsmouth, NH: Heinemann.

Johnson, R. T., Johnson, D. W., & Holubec, D. J. (1994). *Cooperative learning in the classroom.* Alexandria, VA: Association for Supervision and Curriculum Development.

Kagan, S. (1993). *Cooperative learning.* San Clemente, CA: Kagan.

Kameenui, E. J., & Darch, C. B. (1995). *Instructional classroom management: A proactive approach to behavior management.* White Plains, NY: Longman.

Keller, D. (2004). *Feng shui for the classroom.* Kansas City, MO: Andrews McMeel.

Kounin, J. S. (1970). *Discipline and group management in classrooms.* New York: Holt, Rinehart & Winston.

Kounin, J. S. (1977). *Discipline and group management in classrooms* (2nd ed.). Huntington, NY: Krieger.

Kyriancou, C. (1991). *Essential teaching skills.* Oxford, UK: Basil Blackwell.

Lackney, J. A. (1996). *Quality in school environments. A multiple case study of environmental quality assessment in five elementary schools in the Baltimore City Public Schools from an action research perspective.* Milwaukee: University of Wisconsin, School of Architecture and Urban Planning. (Available from UMI Dissertation Services, No. 971742)

Lackney, J. A., & Jacobs, P. J. (2005). *Teachers as placemakers: Investigating teachers' use of the physical environment in instructional design.* Madison: University of Wisconsin, College of Engineering, School Design Research Studio. Retrieved October 20, 2005, from http://www.engr.wisc.edu/

Lee, V. E., Smith, J. B., Perry, T. E., & Smylie, M. A. (1999, October). *Social support, academic press, and student achievement: A view from the middle grades in Chicago.* Chicago: Annenberg Research Project. Retrieved October 20, 2005, http://www.consortium-chicago.org/publications/p0e01.html

Marzano, R. J., Gaddy, B. B., & Dean, C. (2000). *What works in classroom instruction.* Aurora, CO: Mid-continent Research for Education and Learning.

McEwan, E. K. (1998). *The principal's guide to attention deficit hyperactivity disorder.* Thousand Oaks, CA: Corwin.

McEwan, E. K. (2002). *The ten traits of highly effective teachers.* Thousand Oaks, CA: Corwin.

McFadyen, D. (2005, February 17). Trouble in the workshop. *New York Teacher.* Retrieved October 20, 2005, from www.uft.org/news/teacher/trouble/

McGuffey, C. (1982). Facilities. In H. J. Walberg (Ed.), *Improving educational standards and productivity,* pp. 237–288. Berkeley, CA: McCutchan.

McLoughlin, D. (2005). *High trust thinking/teaching.* Retrieved October 20, 2005, from http://www.hightrust.net/

Merrett, F. (1994). Whole class and individualized approaches. In P. Kutnick & C. Rogers (Eds.), *Groups in schools.* London: Cassell.

Mertler, C. A. (2003). *Classroom assessment.* Los Angeles: Pyrczak.

New, R. (2000). Reggio Emilia: Catalyst for change and conversation. *ERIC Digest.* ERIC Document ED447971.

Noddings, N. (1992). *The challenge to care in schools: An alternative approach to education.* New York: Teachers College Press.

Open Court Reading. (2005). New York: McGraw-Hill.

Paine, S. C., Radicchi, J., Rosellini, L. C., Deutchman, L., & Darch, C. (1983). *Structuring your classroom for academic success.* Champaign, IL: Research Press.

Palincsar, A., & Brown, A. L. (1984). Reciprocal teaching of comprehension fostering and monitoring activities. *Cognition and Instruction, 1*(2), 117–175.

Patton, J. E., Snell, J., Knight, W. J., & Gerken, K. (2001, April). *A survey study of elementary classroom seating designs.* Paper presented at the Annual Meeting of the National Association of School Psychologists, Washington, DC.

Read, M. A., Sugawara, A. I., & Brandt, J. A. (1999, May). Impact of space and color in the physical environment on preschool children's cooperative behavior. *Environment and Behavior, 31*(3), 413–428.

Rose, C., & Nicholl, M. (1997). *Accelerated learning for the 21st century: The six-step plan to unlock your master mind.* New York: Dell.

Ryan, K., & Cooper, J. M. (1995). *Those who can, teach.* Boston: Houghton Mifflin.

Saphier, J., & Gower, R. (1997). *The skillful teacher: Building your teaching skills.* Acton, MA: Research for Better Teaching.

Saraceno, J. (2005, February 7). Being Brady good enough for Pats QB. *USA Today,* p. 6C.

Slavin, R. E. (1978). *Cooperative learning.* Baltimore: Johns Hopkins University, Center for Social Organization of Schools.

University of Kansas Center for Research on Learning. (2005). *Strategic Instruction Model.* Retrieved October 20, 2005, from http://www.ku-crl.org/sim/index.html

Walberg, H. J., & Paik, S. J. (2003). *Effective educational practices.* International Bureau of Education. Retrieved October 20, 2005, from www.ibe.unesco.org/

Ward, W. A. (2005). Retrieved October 20, 2005, from http://www.brainyquote.com/

Wheldall, K. L., & Lam, Y. Y. (1987). Rows versus tables II: The effects of two classroom seating arrangements on disruption rate, on-task behaviour and teacher behaviour in three special school classes. *Educational Psychology, 7*(4), 303–312.

Wheldall, K. L., Morris, M., Vaughan, P., & Ng, Y. Y. (1981). Rows versus tables: An example of behavioural ecology in two classes of eleven-year old children. *Educational Psychology, 1*(2), 27–44.

Wise, K., & Okey, J. (1983). A meta-analysis of the effects of various science teaching strategies on achievement. *Journal of Research in Science Teaching, 20,* 419–435.

Wong, H. K., & Wong, R. T. (1998). *The first days of school: How to be an effective teacher.* Mountain View, CA: Harry K. Wong.

Wooden, J., & Jamison, S. (1997). *Wooden: A lifetime of observations and reflections on and off the court.* Chicago: Contemporary Books.

Yeomans, J. (1989). Changing seating arrangements: The use of antecedent control to increase on-task behaviour. *Behavioural Approaches with Children, 13*(3), 151–160.

Zentall, S. S. (1986). Effects of color stimulation on performance and activity of hyperactive and nonhyperactive children. *Journal of Educational Psychology, 78*(2), 159–165.

Zernike, K. (2001, August 5). The feng shui of schools. *New York Times,* Section 4A, p. 20.

Index

**CORWIN
PRESS**

The Corwin Press logo—a raven striding across an open book—represents the union of courage and learning. Corwin Press is committed to improving education for all learners by publishing books and other professional development resources for those serving the field of PreK–12 education. By providing practical, hands-on materials, Corwin PressW continues to carry out the promise of its motto: **"Helping Educators Do Their Work Better."**